THE FLAMING TRESSES OF DRAUPADI

Other books by M. Veerappa Moily (from Rupa Publications)

The Edge of Time

Unleashing India: Agrarian Wealth Creation–Vol. I

Unleashing India: Water, Elixir of Life–Vol. II

Unleashing India: Powering the Nation–Vol. III

Unleashing India: The Fire of Knowledge–Vol. IV

Shree Ramayana Mahanveshanam (Vol. I and II)

THE FLAMING TRESSES OF DRAUPADI

M. Veerappa Moily

Translated by D.A. Shankar

RUPA

Published by
Rupa Publications India Pvt. Ltd 2017
7/16, Ansari Road, Daryaganj
New Delhi 110002

Sales Centres:

Allahabad Bengaluru Chennai
Hyderabad Jaipur Kathmandu
Kolkata Mumbai

ISBN: 978-81-291-4534-5

First impression 2017

10 9 8 7 6 5 4 3 2 1

Printed by Thomson Press India Ltd., Faridabad

Dedication

Oh, mother! Primal source of my strength,
Great fountainhead of my inspiration,
My eternally lit light,
You gave me life in the fiery world and
Filled me with resolution deep,
Made me study day and night,
Taught me lessons of selflessness and renunciation,
Instilled in me that work alone is my righteous dharma,
Made me stay constant there and
Propelled me to widen the horizon of my knowledge,
Became my unfailing spring of
The water of life,
To you
I, your son, dedicate this radiant flower of an epic.
The Flaming Tresses of Draupadi
And I reverently place it at your sacred feet,
Poovamma, my noble mother.
In your motherly love
Accept it and bless me.

CONTENTS

FOREWORD

There is no other poetry in India that has engaged the Indian minds as has been done by the Ramayana and the Mahabharata, especially the latter. Even today, the Mahabharata provides analogies and imageries for the historical events through different time periods.

Jaya, as it was named initially, was of a modest size but grew with the times and, came to be known as the Mahabharata. If this is one side of its growth, the dimension of its growth in other local languages is another interesting factor. In the hands of able poets of various languages of India it had a rebirth each time, influenced by the poet's contemporary society, contemporary men and contemporary polity and, of course, contemporary war. These poets likened the heroes of Mahabharata to the heroes of their times. Pampa, the Adi Kavi (the poet-pioneer) of Kannada language, portrayed his patron as Arjuna, the popular hero of Mahabharata, which of course forced him to coronate Arjuna as the king after the Great War. The examples of Ranna and Kumaravyasa, two other great poets in Kannada, are also there for us to examine.

In Kannada alone, we have versions of the Mahabharata by Pampa and Kumaravyasa. To this great tradition of Kannada Mahabharata, Sri Veerappa Moily has now added another graceful contribution—*The Flaming Tresses of Draupadi*.

As exemplary her traits were, Draupadi's soliloquies in this epic written by Dr Moily tread a different path of technique for unfolding the events of Mahabharata. Pampa said that the incident of Draupadi's braided hair being disheveled unceremoniously by the Kauravas was the seed that lead to the culmination of the Great War. The soliloquies are hers, but they are also of the consciousness that works through all ages against the atrocities and cruelty committed by men against women and also works for getting justice for the latter. This is the spirit that flows as a forceful undercurrent throughout this epic.

Draupadi was not just a wife for the five Pandava brothers, but she was their friend and guide too. She did not know hypocrisy. She was a straightforward woman who had undergone the trauma that remained unhealed forever. She had deep and loving compassion for the suffering lot in the society. She never lost her patience even during severe hardship. More than anything, her love for life and the boldness remain admirable for everyone.

This swarthy lady had a beautiful soul. She was the binding factor of five different energies, flowing in different directions, and with the unfading support and love of Krishna, led her five husbands to victory against the Kauravas. This proves the great inherent power Draupadi had. She had the courage to challenge the evil powers of the society and also had the acumen to protect other women from those powers, and was relentless in doing so.

The poet has wonderfully amalgamated fire, light and water together in moulding Draupadi's character. Readers bow before her for the love, determination and responsible nature of hers. But, more than anything else, her character in this epic is admired for her unstinted love for humanity. Above all, she remains the epitome of virtue.

This is a most valuable contribution that Dr Moily has made to the Indian literature. He deserves our gratitude.

Dr Chandrashekara Kambara

PREFACE

Many well-known critics and literary personalities say that no poet, subsequent to the Ramayana and Mahabharata, has written an epic on a theme that falls outside the purview of these two great epics. Others question the benefit of picking up the same old theme for a new epic. The truth behind their comments is actually that all poets after Valmiki and Vedavyasa look too insignificant in the context of the colossus of these talents. There is no doubt that the epics are unparalleled in the field of Indian literature, and in fact they are the makers of the constitution for Indian poetry.

Historically speaking, neither of these epics, as they are today, were composed by a single hand. The work of culling out the interpolations from them continues even today. These epics are revised, renewed and enlarged by each generation. Valmiki and Vedavyasa gave the oral epics a written form. This tradition has continued till the times of Rashtra Kavi Kuvempu (K.V. Puttappa, the renowned Kannada poet). This is not limited to Kannada only, but has happened in other Indian languages as well.

When a poet chooses a certain theme, it provides only a skeletal form for his work. There are about three hundred versions of the Ramayana in both Telugu and Kannada languages each. Naturally, the theme for these versions are varied, and the style for each of them and the manner in which the ideas are expressed by each poet are different. However, for all of them the source remains Valmiki's Ramayana. Many folk poets had not even read the original Ramayana, but using their creative talent they gave it a form to suit their local readers. Their conviction was that a known theme would make the effort of taking their work to the general public easier. They have brought the ambrosia of original epics in different vessels for the general public. In the process, adding their imagination into that which exhibits the vivid images of India.

Even when a poet chooses characters like Kumara Rama, Kari Bhanta, Koti Channayya—these heroes are likened to the heroes of the Ramayana and Mahabharata. Independent of the source where the poet takes the theme for his work from, it is important that he ensures that in his work the time in which he lives is reflected, the aesthetical aspect is given its due and that his vision is expressed well.

It is not a secret that the protagonist's role in Indian literature is almost the monopoly of men. The woman might have been deified, but she has never been made the central character. Her place as a housewife, companion and associate is well established. At the most she can be regarded as a wise counsel. That is the place which many believe she deserves.

By portraying her as soft and delicate, the civilized society has undermined her personality. This is the main reason behind the discriminatory attitude that she has been subjected to over time. The characters like Ahalye, Kaikeyi, Sithe, Mandodari, Shabari, Tara, Satyavati, Urmile, Ambike, Ambalike, Gandhari, Kunti, Draupadi and Uttare have become ever shining stars in Indian literature, because of these epics. However, each one of them is a character playing a subordinate role to enhance the importance of the protagonist's role.

There might be a few works that centre around Ahalye, Mandodari, Kunti, Gandhari, etc. But I was always pained to see that no work has ever been written without gender bias and by treating both the sexes fairly. As I studied the Mahabharata repeatedly and came in contact with different sources of folk literature, Draupadi's character emerged as an answer to all my pain and discomfort. It shone brilliantly on the mind of the poet in me.

As a result of intense thoughts for decades, Draupadi appeared to me as a character serving all the experience of the Dwapara yuga consolidated and condensed, through her soliloquies. She was the woman who underwent oppression and exploitation more than any other woman in the Mahabharata. But, she did not shrink with fear or diffidence, nor did she blame the providence for that. Not only did she submit herself for the great cause, but was also a powerful influence behind many of her contemporaries. Hers was an exemplary character for the age she lived in and the age that followed it.

The only character which grew to match the towering personality of Krishna was that of Draupadi. Krishna had posited his complete confidence in her. She had the audacity of questioning even Krishna. One can see a blend of the hardness and softness of human character in her, and that was the grandeur of Draupadi. The two boons she asked for following the disastrous gambling, show her political acumen and her sense of propriety. Everyone, including Bhishma and Drona, was fascinated and awed by her personality.

After I completed *Shree Ramayana Mahanveshanam*, I was in search of a theme relating to a strong female character. My wife Malathi suggested that I take up the Mahabharata, keeping Draupadi's character at its centre. In an event hosted for *Shree Ramayana Mahanveshanam*, Sri Narahalli Balasubrahmanya, a prominent critic and a Kannada litterateur, threw a challenge at me to consider taking up a work on the Mahabharata. Again it was Malathi who came to my help. My next five years were engaged in doing research on Draupadi and other well-known female characters in the world and in the study of their fascinating psychology, which made them who they were.

In my life, two women have played crucial roles—my mother Poovamma and my wife Malathi. Though an illiterate herself, when I was a child my mother would wake me up at 4.30 in the morning, light a kerosene lamp and make me study. She would sit on the floor and watch me study. Her expectations would make her sit with me again in the evening till as late as 10.30 in the night. My pursuit of knowledge which began then continues till today. Even when I was the Chief Minister of Karnataka I used to work on my literary works early in the mornings. Even then she would sit in front of me and watch me intensely. My mother was a continuous source of inspiration for all my literary works. I am fortunate enough that Malathi, as my wife, as a critic of my work, and most importantly as a guiding lamp, is leading me forward on the path of achieving my goals. These two women have always been the inspiring forces in my life.

Draupadi did not borrow any of her attributes from men, nor were they a gift of God to her. There is an incident of Shiva telling Parvati: 'What does a woman's virtuosity mean? You are my wife and your character and your inner mettle are in no way inferior to that of mine. You are half of my personality. That is why I am known as Ardhanarishwara. A woman should be measured only by comparing her to another woman's character and determination, and to nothing else.'

Parvati replied to this by saying, 'When all the great rivers (which are personified as women in Indian culture) consulted Ganga, the celestial river, about this, Ganga told them that women always follow women and not men. Hence, a woman can only be compared to another woman.' Ganga, who was present there, added her views: 'A woman is the most powerful person. She, like the rivers, is the propelling force behind the world. All the activities in the world would have come to a standstill, but for her.'

In the Mahabharata, all women characters are central and play a vital role. All men, whether they are emperors, rishis, scholars, or ordinary men, are influenced by the force and energy of women. None could escape from it. I did not venture to analyse and critique the female characters of the Mahabharata.

Draupadi is also known as Yagnaseni, as she was the daughter of Yagnasena, another name for Drupada. Also, it is noteworthy that her character has an inseparable connection with the sacrificial fire. She was born through the sacrificial fire; she had to undergo fire ordeals many a time in her life; she was the embodiment of blazing fire. Her consent was not taken before making arrangements for her marriage. It was simply thrust on her. This gave a decisive turn to her life. Then on, she became the brilliant burning flame and remained so throughout her lifetime.

All epics contain within themselves the values of past and future. This is the reason why they last forever retaining their relevance through time and age. As long as exploitation rules the world, so long will be the need for recollection of the name and life of Draupadi as a protective force. She is the inspiration for all those who fight against exploitation. She is the pioneering force in changing the circumstances that ought to be changed.

For constructing something new, it is inevitable that the old has to be demolished. It is a fact that twenty-one civilizations got erased because of their own weakness. Dwapara Yuga did not end because of the Great War or strife between a few people, but the fall was caused by the social evils such as exploitation of women, atrocities, excess pleasure-seeking, oppression of the weak, etc., the aspect of history that needs to be studied deeply.

Dr M. Veerappa Moily

I. Movement

YAGNASENI

CANTO I

EPOCH-HONOURED YAGNASENI

In the perennially green and beautiful valley of
The sacred Sahyadri mountains, I begin my bardic
Pilgrimage, and the land of the great Kaveri river
With the blessings of the poetic tradition of yesteryears
Which, has a rich variety of themes and metrical patterns
And rhythms and turns and movements of varied verse forms
Which carry the incantatory voice of the King of poets,
Vyasa, extolled by goddess Saraswati herself, and
I plunge into this pool of poetric beauty, and swim.
Look, there it is at the top of the mountains a
Many coloured rainbow, presenting the richness of
A variety of themes and feelings and emotions of man,
And the entire land of Kannada-speaking world
Rises, listens and dances to the new idiom and the lilt,
And to prosodic variations and changes new.
The flow of light and song floods the life of man
And, brings into view the great Draupadi
Whose rich and sacred tresses of hair
When loosely plaited together send forth resounding,

Drum beats which echo and re-echo from the caves
And hollows, and raise issues of *dharma* and *karma*
And make the world alive to these.

The vibrant echo said that the world was in its
Womb and that the great epic was piecing together
The spirit emanating from deep down the earth and

There was the dazzling beauty born of a thousand suns,
And unveiled a wonderfully effulgent creation of Nature.
It had forms many, and sprang from the fire within
The depth of the earth but with it was the soothing light
Of the new moon in all its brilliance, and made a
Word full of terrible music and beauty and magic and
I, on the back of the winged mystical horse, played in the
Spring water of the flowing Saraswati, and I was
Bathed in the sounds of poetic beauty.

The second epic of mine born in the heart of
My wedded wife, Malathi, and gushed though my
Being like stainless pure water of the Achhoda
Lake, and the cool water rippled down and bestowed
On me the nectar of a poetry of high order
And filled I was with the mystery of her love;
And the presence of my great teacher, Anantaramu,
Saw to it that my mind did not get deflected by

Passing worries and crises which made me work
Like *Stithapragna,* a man of total poise, in the garden of poetry;
And like the spring season itself
Kabbinale Vasanta Bharadwaja in much happiness
Led me through the mazes of poetry and then, ah,
Descended my creative upsurge like
Bright stars illuminating the night sky!

As from the one incarnates many, multiple things,
The world, richly plural and diverse, appeared
As if it was one single entity and then I saw
The great epic of the flaming, auspicious saga
Of the tresses of Draupadi.
And made me see the fecund and endless creative
Urge of Nature covered in the sweet fragrance
Of the waters of the sweet-smelling mountains.
In creativity is there a match to nature?

On the sea beach a temple whose spires

Look like they are kissing the sky, and beside these,
Stars appear like lamps of love, and when the
Sun rises in the east, cool breeze moves
Around, and the pools of cool water give birth to
Laughing lotus flowers, and bees sing sweetly
And the chakravaka birds in intimate love
Make pleasant noises, but you, caught
With five wedded husbands, feel lonely.
And alone, don't you?

You belonged to none and your pulsating
Feminity, deprived of the dream of
Rounded fullness, you continued to dream:
Your womb in pain and in travail shook,
Yet you remained quietly suffering
And in silence. You the auspicious-looking one,
Stood, and in your moment of humiliation,
You begged aloud for help but your
Five husbands came not to your help;
The other tugged and pulled the saree you wore
But Bhisma and Drona and the rest
Remained silent spectators, and then from above,
From the sacred firmament, from the blazing
Sun's orbit, fell unfathomable feminine spirit,
And it surrounded you like the many-armed giant and
Stood like an immovable chain of mountains.

But the storehouse of righteousness, Yudhisthira,
The world-renowned hero, Partha, anger-incarnate and
Terrible Bhima and the two unmatched heroes,
Nakula and Sahadeva—all, and each one your
Husband—could not stand up to protect you;
With downcast looks, and paralysed as if they were,
They fell struck by their own righteousness!
Did then *dharma* lose its strength and fail?
Once you stood rock-like as virtue itself and
Then moonlight descended in showers.

You are the virgin daughter of the fire-god
And like the fire itself shone in full splendour.
You are the image incarnate of self-confidence,
Of soul strength and of resolution complete.
It is you who in the light of your own
Awareness stood straight and erect and
Defeated sorrow and pain and rancorous rumour
And blame; in the fiery furnace you stood and
In righteous haughtiness dismissed purile questions
About the holiness of woman, and snuffed out
Taboos laid down by the strong-armed menfolk.
Stepping out of the circle of enforced coyness and modesty,
Unafraid and with a mind in steadfast equipoise,
You stood up in the brilliance of your intellect and
Stamped out a docile traditional attitude and created
A new world of equality, and fought a war for the
Liberation of all womankind!

Bravely helping the helpless wedded women,
You, through, your woman-words, have leaped
Over and with determination pushed aside the age-old
Feudal rule and mauled and put down the arrogance
Of the male world, and became she who destroyed
Sexual exploitation, and pulverized wicked male passions.
You mastered your great five husbands and became
The symbol of woman power and achieved a
Persona beyond the world of wedded wives. You
Promulgated a new law which without erasing the
Age-old rich tradition became the pillar of high
Self-respect, and fighting dissention within and without,
You stood. The wife of five men, you, who through
An ethic new and daring, put an end to the
Tragic life woven round you; and the world of
Men trembled and cogitated over but you are
The one who commands and orders others to do away with

Cruelty and humiliation and exploitation of women

And rose in the new world created by you an
Image representing the equality of the sexes.

You know without the help of words spoken, and
Your speech is sweet which helped you gain ascendency
Over your five husbands with unmatched skills and art.
In the ancient annals of ancient India, it is you
Who made the impossible possible!
With love and devotion and friendship and composure
Weighted feelings and thoughts and emotions as
Becoming the daughter of the fire-god and wedded wife of five men.
You attained true glory and as the daughter of the king of
Panchala and the daughter-in-law of the Kuru clan.
A friend dear to Sri Krishna himself, you,
In life, suffered many trials and tribulations and
Pain and humiliation and yet you drew strength
From your own indomitable self and rose truly like
The daughter from the pit of sacred sacrificial fire,
You remained Yagnaseni!

Today you rose and stood up to dispense
Justice to the women of the world and you,
Did it, carrying flowers in your hand, and with
Love, made them into a festoon and
Likewise made womanliness a full feminine world,
Representing the subtle feelings and emotions of a
Being sensitive and aware and in doing so, you became
Yourself a picture of culture and virtue and large-mindedness
And of harmonized complex thought.

You the primal daughter of the energy of
Creation, you the daughter of primeval fire,
You, Sita and Draupadi, you really are the
Great daughters of this earth.
No, no, not lovely daughters but women born of fire!
Janaki, the mild, had to be beside her Rama
And without him she could not live and that is why

She, unable to live by herself, found refuge in
The bowels of the earth.
But you, with eyes spouting fire, you, great
Daughter of Drupada, you Yagnaseni, you Panchali
Bowed not and refused to tow the line of Sita and Savitri.
Revolted against the age-old tradition and history,
And tore apart the accepted view of modest women and
Breaking into pieces like the god of destruction, Rudra, you
Became the voice and persona of women's true awakened
Nature. For a while you were depressed because of strifes
Internal, but again in steeping yourself in sweeping
Anger, your true nature, blazed forth like a live
Ball of fire but feelings subtle, and sensitivity
You lost not, and yet gave the husbands your fellowship,
In sorrow and pain intense, and suffering rejection,
Humiliation and exploitation total.

In immovable self-confidence you pushed aside all notions
Of inferiority, and at that time itself called out
Loud that the son of Yama, Yudhisthira, who put all his
Faith in fate and god, was but a man luckless and
The worst of men.

You grew in maturity and strength of will and
Slowly, relentlessly kept the fire of war alive in your
Five husbands and taunted their mannish arrogance
And broke down the strong fort built around you,
But felt the uselessness of five husbands who were
With you and also facing unimaginable emotional strife.
You fought the war within yourself;
You stayed silent but within you raged
A righteous war of propriety but like the five
Fingers of the five Pandavas you stayed true and
Were busy building cloud castles.

Though caught in the many inner crises and conflicts,
You stood upright and won all the fights and crossed
Dilemmas of virtue and immorality and although

Buffeted by the waters of the wavering conscience
You bended not and cared but little for loss and gain
And tasted unmoved all that came your way.

Yes, in that swayamvara, the game of the choice of the bride,
Partha bent a bow which none had been able to and
Won you, but you bent the world of men and made them
Bow to you; and in the granary of reminiscences
Kept the warmth of women's feelings within yourself
Without getting lost in the whirlpool of feelings contrary;
You, through your willpower, teased the consciousness
Of Yudhisthira and though the honour of the family
Was questioned you stood without becoming or
Belonging to anyone and you stood by your own
Self and although they pushed you into the
Pit of humiliation you stood like an angel of strength,
Beside the son of the wind-god, Bhima, and truly like the
Daughter of the fire-god you inflamed his anger and kept it
Burning and his strength doubled and he responded
To the conflicts within you.

Sweet, fragrant breeze cooled your burning anger,
And the coming together of the two made you the
Universal feminine principle and through your love, pure as
Ganga, became Krishne to Krishna and in a new
Bonding, in the newness of a new feeling, in great
Love became a friend and a devotee and a disciple
To him and in mutual affection sprang a togetherness,
Transcending the physical and you offered at the time of
Your wedding a fresh garland born of this new
Fellowship. And thus was born your soul-
Relationship with Krishna which created a new love,
Unknown till then to the men and women of this world.
Far outside the frame of wedded love and bond
Sprang a fellow-feeling which transformed you
Into a woman of new universe with a fragrant
and universal touch.

The sweet sound of
Krishna's flute softly swept into
Your sensitive inner being and purified you, and
Made you a full and loved friend, and your life
Blossomed. You developed a strength that could draw
The world to you.
Yet you stayed like ash-covered live-coal and
Who knows who will awaken it, who will get burnt,
And who will use it to light up the world and who
Will see to it that it won't ever be put out.

You, it is, who have saved countless lives and made
Rain and sunshine and spring breeze move as per
The divine ordinance and it is you who woke up
And stood against the unrighteous Kaurava who did not
Want peace and hungered for destructive war and
A huge number of men caught in the war of fire
Have died but
Where Krishna is, there is righteousness and where
Righteousness is, there is Krishna, and as in the
Peepul tree a million green tender leaves spring up
Only to fall during the hard winter months and
Leave the tree naked but the underlying spirit of
Nature makes the tree, in the spring, put forth new,
And green and light crimson-coloured leaves in millions
And it proclaims the forever-prevailing truth
Of the green earth.

CANTO II

MYSTERIOUS CHILD, THE FLOWER OF AEONS

In the city of Panchala, Drupada, a king noble,
Yearning for progeny performed a *yagna*, a holy
Ritual sacrifice, and from within the holy fire
Sprang in burning glory twin infants, and amazed,
The assembled ones in unison cried out, 'Whose
Children are these?' None knew and each one
Asked the other for answers right, while the king stood
In stupefaction and wonder.
Then rose one from among the assembled revered sages
Who said, 'Oh, king, be not afraid. Be not worried.'

In your desire for progeny you performed this ritual
And here are the glorious infants and receive them as
The sacred Vyshavaagni, of the Puranas;
One is your son, Dristadyumna and the other, a daughter, Yagnaseni!
To his heart, he pressed his little daughter of
The hue of blue lotus, and she shone like a dark
Diamond and he said to himself: 'The good fortune
Of which age has flowered and blossomed and is
In my arms! This child is truly the flower

Of our age and is asleep in the form of an infant.'
Its hair, like the dark, flowing waves of the ocean,
And its eyes large, and like windows of knowledge and wisdom,
Shone and dazzled those who looked at the child.
She looked as if Brahma, the creator himself, had with skill
Sculpted her without blemish; and beautiful as she was

Her face radiated charm in waves of bright light everywhere,
Lightning itself felt shy when it compared itself with her
Striking brightness and drawn by the sweet fragrance of her body
Bees, deceived, hovered round her and the sages and
ascetics who were
Meditating on god felt distracted by her appearance
On this earth, and their lips which were murmuring god's name
Fell silent without their knowing it and the flames which
Rose from the sacrificed fire stayed still as they saw
The beauty of the child and even leaves of the peepul tree
Fell silent and stirred not, and the audience wonderstruck stammered
As they were unable to overcome their wonder,
And exclaimed: 'The wonder of wonders! How does anyone
Describe it: this fascinating beauty incarnate exceeds all the
Thousand similies found in a great big epic and her smile,
indescribable, whose charm was uncommon, hither to unknown
It was to the universe.'

As she grew, she thought and rethought, and asked
Herself: 'Why should I strive to protect righteousness,
Dharma, and keep fighting to put down unrighteousness,
Adharma? And a life which vanquished not *Adharma*, is it
Life fulfilled? Why live if one cannot save women, my
Sisters, from suffering endless pain? In a series,
As it were, humiliation and unrighteous accusations and
Injustice have come my way and if I have strength,
Not fight them with god's help, why live at all?
Why did the king of Panchala name me Yagnaseni?
And should I put out the fire of humiliation kindled by
Drona, our teacher, with my tears flowing endlessly?'

Then, at that point, came the father, Drupada:
'Ah, my child, do not fear. I also named you as
Krishne! And surely He will take care of you.
The world's greatest person he is, and surrendering
Yourself to him you will regain the self-respect
I lost because of Drona. My life will be sanctified then.'

The utterance of the name of Sri Krishna instantly
Touched her body and mind, and there swept through
Her being a divine breeze that thrilled every hair on her body.
'Oh, the establisher of *dharma*, great and strong warrior!
Who would not wish to be with you and who would not
Desire to surrender their all to you and feel richly
Rewarded, Sri Krishna!

I am but a basil leaf and I "Krishne", wait for you
In yearning; and the sheer wait of expection has made my
Eyes go visionless, come, oh you, the noblest of men
I cry "Krishna, Krishna" and "where are you?"'

In the company of her dear friend, Nitambini, as
Ordained by Krishna, a cool breeze from Brindavan,
Streamed against them and it asked her,
'Dear maid, who is this Krishna Govinda Hari?'
'Does it matter who it is? Why worry without cause?'
And I, in deep forgetfulness and earnestness, said again:
'From father I know who Krishna is. He it is who has put
The world under his *maya*. He is the one who mermerizes
All and is handsomeness itself.'

'What has this Krishne to do with that Sri Krishna?'
Teased Nitambini, and softly touching her chin she
Said, 'He is an impossibility, friend! Forget him.
He is a sorcerer, uncatchable, why adventure now?'

'Why? What has happened? Is he unattainable?
Why this sharp speech? Say, what game is this?'
Holding her close to me I told her:
'Listen! Wise he is and as a man is an ideal,
Human being. In the game of politics, he is
A past master, and intelligent and a tested and
Reliable leader, and clean he is, and grants whatever
Is wished for by the devout and is the very image of
Humanness. He is like those who receive a little but grant
Lavishly. Rich he is and discriminating, and is wisdom itself.

He can be compared only to an ocean which can be compared
Only with another ocean. None is anywhere near him. He
Is the Lord of this world.'
'What else, and what more, tell me his story.'
'Yes, loose and licentious he is and, skillfully managed to win
The love of sixteen thousand young, innocent maids and winning
Their hearts, he moved away but attracted by his enchanting
Music he played on his flute, these maids, deprived of wedded bliss
Still sit forlorn on the banks of the Yamuna and shed
Hot, scalding tears. Theirs is a story of
Shedding sad tears and would you like to be one of these
Heartbroken young ladies? No, give up this thought,
You are Yagnaseni and don't become the dry stick
That priests ritually drop into burning sacrificial fire,
Trust not a heartless man and remain a jilted maid
All your life. Wake up Panchali, do wake up. And
Don't you hear everywhere, on the earth and in the skies,
The murmuring of the name of Krishna by thousands and
Why would you like to add your voice to the terrible
Music, the depressing music of tears of thousands of women!'
'But I could not dislodge the image of Krishna which had
Stayed with me in the room of my heart, and if I, in love,
Dedicate myself to Krishna, what fault would be there in
Him? He is blemishless, beyond good and evil, and
Boundless he is and can't I see him but once at least?'
Hearing these words, Nitambini, immediately, in much anger,
Spoke harshly. But I unable to restrain myself in my love
For him, I said: 'Tell me more about him.'
'What shall I say, how shall I describe the grandeur
Of that ancient myth? I do not know whether it is
True or not, but to see beauty in life is life's harvest.'
Then Nitambini, in ways pleasing to the mind, began to
Narrate the story of Brindavana:

'There was a Radha who in divine empathy and ecstasy,
As if inspired by the primeval power itself, steeped herself
In the waters of devotion to Sri Krishna and grew in herself

A love, godly and worshipful and in such a way that he,
Krishna could not be by himself but always beside his

Young, yearning love and she too was with him all the time,
From within her being.
And where she was not, he too wouldn't be there; and
Where she was present he too would be present or vanish she would.
It was like the coming together of Shiva and Shakti or like
The variegated hues of the rainbow coming together and becoming
But one.
If he was a poem she would become its music or put it in this
Way: Radhe is the leaf of love which the tree of Krishna
Allowed to sprout.
And in the music he played on his flute, she it was who became

Its tenor and movement and ecstasy and it was rather like
Divine music becoming blended with great soul-pleasure.
Did she yearn for him? Blissful Radhe where is she?
Is he in her mind or in one of his incarnation?
Did she become a river or a hill, and moved looking round
For him? Or did she bathe in the music of the flute or
Did, like the moonlight fleeting, she in friendly feeling for
Him radiated warmth and yet was within cool and in the
Presence of his loved one she flowered into a rich green tree
And made him her prisoner and swam in the flowing

Love of Krishna for her.
Creepers wave and spread and form a net but
Some grow straight and some create a green frame
And make one feel caged and something, unknown
Frightening and continuously, causes unknown pain, and
In love separated, Radhe said within herself:
"Ah, time! I think of calling Hari today but I know
He isn't here and there's none to listen to my prayer.
Mine is a cry in the wilderness! The world shrinks
With the poison spouted around and life itself retreats,
The richest of youth, like the sailing clouds in the sky,

Moves away fast and the wind disturbed, like a
Drop of water on a lotus leaf, which keeps running hither
And thither.

Nothing stays firm and what we imagine to be strong
And has staying power, moves away as even long
Streaming rivers go dry as does the river of love which
We thought would flow ceaselessly. And life stays on the banks
Waiting for a mystery, a mystery which would bring back
The green garden and make the desert disappear but the
Cool breeze of Srihari's love, its caressing touch isn't there.
Is there bright light within the darkened mind? But will

What is not present today be present tomorrow and dispel
The darkness that envelopes me now? I don't know.
Or is it saying that accessing happiness in this world is
Next to the impossible or what message is it conveying?
Where is it gone, the consciousness of the unity of the
Universe? He, the appointed man of the age which is
To see it right, where has he gone? Why is there this silence?
The world sings your limitless goodness and says that

It stays within the heart of man under the large, spread—
Hood of Adishesha and it looks like the rising image of
The sun god and heralds a deity who triumphs over death,
And that is how they praise you, the one who saved and
Protected the universe.
You teased us like the mirage in a vast desert or
Rather like the faint light of a star for above the world.
Will you not allow all sweet sounds to fuse sweetly
And pour it through our ears into our heart?
Make all our harmonious feelings and thoughts
come together
And see they stay richly and steadily in our mind.

When will the moving bird of love come and stay on
The bough of my heart's tree?
When will the scorching heat of my body be cooled

By your affection and when will I, singing sweetly,
Move on the waves of the ocean of life.
Come, before the peacock living in my body flies away disappointed.
Oh, friend, hold your magic flute to your lips
Sing and make me dance on the floor of my heart.
You are the famed one: it is said that you never let down
Those who sing of you in devout devotion.

The fire in my belly is burning like the wild forest fire,
But where have you gone?
Giridhara, to rid me of my burning pain,
Come holding feathers of the peacock in your hand.
Oh, you who play the flute and are mine, please
Come, be kind to me, and in kindness allow me a
Glimpse of your face: I shall again and again
Plead and quarrel with you and wait in the way
In which flocks of birds dying of thirst

Look for the season of rains which makes the peacocks dance
In happiness and which also impels my friends to go to
The flowing river in Bhadrapada month and wait with hope for
The rains in Ashwija month which makes pearls happen in cowrie shells
You alone are my god and therefore who else can I
Worship and adore?
You disappeared from me when the earth was covered with
The mist of *Pushya* month and you gave me the slip when
The water fountains sprinkled cool water all round and
During *Phalguna* month when the world of women play the

Colourful *Holi* with varieties of coloured water but burns
The body because of sun's heat. And in *Chaitra*, the
Spring season, when flowers bloom and Koels in numbers sing
And make the feeling of love surge up and cause pain.
I, in the desert land, lonesome, with my face gone white
And pale, am fallen like a withered flower.
Don't the waters of kindness spring in your heart and
Make you came to me who in deep burning memory

Wait for your return, you who play on the flute!"
In this fashion Radha remembering Krishna

In dream and in wakefulness shook and trembled and waited.'

CANTO III

THE CALL OF THE FEATHERBED OF IMAGINATION

For a moment, her companion stopped narrating the fascinating
Story of Radhakrishna and, as if, the flow of feeling had
Snapped suddenly, I forgot myself and was lost in his heart.
But consoled myself saying, that he would forever stay in my
Heart and was afloat again in the world of emotions sweet, and
Began again my voyage in the boat of memory and while
Awake and while forgetful the form of Krishna I saw
Wherever I looked and with him I journeyed away.
With my companion I sat on the swing of creepers green
And watched the setting sun around whom played clouds of
Many colours and for a while clouded the moon and
The sky looked as if somebody had played with colours—a
Veritable Holi evening it looked like.

Listening to the description of Krishna by Nitambini, my heart
Danced like the peacock with spread feathers, and my mind
Could think of nothing but him:
What does Krishna look like? Is he like the dark-hued leaves
Of the Tamala tree? Are his eyes like the eyes in the peacock
Feathers? Are his lips soft, like the petals of the lotus flower?
Are his feet beautiful like those of the swan?

And his fingers like the buds of a flower? Is his broad
Chest like the blue sky and does his voice make the
The koel think it is spring? And is his body fragrant
Like the heavenly flower, Mandara?

As if drunk I slept in the lap of Nitambini and my
Heart desirous of emotional unity got flooded with the
Flowing love for Krishna.
But oh God! Where are you and where am I, and won't
You stay in the temple I have built for you in my heart?
In the sky and in the earth there is heavy downpour.
A flash there is of lightning.
And I, with the strength of the god's name in my being
I stand.
And, as if waters are gushing through sluices, the divine voice
Resonates in every single, tiny drop of water and
The moment I am blessed with a vision of yourself,
My fear of life and death wash away
And confidence floods through my every pore and
I shall live life trusting you, and this alone is truth.

Nitambini paused for a while and then described the
Pleasant, happy pain of separation of Radha.
'Oh! dear friend. In the home of my mind I see
No limits to my happiness and I see him wherever
I look and in everything and everyone I see your
Being but how is it you have forgotten me!
Thinking you would be in the shrubbery of Brindavan,
I looked for you there. But you weren't there I heard.
But I felt your lips kissing my cheeks or I imagined so.
Where are you? Are you lost in Maya? I saw within you,
A mine of gold and diamonds and there, within your body,
Was bright light indescribable; and everywhere in Brindavan
There are flower-bearing creepers in full bloom and there sweeps
Across a divine, sweet music and in the firmament of my
Mind flocks of swans move round and in the strength of desire for
Your name I have put my faith, and though my soul is heavy
like stone
It can with help from your name divine it can float in the waters.
A feeling which nothing can destroy I have, and it stays
Strong beause it lives on the vital strength of your
Name, divinely powerful, and it fills me with happiness and raises

My spirit to heights great; and the door to the granary of
Of spiritual strength is open today, and the spiritual
Love, on the strength of your name, floods and in
Great force sweeps my being and I find again
My lost strength in the strength of your name!
Oh, Murari, come, let my eyes have a look at your face,
Who else can I take refuge in but within yourself?
Without the sun appearing in the sky, the lotus won't bloom
And the sky without the moon brightening it, looks not bright,
And I in both day and night cry in anguish and I sleep not

And my eyes refuse to close in sleep and, my lips gone dry,
Won't narrate the sad story of mine!
Words unable to speak of my desire stay in silence,
Why won't you put out the fire of love which burns me
All the time? Are you that innocent? Be kind, please,
And the deep sorrow within me, come and allay it, through
Your kindness. Protect me.
Why this cruelty, Krishna? Is there no room for kindness
In your heart?

Ah, look, there comes the lifter of the Govardhana hill,
And all the forest looks green, and from the skies leaps
Rainbow of dark clouds and in come the young maidens
Bathing in it all! Here is earth's fortune truly!
Shyama, the cloud-coloured with ringlets of hair on
His brow, he, the tall one with arms touching his knee;
His lips are tender like the newly-sprouted leaves and
His smile is like that of new-bloomed jasmine and
From his eyes speak the brightness of young youth.
His whole fascinating figure radiates charm.

Looking at Govinda, the many-faceted god, a
Conglomerate of all that is good and positive and auspicious, and he
Who is beyond all this and who in the sweet waves of music
Fills the heart with all that is sweet and fulfilling, her heart
Beamed in ecstasy of feelings.
All that is creative and releasing, the very voice of the eternal,

Beautiful spirit of Bharata is here spread on a couch
Of imagination and calls, loud and clear.
The waves of the music of the flute which speak of
the heartbeat of Hari himself,
Draw and capture the world spirit!
The incarnation of courage, of wonder-inspiring bravery, the great
Hero with whom moves the quest of the universe for a sense
Divine and absolute.
Oh, you, the fiery-tester that you are, won't you with
Your smiling countenance, make me the un-enlightened, the
one without inner light,
Take a dip in your ocean of life and make me satiated?
If you come not, if the nectar of your love does not flow
Into my being, my life will burn and turn into ashes
In the pit of sacrificial fire, for what other way is open
To me, tell me.
See, all land has gone dry and cries for life-giving water,
And as a child in great distress runs towards its mother,
Looks for relief, hoping for cessation of all pain, and
Waits, so am I now.
Saying so, I again slept in the swing of sweet scented
Swing of creepers and in dream-like state, I walked
In the world of dreams and wherever I saw, wherever I
Looked, I saw but the cloud-blue form of Krishna and he was
There in my mind, in my soul, in my body and in the whole of
The world and then, there arose, the great yoga,

The Advaita, the undivided yoga of love divine?
When Nitambini went to fetch water, from the sky, the
Clouds sent down a light shower, and as it fell on the dark leaves
Of the tree, there sprang up designs of various hues, and the
Peacock spread its tail and danced and then I wondered what
Nitambini thinks. And wondering so I stood while she came with
Twin flowers in her hand and I said to her:
'Oh, why did you pluck the flowers when it is still dark?
Those flowers which drank the moonlight and were laughing,
These you have, heartlessly, plundered, why, my friend?

Do not stop narrating the heavenly narrative of Brindavan.
And deprive me of genuine aesthetic pleasure, please.
My feeling are all strung up and therefore describe
To me the climactic phase of the divine love of Radha and Krishna.'
Then Nitambini went back to her narration;
'Who knows what games he played in Brindavan!
Radhe and the Gopis became dry leaves tossed about by a
Gusty wind, and they disappeared: and in the whirlpools of
The Yamuna, deep down, in caked earth they became part and
Parcel there. Their pitiable lives and stories of those lives
Became part of the infinite atom of the earth, and
Got transformed into manure and again, was absorbed into Nature.
Each grain of sand on the banks of Yamuna
Tell a sad story of the circular and fruitless fortune of
The ones who loved Krishna and of those, who perforce had to
Live in a world imaginary, and confusing and those
Innocent maidens, like flies attracted by a burning lamp,
Are tired and live a listless life.
Krishna, with his melodious songs on his flute, to which
They desired to dance, has not come and all their desires
Have turned into insubstantial and rhythmless flow of
Waste water. The eyes of the maids desiring too much
Have gone dry,' and such stories, sad stories of the
Brindavan of Krishna she placed before me.
And as she spoke of these tragic tales of love,
My mind, went limp in sorrow and then I asked
Within myself: how come you squeeze the life out of newly
Sprouted buds but spread the sound of your wonderful flute?
How could you stand there silently, and in cruelty hard?
You smothered the soft breathing of the dark lotus flowers
And stood there unseeing and unseen? Did you in happiness
Terribly dance while piping songs which dropped drops of
Sweetness and you moved on, destroying the fresh green
Leaves freshly sprouted? Did you disappear dancing,
And danced away?
From the soul-breaking cries of the Gopis of Brindavan, the

Place has all but vanished.
The cool moonlight has turned into a killing avalanche and
From the sky flash lightnings and frightening thunder,
And did you, deceiving them all, disappear like a
Magician? Did you, without realizing the wrong done
Move away from Radhe and leave her on the burning sand.
Of forlorn love? Keeping all the fragrance of the place,
Did you walk away?
And I, and my spirit, were flooded by the waves of the
Sad tales of Radhe, and I begged Nitambini to continue her narration.
'Krishne, listen, Murali, the player on the flute, who left
Brindavan that day did not return. The maid removed
The coral garland around her neck and threw it away but
By then Krishna had gone far away with Akrura—the one
Without cruelty! He turned cruel as he took away Krishna in his
Chariot and the whip he held whipped Radhe and
Raising clouds of red dust the chariot moved away, and
The wheels of the chariot crushed into mud the flower of
Radhe's love!
Within the heart of Radhe and Gopis, Krishna
Flowered and softly whispered in their inner ear thus:
"Do not forget to make your life all gold; forget yourself
In meditation and getting lost in it, be free of constricting
Passions and if I am away from you, I am away for
Your own well being, and fulfilled I feel in your intense
Love for me. And wherever I am my song of love
For you shall stay with you and your love surely will be
My *Sudarshana Chakra*, my invincible discus, and
Therefore blame me not. You are the breath of my breath
And your Krishna cannot live without you for you have
Surrendered yourselves to me in love and so have I to you.
Your souls will move with mine in my quest always
For the quest of this age, and forget I shall not, you and
Your ecstatic love. Does it matter where I am, for the lamp of
Your love will always brighten the path of my life."

The Gopis stood in a circle and holding hands

Looked at the sky with expectations and intense hope
There they witnessed a bright, rising moon in full splendour
And wondered at what they saw and as there saw there sprang from
Their hearts, and flew away, the birds of their egos as they had
Surrendered themselves fully and were left with nothing that
was their own. The *leela* of Krishna with his divine music,
had transformed their world, and each Gopi looked a Krishna
To another Gopi, and each thought Krishna was for her
ownself and danced; and it rained and the sky resounded.
With music from the heavens, and the Gopis in happiness
Sang, and danced, and all the notes of music came together and
The Gopis with Krishna swam in a world of music and
Love, and each springing on to a swing made of creepers sat
With her hands around Krishna and in ecstasy entered
The world of mesmerizing, sacred love.
As the hanging ear-ornament moved this way and that
She placed her cheek against his and struck a dance
Pose and the moon stood still in the sky watching this
Sacred *Raslila* and the faces of the dancers shone in the
Light of the non-ego and each, in a mood of ecstasy,
Sketched the handsome Krishna in her innerself and in this
Way, love profane and sacred came together in ways unknown.

How can anything separate the love divine of these two souls?
The sky turned orange-red, against a blue sky
The stars, it drew designs amazing, and the music of the
Flute made the dancing pair dance and dance; and it looked
As if the Universe was moving round the sun and the moon
And the spirit of life in the form of truth and beauty
And their oneness made the form of Krishna without
Radhe, melt and showed the universal truth of love.
When she sprinkled some water on my face I turned
Silent, and was ashamed a little, and there was also sadness
As my companion had plucked a flower but Nitambini
Touched me with the petals of the flower in her hand and said:

"I know without a touch from the lotus-like hand of

Krishna, the lover of Radhe, your heaviness of heart, your
Worry won't go. But where shall I find the King of
Dwaraka, Krishna. But I shall do this job for you:
I shall recite the incantatory name of Krishna and then
Place these petals invoking his presence and
Then within you will spring a new rejuvenating spirit. There is
No need for a doctor for your illness as yours is illness
Associated with intense love," saying so she placed the petals
On my chest and I felt better. But she did however
Convey my state of mind to my father, the King of Panchala.
I, in anger, looked at her and then covered my face with
My veil and became silent.'

'Krishne, you be a doctor unto yourself, and be brave,
I do not know why Nitambini enacted this play in
Front of you. You do not need a doctor nor medicines.
Say, "Krishna, Krishna" and all your worries will fly away;
And now see! Hearing you call, Krishna has come,
He is here, place these flowers at his sacred feet.'
Those feet, which no great poet could adequately describe,
I saw and felt I was blessed immensely and with the flowers
Of my overflowing tears of happiness, I washed his feet.
At the very instant my eyes got riveted there and
With what words can I describe him!
With arms touching the knees and a chest large and
Full of love—the sight flooded me through and through.
I was a witness to his auspicious form and he stood there and that
Auspicious feeling—how can it be described? With what words,
Culled from how many dictionaries?
No, there is to this divine picture no beginning and no end
Its transfixing beauty cannot be translated into any language.
Its sublimity is incarnation of all that is sublime,
All that is vast as the sea and the sky, all
Limitless, beyond all limits.

CANTO IV

DARK-BLUE IS NOT BLACK, IT'S SYMBOLIC OF THE VAST UNIVERSE

Once Sri Guru Vedavyasa spoke in this way:
'The word Trishna, meaning thirst, looks more beautiful
Than Krishna, but this unique young maid's hunger for
Knowledge nothing can quench—no, not even in thousands of
Years, in life after life.
Thirst can be quenched with water but as the burgeoning
Hunger for wisdom asks for more and more, the hunger
Exceeds, it goes beyond encyclopedic knowledge.'
'But if one is thorough with all books, what is there left to learn?'
Vedavyasa, the seer, smiling said:
'How could there be a want of good, ennobling books?
The world itself is a moving and overflowing storehouse of
Knowledge, truth eternal, individual and communal; it
Is a book unending, its pages full of experiences, and
Replete with extract of wisdom. And whoever reads here
Finds poets and scholars and virtuous, gifted women,
Who too, were unable to unravel the truth of life immensely
Complex. And, therefore multiplicity of works by many
Is a necessity which is needed to understand the
Meaning and the goal of life.
For you alone wait many situations and contexts, for
You alone are to respond to and find solutions.
And the finest work that is to be read is the book
Of knowledge about this wide world.
You be prepared, you be ready to prove that you are,

That you would be, the invaluable treasure for this universe.'
It was the finely strung thought-series of the great
Badarayana and, in this world of magical revelations
And structured imaginary reasonings, I, freely and
In pleasure, swam to my heart's content.
Nitambini stood in surprise and watched as the
Teasing of Nilamani, the parrot, went unchecked.
And to add to it Nitambini tried to put flowers
In my hair. But Nilamani in an enticing voice
Repeated the name of "Krishna" and I wondered
What this new game was, and asked in excitement:
'Who taught her the name of Krishna? Why is she
singing his name.'
'I do not know why you blame without cause, Nilamani!'
'But why is she playing with the name 'Krishna?'
'You are daft and you run down Nilamani.'
'Why are you shielding Krishna and his play acting?
It is he who taught Nilamani to say "Krishna! Krishna!"
And it is he who has done it. Why do you
Hold me responsible? I do not know a thing.'
You, here repeat his name, "Krishna", "Krishna",
And this message Nilamani conveyed to Sri Krishna and
He, again, taught the same name to her and sent her back here!
Why this hide and seek? I do not believe you.
The peacock feather here tells me a thousand love stories.
The surrounding here smells sweet with fragrance
Sweet, and therefore why this idle talk. Don't you
Make our love play more explicit!'
'Ah, you are again at it and without respite
You make fun of me!'

But within my inner eye as Krishna walked around,
I stood like a sculpted figure, but wondered within
Myself: in his mansion are Rukmini and Satyabhama.
Both beautiful, and so why would he think of me, me
The dark one! I do remember him the way millions of
His devotees offer him millions of garlands of fresh flowers.

As I stood lost in thinking about Krishna, the bell-like
Voice of father called out, and I listened and looked
At the east from where the sun rose and a soft voice
Very musical and soft, called 'Krishna' 'Krishna' and I
Stood their savouring the name called lovingly in whispers.
I listened and the name of Krishna tapped on the
Door of my heart and the divine sound of the flute opened
The shut door of my consciousness and I felt as if the
Sun god was waking the world up in the morning, and the
Name of Krishna floated through air and water, and my
Nilamani in lilting tone repeated the sacred name and
The pages of the history of the love of Gopikas and the
kidnapping of Rukmini opened up
And there appeared the loving husband of
Satyabhame and Rukmini, he who was the protector of *dharma,*
And he who had stolen the heart of women and I, dusting the
Cage of Nilamani, stroked her and she repeatedly parrot-like
Recited the name 'Krishna', 'Krishna' and my love for the god
Came in a flood, and thanking her for revealing the secret of
My happiness, and yet in pretended anger, said,
'Oh, Nilamani, stop this play-acting.' But like the sound
Of *Omkara*, the primal sound, it rolled on and on
And echoed and re-echoed from every corner and
I begged her to stop singing of Krishna; but without
Paying attention she continued and the song of love flowed
Unchecked and looked as if it would wash away the palace
And the city of Panchala itself, and then Nitambini said,
'Friend, why blame me! It is your pampered Nilamani!
Ask her to keep her mouth shut.'
'I have asked her again and again, and yet she in nonchalance sings,
And says, "it is my heart which sings without a stop
The name of Krishna on the *veena* of my heart," and
This is high Ananda Yoga of the whole world.'

'Ah, friend, I do not know from the moment I wake up,
And all day, I cannot keep away from Nilamani who
Roams freely the world of Krishna and observes everything most

Minutely and sensitively. Don't I know how to read your
Face, your emotions, which flow in great speed like
The Ganga and the Yamuna? Please do stop this play
Acting, please.'

Saying, so Nitambini, without a stop, teased and
Teased and I, because of my modesty, biting my lips,
Began a conversation with her.

'How do I stop playing with my loving Nilamani?
It is a bird you named and took care of.'

'True, it is I who in love named her Nilamani.
I do not know why I named her so, but among the
Names our court-poet listed, I found this right
And therefore I named her so.
What is wrong with that?'
'Ah, crown princess, how well suits you the name of Krishna
And when the word Nilamani escapes through your lips
How lovely does it sound, and how sweetly!'
'What newness do you see here? Nilamani, Nilamani,
I always say, why does it sound new to day?'
'This is not new to me, yet today it sounds very new,
And I, here, staying at the place of a guest special
Have my sleep disturbed because of the name, and
How shall I suffer it?'
'What shall I say? Why do I disturb people's sleep?
And why should I send Nilamani to do it? But
When Nilamani in friendly liberty says "Krishna, Krishna,"
It gets echoed and re-echoed from corners four
And spreads a fragrance sweet, and she makes me
High strung and worried, and I do not know how
I should face Krishna!'

Opening the door of the cage, I said,
'Go now and do not ever come back and bother me,
And she flew away into the vast blue horizon of the sky.
She went away but now, without Nilamani, how do I

Spend my time? With whom do I share my thoughts?
The veena of my heart, its strings are cut and where is
The veena-player who will make the broken veena right again.'
Understanding the feelings of Krishne, Nitambini spoke
In this fashion:
'Panchali, do not be sad, Nilamani does not worry you
Nor does she deceive. She thinks not of gaining a friend,
It is not in her heart. Sleeplessness has made your eyes
Red and it has taken you far into a world of dreams.
Come out of it. Nilamani will surely come back. Do not worry.'
And as Nitambini, smiling, tugged softly at the pallu of
My saree and mischievously looked at me, I missing
The song of Nilamani, unable to hear the repetitive name of
'Krishna' 'Krishna', and, ah! She flew in and flew around
and touched
My long dark hair and woke up the song of my heart, 'Krishna!'
I know not what good fortune brought me close to
The cloud-hued Krishna but even before that
I used to stand before a mirror and run him down
For bestowing on me a dark hue, and for discriminating
Against me. I, to get over it brought mainly roots and herbs,
And making a fragrant paste of these I used to apply
To my face. But nothing changed, although I doubled
My efforts. I developed an inferiority complex and
Rued within myself.
But when I saw that blue was the colour of the world
Adored and when I heard him say so, the words
He spoke removed the film from my eyes:

'The black that you are worried about is not black.
It's blue which is symbolic of the vast sky and of
The vast sea, and therefore why feel small or feel
Discriminated against? Do not be short-sighted but
Think sensitively and subtly.'

Those words I heard gained more meaning
When I remembered that it was this Krishna,

Krishna, the blue-hued who had won the love of thousands
Of Gopis in Brindavan. How then could this blue-black
Colour be inferior to any other colour?
Is his sky-blue colour less to any other
When compared?
The marvel of his colour became known when he was
Still in his teens and he was the one who transformed his
Age he was born in and that is the real wonder of his colour.
Do not therefore look with doubtful gaze
For beauty is but truth and auspiciousness.

CANTO V

WHO ELSE BUT YOU WHO WILL LEAD ME BY MY HAND

One day Drupada, with his family, set out to visit the temple of Shiva.
I tried hard to stay back but
Dristadyumna dragged me by force while people
Stared at us. I was unhappy but my companion
Dressed me in fine silks and as I went along with the
Procession, people who had gathered there praised me and
My beauty and to allay my disturbed mind there floated
The mesmerizing music of Krishna which awakened in me
The latent feeling that I truly was fire-born, and it said:

'Do not forget that you are wonderfully unique in
This world and that you alone, are gifted with the
Power to create a new woman-world which would
Possess, through hard means, both physical and intellectual strength.'
Speaking so and calling me in affection 'Krishna', in both
The senses of the word meant that I was dark-hued, but
A friend to him; this is what the fascinating, floating
Music of the flute whispered to me! And this whispered advice
Stayed in my ear even after he left for Dwaraka!

One day there was in the palace a sudden heavy
Air of amazement, and all were terrified and in great
Confusion as an eunuch descended on them. Each was
Asking the other 'Who is this?', 'Who is this?' and there he
was: born a man he had, for twelve long years, lived the

Hard life of an ascetic wanting to be known as the greatest soldier
But had been turned into a half-woman by the Unknowable
And news was brought that this eunuch wanted a meeting with me!

When my own mother told me this, my curiosity trebled and
I waited in suspense but was all compassion for the
One who had lost her femininity and I waited to meet my
New sister and wondered within myself how she would look:
'How do her arms, with cuts from many weapons, appear?
How many wounds, and how did she live for so long in the
Forest, alone! Or did her father, because of some heinous crime
Committed, drove her away from home?
Why does she want to talk with me in private?'
I waited with bated breath for the arrival of the new-found
Elder sister and she came, stalking like a female cheetah!
She had spoken right. Although born a female she had,
While growing, had become a male:
Wearing a dhoti, bare chested, she came in and
Leaned the bow she was carrying against the wall and stood boldly;
Her eyes, large like red lotus and round her neck a garland of
White lotus flowers, and the moment he came in he patted my
Cheeks, and quickly pulled back his hand, but within me
because of his touch,
There was a tingling feeling of fraternity and as we were
Of the same height, he bent and kissed my forehead and said:

'Sister dear, in pleasure I thank you for your warm welcome.
I have struggled for years to have a meaningful life.
But, surely you have heard of the story of a donkey which, to
Keep the teasing criminals, wore the skin of a lion and likewise
A wolf wore the skin of a sheep and they both lost the
knowledge of their real selves.
In life, I was uninterested and prayed fervently to a Yaksha
Who came, and with a burning sword stabbed me and the pain
It caused, made me unconscious and when I regained consciousness
I, with a shock, became aware that my femininity of mind I
had not lost

But still was a man!
I became a man to fulfill the desire of my father, which was
To kill the man who had insulted my father, Drona, by name
And during the offering of sacrifice I lost my female form
As desired by my father.
This is a cruel world: Acharya Bhisma who destroyed my
Father's ego, and to get out of this tangled male egos,
I was made to don this strange form.
Ashamed of my broken form and to save his citizens from
Witnessing this ugly transformation, he, through royal edict,
Drove me out of his kingdom. Tell me, are we only symbols who
Are used to satisfy their anger and humiliation?'

One day King Drupada came and said:
'Come, dear daughter, we shall go and have darshan
Of Sri Krishna, and be blessed by him.
We go now to Dwaraka.'
Immediately I readied myself, collected flowers I know
He liked and made a garland out of them, and choosing
A green saree and blouse, stood before the mirror;
Not satisfied with myself, I chose another saree and
Another set of jewels and then called Nitambini and said:
'Oh, friend, how do I look? Is everything right?
I do not know what Krishna would like to see.
Which saree is right and what jewels, tell me
What I should wear.'
When she heard me speak this way and mention
Krishna, she held out her arms, embraced me and
Said: "Oh, princess, among the universally beautiful,
You are the most beautiful and he, the king of Mathura,
Is the most handsome. Why do you worry, then?
If Krishna is cloud-hued you are the one
Who shines bright like the dazzling twilight;
If Krishna is blue like the waters of the pool
You are like the lotus reflected in the clear water;
If he is like the pacific blue ocean, you are like the rich dark
Foam that covers it, of you two which is less in beauty?'

In this way, Nitambini continuing, in ways fascinating, described
The Dwarapayuga, and as she turned page by page the
History of those days, Krishna appeared and they heard the
auspicious sound
Of the conch, and both hurried to go and see Krishna and as
they hurried themselves,
Panchali saw that on her stainless white saree, at the back,
There was her rich thick dark hair flowing in ringlets.
And she wondered how she was going to plait it and make it
Presentable to her love, the King of Dwaraka, Krishna: then
Her friend Nilanjane came near her and said:
'The creator has sculpted you from a mine of beauty
Why would you need gold jewellery or silk saree? This
You can do without. And the saree you have on you will
Surely catch the mind of Krishna, and once he sees you he
Won't go back to Dwaraka. Now without anymore delay you
Go, have his darshan.'

What shall I say? Before I was ready, there was
News of Krishna arriving at Panchala city!
While there was serious discussion going on at the court of
Drupada, I hurried out to have the long-waited
Darshan of Krishna but did not have the courage to raise my head
And look him in the eyes. But before I could do it came
Floating the resonant voice of Krishna himself:
'Krishne! You are born with immense courage in order to
Put down the arrogance of the wicked; you are, like the
live volcano,
Born to protect righteousness and therefore I came to see you.
I wanted the meeting and I told Drupada,
And I, bound to preserve *dharma*, am here to mingle my
Strength with yours, and I see in you
The momentous forms of resolution great.'

The words thrilled Drupada and he said:
'That is why I named her Krishne and this is the flower
I place at your sacred feet. From the day I named her

I waited only to offer this gift to you. Accept her,
She is no ordinary being. She is fire-born and is a live
Flame, and therefore who else but you can protect Dwaraka.'

She bent her head down, folded her hands in reverence,
And stood lost in reverie and Krishna patting Drupada
Said: 'King Drupada, do not think she is a simple woman,
Hold her swayamvara and let the noblest and the best man
In all Aryavarta wed her. Do not give her away to a
Common man. Without giving room to any insult,
Look for the bravest of the brave who alone is fit to hold
Her hand. Think not of others.'

The king in surprise and, with much anxiety, said:
'Govinda! Tell me in the whole of Aryavarta is there a
Better groom anywhere? Our cousin is you. Who else but
You are fit to wed her? Yes. You are the greatest
Hero of our age, and you come as one without any name
And wed! That is the hero you are!'

Listening to these words, Krishna laughed and Drupada
In greater anxiety spoke:
'Who else but Krishna who will wed my Krishne?
Who else can be the lord of her heart? Oh, god.
Do not, as you did with the Gopis of Brindavan
Play with her feelings and break her heart.'

Krishna unperturbed said:
'The powers of Hari Hara Brahma and Indra have come together
And is born as the middle Pandava, Partha, who is my
Nephew, and he is younger to me by a year and belongs to my own
Clan and we are not different from one another: listen,
Yadu, son of Devayani, the daughter of Shukracharya,
Had a brother, Puru, who is the most senior among us all,
And from him were born the Pandavas, among whom is Partha,
Who is like a brother to me and is my soul-friend,
And we are two separate beings in body but truly are one,
And if Phalguna becomes your son-in-law, your fame will

Rise sky-high and he would be the one to fulfill your vow, too.'

Drupada hearing that Drona's own disciple was going to
Become his son-in-law was more than happy, felt greatly
Fulfilled in his heart and was sure that Partha would trample into
Mud the arrogance of Drona and that his vow of vengence
would be
Fully accomplished and that he could walk around again
With his self-esteem restored, and swaying in pleasure he
Said to himself: 'What if it is Partha? He is surely as heroic as
Krishna and he has the strength to defeat Drona and when I
Have Partha to my right and Krishna to my left
Who can stand up to me as an equal?'

As, Drupada sat dreaming of his soul-satisfying victory,
His daughter, without a deep understanding of the spring
Of love in her heart, was taken up with her own thought
And wondered what meaning her life really had for
Her ownself as she thought she was to become a dry piece of wood
To be offered as a sacrifice to satisfy some one else's ambitions.
Why live if someone determines your life for you?
From where did I come and what meaning is there for
My life, why live, and to achieve what?—knowing the
Flow of my thought Krishna spoke thus:

'Devi Draupadi, you have taken birth only to destroy
Your enemies, but before you think of achieving it
You have to defeat that tangled emotional problem that is
Within you. I am no enemy to your father, and to give up,
To sacrifice yourself in order to realize your father's
Dream is life's great objective—do not forget it.'
Listening to the words of Krishna I said to myself:
'Oh, Krishna, what work I perform is not really mine.
The fruit of that work, I do not know what it would be.
You are assigning me great tasks. I surrender to you;
You are on a chariot of idealism; I am its charioteer;
And yet within me are anger and desire; but
Since you have the power to steer all right I may access

Woman-power of an unusual kind.
Could I have the strength to rise from strength human
To strength divine? Would I have that power?
The garland of flowers round my neck is wet with my tears
And since I cannot put it round your neck,
Shall I leave it at your sacred feet?
My youth has been awash with my own tears,
And I received not pleasure in my young years,
And therefore wetting Krishna's feet with tear drops
I have to perforce place Partha, his friend, in my heart?
There isn't an alternative course and I have to
Fight in whosoever hand you place me.
You are the one who directs this universal play,
You have all the strings in your hand and since
Yours is the last word, do we have any freedom?
And I bid you goodbye.' Hearing it Krishna said:
'Ah, the mad rider who sits on the back of a mad horse
Called Krishna and keeps saying; "Krishna", "Krishna."
What rules or options are there, tell me? But this is true,
Whoever trusts me leads not an unworried life! Those
Who gave me their hearts, so many of them, how much
Have they suffered and wept! I am myself, a man
Who has sacrificed himself for the sake of a great purpose.
Whoever you trust, whoever you love, all that is to be
Dedicated to the wellness of the world. This is but the
Desire of the age of Dwapara. And you know its soul,
Therefore, respond to its urges, you, a goddess, have to
Destroy the tree of love that has begun to sprout
And in that act rests the safety of the age. We all are partners
In the victory and defeat of Partha, I have become a bonded
Slave to his intense affection but this, you remember:
The relationship between you and me is eternal, and subtle,
And is beyond the love of man and woman and the sacred
Thread which binds us can never be cut. This you
Understand, Devi' saying so the lord bid goodbye.

CANTO VI

WHO WILL STRING THE BOW OF MY SOUL?

For the wedding of his radiant daughter to go smoothly,
King Drupada took many vows and offered worship to gods at
Madhure, Rameshwaram, Kanchi, Palani, Guruvayur,
Kateel, and Bappanadu, Mookambika and Mangaladevi, and
Udupi, Murdeshwara, the Lord of Kadire and the lord of the
serpent gods
And offered to these gods savouries made of many kinds and
As maids-in-waiting waved softly fans made of yak tails
The shining Draupadi sat in a palanquin of silver and as the
people saw
This radiant-looking young lady they spoke among themselves;
'Is she the image of all that is beautiful and enchanting or
Is she the image which sprang from the ocean of milk when
It was churned?' and exclaiming in this manner, the men gathered at
The palace and gazed open-mouthed, and lapped up the
Moonlight she spread.

'No, I was not thrilled by the swayamvara organized,
On the contrary, I felt like a decorated sheep ready to be
Offered as sacrifice, and led towards the sacrificial fire;
Men in their pandering play of desire, as if in a gambling game,
Have made me their dice and are tossing me about whichever
Way they desire, and are caught in this deceitful game.
I do not know how this swayamvara will go and I do not
Know who is going to be my husband; it all looks like a
Farce directed by fate and am being made the sport of a

Male-dominated world which gazes at me with lustful
Eyes but makes a show of a test of male prowess: like
Small fish pushed into a pool, and then caught and cooked—
That is the way I feel. I know not whose servant
I am going to be!
In this game of frightening chess, I am here a captive
And I do not know whose lust I am to satisfy.
I am a deer caught in the net of my father's anger
Against someone but who will listen to my tale of sorrow?

Since my father knows the bravery and unmatched skill of Partha.
He has, with a double view, arranged this swayamvara for
He knows that only Arjuna can win, in this designed contest:
And therefore has erected this tall pillar at the top of
Which is a wheel with a fish in its spokes and which keeps
Rotating fast all the time and through the narrow hole the
Archer has to shoot the fish which can be seen only in the
trough of oil
Which reflects the fish and the archer looking at the reflected image
He has to bring it down and who else but Arjuna can do it!
Father has deliberately created this new, subtle and hard
Contest to get me trapped in the game of wedding.
And it is all to achieve his selfish objective!
What is it I can do? What new game is this? I have not
Even seen Partha and why is Krishna pushing me into this
Great whirlpool, and I am tossed about in its unstoppable currents.
But there was, in Panchala, in every nook and corner,
Big celebrations going on and the rich and the poor alike moved
Round in great glee and there were lit thousands and
thousands of lights
And the entire city plunged into a revelry of song and dance
And I silently watched it all thinking that it was all a play of
Destiny! Caught in the net woven by men with selfish ends
I said to myself
That if I was rather to wed this way I would choose total
celibacy.
In case you want to wed me, hit right the eye of the fish,

If you fail you are not fit; the bow has its own strength and is no
Toy and the achiever has to, with resolution, perform this task.
As many came, attempted and failed
To lift this weapon of goddess Durga herself!

Many kings arrived at the place of Drupada and, thinking of
The lotus-faced Draupadi, there was on the face of each a
Happy anticipatory smile!
And, there was Panchali sitting troubled, by my many
Anthills of worry, as there was no news or sign of the coming of
Phalguna, and she saw only a forest of darkness surrounding her
And wondered within herself:

'Helpless I am and am groping in this enveloping darkness;
Who else but Partha who can string the bow and hit the target?
Those who put their trust in Vasudeva's son are sure to
Suffer humiliation, the way the five Pandavas did! He who said
I shall protect the righteous, did he save them from going into
The forest and suffering awful disasters? In the broad field
Stand princes many who practise archery to win this swayamvara,
Who will come to my help? Arjuna I know not, would he be
Able, in the swayamvara court, to string the bow and the
Bow of my soul? I do not know. Why did the stealthy Krishna
Put me into this situation? Have I become a toy in his
playful hands?
The other day, the day Krishna came into my mind, he said
Partha is his own self, his own double and was equal unto him.
And I, bowled over and in absolute surrender, kept crying
'Krishna, Krishna!' Ah, my dear brother, won't you be able to
Stop this swayamvara? Who else can come to my aid, except you?'

In sorrow Drishtadyumna spoke, standing close to her:
'Dear Sister, how can I stop this swayamvara?
Our first cousins Duryodhana and his brothers, and Maghada,
Karna, Shakuni, Kritavarma, Satyaki, Shalya, Shishupala,
And numerous great heroes have assembled here and the
Palace guest house is overflowing with these and their retinue;
Again, Bhishma, our teacher Drona, Kripacharya and Balaram too

Are here along with kings of Anga, Vanga, Kalinga, Chola,
Pandya, Kambhoja and Gandharva and with them have come
Great scholars and poets, and if we insult them by calling off
The swayamvara, it would be an insult to our own country,
Panchala; and, remember if we attempt anything like, this,
The kings assembled here would wage a terrible war against us
And our father Drupada would surely in humiliation will commit suicide,
No, we do not have an option. Let the swayamvara take place,
Bow to time, comfort yourself and be a goddess to
Protect all of us, and be a light unto us all.'
'I do not know what you are saying. I do not want to

Get married but I shall stand here and see who will observe
The rules of swayamvara; and whether it will be a war
Or an event without the wedding, I shall see,' with those
Words she became silent, the stream of silence went dry!
'I shall live the life of an ascetic, Brindavan has disturbed

The dream of my heart, and waves of emotion fill my
Eyes with tears, see the way they flow down my dimpled cheeks!'
The brother with a heavy heart tried to comfort her:
'Krishne, come, father is waiting and Krishna is about to arrive.
And we have to welcome him, who is partner in our sorrow and happiness'

I, checking my tears, said: 'Ah! Who am I? How do I face
Him? Me, the unfortunate one! I am a tragic heroine
Who is to wed his dear friend. No, forgive me, I can't come.'

As tears trickled down her cheeks, there appeared, before her
The wonderful, divine figure of Sri Krishna:
On his forehead the tilaka of musk and in his hand the flute;
Dressed he was in fine, orange-yellow silk and on his chest shone
The kausthuba diamond and his body in sea-blue hue dazzled
Everyone; I and the liquid compassion of his eyes drove away all
That had clouded my mind and heart as he, in speech

Soft and sweet, addressed me, and mesmerized I stood:

'Ah, you innocent one, your face, because of heavy anxiety,
Has become more beautiful. The news of the passing away of the
Five Pandavas, I don't know if this is true or false, but seeing
You, all my sorrow has gone away from me.' 'But I said
To myself this is a strange way of appearing to be happy?'

Looking at me straight, Vasudeva said: 'The moment I saw
You, I knew the Pandavas were alive. They aren't fools to
Get burnt in the palace of wax. If they did, I would have been a
Bigger fool. If I am not a fool, how could they be dead?'
Hearing him I knew that Arjuna would come and save me,
More so as Krishna himself said he had prayed to goddess Parvati.
The day of the fiery test has arrived and therefore
Waking up early I had my bath and with my maids
Went to the golden temple of Parvati, unadorned as
I was, I left my hair free on my back and prayed to the
Goddess who shone in the light of lighted lamps, and in
Silence I prayed:

'Oh, Goddess, you who entered sacrificial fire to save the
Honour of your husband, your way is to me, too, the
Honoured way. I appeared from out of the womb of fire,
And if I see dishonour attending on those I admire,
Would there be any sense in my being alive? My father
Is ready to accept him as his son-in-law whoever wins this
Test, but should I do it too? If there is righteousness in the
World, and if I have ever worshipped you devoutly,
Bless me, ah! I see a flower falling my way, from your right shoulder,
And that to me is a sign of good omen. True, within me
Remained total emptiness!
Whose wife and whose daughter-in-law am I going to be?
What has destiny kept in store for me? Would all my
Wishes go unfulfilled? Whom shall I blame and whom
Shall I remember?—At that point came my brother,
Lovingly patted me on my head, drew me to his chest,
And in maternal tones said:

"I hear that by vile means deceiving the Pandavas,
The Kauravas drove them away into Varanavata, this
News reached me just now." Hearing it I became anxious and
Asked: "Why, what has happened at Hastiravati? Tell me."
And he said, "What shouldn't have happened has happened.
Deceived by the Kauravas, the Pandavas, along with Kunti,
Got burned to ashes in the wax palace that had been built
For them and the great lamp of righteousness is now put out."
Hearing this terrible news I feel as if the main pillar
Of the great building erected for swayamvara had collapsed and
That Krishna had deceived me by placing before my mind's
Eye an image of Arjuna and had me as the sacrificial lamb at
The game of self-centred politics.'

No, Arjuna will come, he is sure to come, miss he
Won't and as I listened to the story of the
swayamvara of Rama and Sita in my mind's mind
I felt that she was my ideal of womanhood but then,
Arose the doubt: Could I be as fortunate as she was?
Where is she who is goddess-like and who was the chosen
Wife of the best of men, and what am I?
What is it I can offer to Sri Krishna, except the great
Sadness I feel. Who else is there to save Yagnaseni?
Tears flowed down my face, and brimming over they joined
The compassionate, the all-accepting ocean of Sri Krishna.

CANTO VII

WHO ELSE BUT SAVYASAACHI?

Reaching the centre of the swayamvara hall, Dristadyumna,
In a resonant voice, resembling thunder, addressed the gathering of princes;
'Please listen, those brave, heroic ones who looking into the trough of oil
On the ground, hit the mirrored fish circling above at the mast,
Will be chosen to wed my sister, Draupadi,' saying so
Patted softly on the head of his sister and told her:
'Krishne, look, there you see the Kaurava and Dushyasana,
Durmukha, Yuyutsu, Satyaki, Karna, Shakuni and
Akrura, Virata, Shalya, Balarama and kings of many
States,' he stopped for a second and with his index finger
Pointed out, 'See, Krishna is there, the greatest of the
Yadavas, who is like a wild elephant to the plantain grove and to
The wicked and he, the great hero that he is, he it is
Who destroyed Kamsa and who is again the one who is
Home to all the virtue and goodness in the world, and
Handsomeness itself.' The moment I heard the words
I swam in a pool of devout devotion and silently greeted him
With folded hands. But Dristadyumna continued:
'To wed you, they have come in great eagerness and are
Rearing to hit the rotating fish in the eye and among these
Are brave ones who are pastmasters in archery and are from
Noble houses, and there you see princes whose values and good looks
Outshine the sun himself and here the master of ceremonies

Has got out the great bow and the quiver, and the rotating fish,
In the mechanical contrivance, shines bright and whoever hits the
Target, he will wed you,' and as he spoke these words, the
royal helpers brought
The great and sacred bow and placed beside it sharp arrows, and
Then the weapon was offered worship: they lit lamps and
Decorated it with flowers and waved aarati and then the auspicious
Musical instruments including the conch and the drum and
the flute
Were played and there the bow lay inviting the contenders
for the test.

They, the contestants, tried to lift the bow but they could not even
Raise it from the ground and in their attempts
They broke their bracelets, and the pearl garlands they wore
Got torn and the beads spilled over the carpet, and
The women seeing the futile exercise clapped and laughed;
The princes, crestfallen, slowly returned to their seats
Heavily sighing; and the crowd with bated breath waited.

There was an air of rustle and bustle and with it
Entered the King of Maghada, a big wrestler he was;
He came, stood near the bow, loosened the bracelet on the wrist,
Bent down to lift the bow and seeing him attempting,
The crowd wondered whether the old man would win the
World's great beauty; and Draupadi's maids asked themselves
Whether Draupadi would say yes or no and as this was going on
The King of Maghada bent forward, bit his lips and with all his
Might he tried to lift it but no he could not even nudge the bow,
And the effort made him sweat heavily, and his breathing became
Hoarse but without giving up he tried once more and lifted
the bow,
It came chest-high but he failed again and the
Laughter of the womenfolk filled the hall and the king in anger and
Frustration gave up the attempt, covered his face with his
shoulder cloth
And walked away.

Seeing this Shishupala became wild with anger and saying
'Ah! Did this contrivance defeat the heroic Maghada? I shall
Now go, hold the laughing Panchala princess by
The hair of her head and win the contest' and he ran to the bow,
Held the bow-string and attempted to lift it but he returned
Humiliated as the womenfolk saw his vain attempt.
The next moment King Shalya in great anger said:
'This King of Panchala, Draupada, is wicked and has crookedly
Designed this test only to humiliate kings and princes,
And I shall not allow this to go on and I shall show how,'
With these words he moved towards the bow, did a few
Exercises and grabbing the bow, and holding it tight as
Adishesha did the Mandara mountain, he tried to string it but
Then fell face up, displaying his bloated belly; his clothes
Got muddied and then said that this was a trick of Drupada to
Humiliate all of them and strode away and then the onlookers
Wondered who could pass the test and wed the princess?

It was now the turn of Suyodhana, the Kaurava chief, who got up
And treaded the earth like an angry lion, and his fuming anger
Made the earth shake, and all thought he would succeed.
The Kaurava in confidence great lifted the bow and strung it
But the next moment under its weight he fell down, and
the crowd cried out in horror.
The same moment Karna ran in to help his
Dear friend and looked askance at Draupadi in flooding anger
And announced that 'he would emerge victorious in the contest,
Win Draupadi and gift her to his benefactor, Duryodhana.'
Resolutely he rushed forward, and the throat of Drishtadymna
and Drupada went dry,
And they stood still, struck as if by a bolt from the blue,
And Draupadi, surrendering herself to the compassionate Krishna,
Watched it all, and was still, and Karna lifted the bow, strung it
and said: 'You, woman, watch, I shall hit the eye of the fish,
And what if my friend has failed, I, his faithful follower
Who has eaten his salt, will win you, and drag you by the hair of

Your head and will gift you to him, and from then on
You will be his call girl, getting on to his bed whenever
he orders you to!'
And with those stinging words he, like a live volcano or
Like the fire in the womb of the ocean which drinks up all the
Water or as if the three great trinity, the creator, the destroyer
and the restorer,
Incarnated all in his own self, he stood ready to hit the target,
Then, the enemy of demons, Sri Krishna, sprang to his feet
And in a thundering voice said: 'Hey, you stop this
Childish prattle. It does no credit to you, and of winning the
Lady and offering her to your friend again is shameful;
She is not a thing to be bought and gifted, she is no merchandise!
This is not a game of dice. It is a swayamvara and if you
In a fit of loyalty try to touch the end of her saree, I shall
Not let you live.'
'Hearing these words Karna and the other
Kings sat down in disappointment and frustration deep, but then
Rose Balabhadra, Krishna's brother, and shouted: 'Hey, is it
Possible to put up with the arrogance of this cocky Panchala King?
What humiliation! What insolence! I shall destroy these haughty
Kshatriyas and breaking this artificial bow I shall drag
The daughter of Drupada by her forelocks.' As he moved
towards the bow.
Krishna, the enemy of the wicked, pulled him back by his
hand and said:
'What is this? Where are you going? Why this impatience?
Kunti is your aunt, her sons are your nephews and their wife
Is sister to you. Don't you see this?' Balarama with a finger
On his nose said: 'Krishna, what are you saying? Where are the
Pandavas? What do we know of them? Where are they and what is
This Panchali to them? They got burnt alive in the wax palace!
Please, keep quiet. Don't stop me from teaching this arrogant
Drupada a lesson.
Don't egg him on to go with this deceptive game.'
Krishna smiling said: 'I do not know but Drupada for sure knows

That Pandu's sons alone would wed his daughter and therefore
Thought of this mechanical contrivance but this I swear
And on the name of Vasudeva and Devaki.'
The weilder of the plough, Balarama, said: 'Aha! What is this
I hear! Will the dead ones be back but if they do, it is good.
Let them be back and rule the earth,' and sat down in a huff.

Drupada, however, was lost in a sea of worries and he
Said to himself: 'I do not see anyone who would be equal
Or good enough in bravery or skill or archery to wed my
Daughter. May be I shouldn't have pushed her into this kind of a
Contest. For whose happiness? In my act, an indiscriminate,
A plaything I have made her and somebody plays with her!'
As he sat thinking so, Drushtadyamma stood up and said
'Gentlemen, listen, there is none here who could win this contest,
Kings and princes have tasted only defeat. If there is anyone
Else who would want to compete in this test he is welcome
And of course my sister will wed him, this I promise.'

Royal suitors got wild and gnashed their teeth crestfallen,
But those from a group of Brahmins whispered among themselves;
'Why should we worry about the lotus-eyed beauty! Who are
We and what are we to them! We need but adequate gifts of
Money, good and tasty food. The Kshatriyas are good fighters.
We are good with use of words and at scholarly discussions of
Principles of abstract philosophy and analysis of abstruse thought,
Skilled we are in music and in composition of poetry but we
Rush not into this contest and we know not who will win the jewel of a lady!'

Drupada and Drushtadyumna sat depressed but
Krishna looked at the crowd of Brahmins and with his index finger
Gave the sign and from that part of the hall emerged a form
Brahmnical, wearing a dhoti and making right its pleats, came
Forward with a visage serious and impressive and looked at
The gathering as the crowned kings and princes jeered at
Him in irony and fun and said: 'Ho! Brahmin master! What

Are you looking at or and, thinking, in what direction?
Are you looking for free food?
You too would want to wed Yagnaseni; Ho! Ho!'
And, the crowd of Brahmins went near the one who had
stood up, saying,
'If you want to get married, tell us, we shall look for a
Bride proper for you and chant the right mantras and get
You wedded. But do not here attempt to lift the bow and
Put us all to shame. And you yourself will fall into a deep pit
Of depression and dejection.' The Brahmin, however, said:

'Please have some patience. Do not rush into a hasty decision
And then burn yourselves in the fire of repentence.
Bless me, please, and with your blessing maybe I can
Hit the fish in the eye and wed the lady. Why come in the way?'

Then the Brahmins spoke: 'No, to get into space reserved for
Them traditionally, you should not barge in; this does not
Bring us a fair name, rather it spoils ours.' As this
Went on, some tried to stop him, some encouraged him, and some
Said he was right in appropriation of their space and pushed him
Towards the bow and then the Brahmin, with the sacred
thread on his shoulder
And the caste mark, namam, on his forehead and a small
bundle of
Kusha grass in his arms, stepped forward, tied his dhoti
Tightly around his waist and in obvious nonchalance came near
The dias; and the ladies around Draupadi jeered and said:
'Ah! Come, you the tufted handsome one, you with the Kusha grass,
Come, deer-skin wearing cupid, come, wed Draupadi, look
Draupadi is shy, and come. And, you Draupadi,
See how shameless men become with lust.'

Panchali simply stood with downcast looks and then Krishna
Called to his brother, Balarama, and said, 'Ah, brother,
Look, the middle Pandava is come in the form of a Brahmin.'
And he in surprise stood up and said, 'Ah, how magical!
The one burnt alive in the wax house is now risen

From the ashes,' and stared at the Brahmin in wonder:
The Brahmin, tall, with arms touching the knee and the face
Beautiful and peaceful, and the eyes bright and dazzling, he
Looked as if he was incarnate with a new seed of life and then
Sprung in the barren land of hope of Drupadu a new spring;
In silence, he reverently saluted Acharya Bhisma and his teacher
Drona and Kripa and Krishna, the King of Yadavas and then
Ganesha and lords of the eight directions of the earth and then
Bowed to the bow and remembering the sacred feet of Narayana,
Turned towards Krishne and he said to himself
'Cloud-hued, Krishne,
You represent Durga, you are the symbol of my sadhana, I need
Your goodwill and best wishes' Krishna observing it all said
'This is true humility. This seeming Brahmin, has done his culture
Proud and has rightly honoured the womankind without
thought of caste or creed
And he knows within himself that a woman is born with
Discrimination and wisdom, and those who laugh at the
Brahmin, what do they know of Indian culture?'
Looking at the luminous face of the young Brahmin, within
Me sprouted the germ of admiration but then I wondered why
Krishna was so kind and solicitious about him but my
thought came
To a stop as ear-splitting noise of clapping hands of the gathering
Struck my ears.

The young man came, undid the bundle of arrows tied together,
And ah! What skill did we see! His deft hands
Lifted the bow and with aim unerring he shot the eye of
The rotating fish above and the next moment the gathering
Went mad with unexpected joy and shouted and
Clapped their hands and said:
'Ah! He is truly a Kodandapani, Sri Rama himself or he is
Tripurari, Lord Shiva himself, that is for certain and to
Which city is the lotus-faced lady going to go, and shall
We be fed?' with these words the Brahmins danced in glee.

At the other end, the group of ladies, with fingers on their
Noses were lost in a sea of silence and were in shock and surprise
But she felt she was helpless and although she knew she could
Wed none but Partha, still lost she was in confusion and
Told Drushtadyumna how she ever could marry this stranger.
And he in answer said: 'You are born to uphold rightenousness,
And to that righteousness you sacrifice yourself. The way
Sri Rama went into wildnerness to honour his father's words
You too have to honour father's word. He who protects *dharma*,
Dharma, righteousness, itself protects him. Think this Brahmin
As equal to Partha.' She, caught, in a dilemma, said:
'I have already given my heart to Partha, and now how do
I wed this man? Who else but a brother can save me?
Oh, Krishna I see you everywhere, tell me, should I
Wed this Brahmin?' Krishna smiled and the smile cleansed me,
The way the west wind drives away the dark clouds, and said:
'Krishne, raise your head and see him and, recall
What I had told you; I knew he would come seeking you.
Listen to me and without a second thought put the garland
Round his neck, you have got him whom you wanted.'
Yes, true, he is a spitting image of Sri Krishna, he is, of course,
Partha, who else could he be? It is his own splendour, his own gait,
His own handsome features and therefore why delay, thinking, so
I collected the garland, and the gathered priests, in resonant voice
Recited auspicious mantras and people felt happy and
contented, but
The princes and kings reluctant to accept defeat readied to
Assault the Brahmin, and my maids and royal guards
surrounded me.
And I, shyly, stepped forward and lightly perspiring and
Setting right the pallu of my saree went near him and
Put the garland around him who gracefully bent his head
And then the others, defeated ones in a group came forward
To take me away by force but at that instant a big,
Majestically built person uprooted a tree nearby and with its
stem in hand,

He drove them off. Duryodhana and others gnashing
Their teeth said: 'Ah! See, how this Panchala King
Has insulted us. He allows his daughter to wed a Brahmin!
Isn't this an insult to men? We should together teach a
Lesson to the arrogant Drupada and this upstart Brahmin.
Come we shall join our forces and capture the city.'

The assembly broke up and men and women ran helter-skelter,
The Brahmins took to their feet but the Brahmin
Getting off the dais said: 'Don't be scared. Get me
A bow and sharp arrows and I shall take care of all of you.'
Even before he had stopped talking, arrows in numbers flew from
His bow and men fell in a heap, one after another,
And blood flowed like the monsoon rains and there were
Everywhere cries and groans, and another, along with Partha,
With the stump of a tree in hand, began pounding the soldiers
Who had accompanied the suitors and then, the King of Madra,
Stepped forward and said that it was beneath them to fight
With Brahmins and that they should, collectively, attack Panchala
And wreck vengence on him, and he also said that
Fighting Brahmins could bring bad luck and inauspicious days
for them
And with that they all went back to Hastinapura.

CANTO VIII

SHARE EQUALLY WHAT PROVIDENCE HAS GIVEN YOU

The celibate Brahmin spoke to his four brothers:
'Without the blessings of Mother at Ekachakra Nagar, how
Can the ritual of wedding be gone through, no, this
Won't do at all.'
Listening to this, Drupada and Dristadyumna
Got five chariots ready but the Brahmin continued:
'We live by begging, why do we need these chariots? And
Such luxury is prohibited to us and Krishna knows it all,
We shall walk our way, although this is new and tiring to
The princess but it is the duty of the wife to accept the way
We live, and to us this is nothing strange as we are used to
Walking in the forests.' Dristadyumna got wild and said:
'Without palanquin, how will she go? Her feet walk
On soft carpeted floors! How will they walk on roads that
Are thorny and full of sharp stones? No, it won't do!'

I then stopped my brother and his remonstrations, and said:
'Brother, it is the duty of the wedded wife to go with the
Husband as co-traveller. Have you forgotten the immortal story of
Sri Rama and Sita? In righteous fashion, for fourteen long
Years they walked the rugged path in the forest, and
Upheld *dharma*. And to preserve and sustain *dharma*
I shall not fear entering into the fire, for in *dharma*
Rests the well-being of all. Do send me with him, in love.'

All, for a moment, were silent and tears flowed down their

Cheeks and the deep-rooted tree of ambition in Drupada
All of a sudden fell and turned to dust and ashes!
The fact of a celibate Brahmin becoming his son-in-law
Wrung his heart and although his hot sighs burnt the Panchala princess
She, bowed before her father and pleading softly said,
'Father, why feel disappointed? Your son-in-law is the strongest
In the whole of Aryavarta and therefore don't feel depressed
Your blessings alone will see me through life. Your affection is,
My strength, bless me, I shall walk the path of virtuous fame.'

Then flowed hot, scalding tears of deep repentance
Which burnt up his heart, and repining he told himself that
Unfortunate it was to forget the middle Pandava and to have
Given his daughter to a poor celibate Brahmin, that it
Was he who had created all this suffering for his daughter.

I followed the brothers walking and as I stepped out
With them I wondered: 'How will my mother-in-law receive me'
When she sees me decked with all this gold and diamond
Jewellery? Will she ask me uncomfortable questions?' Then
Putting a stop to such thoughts I told myself: 'If the
Mind is firm, the will strong, it can pound to powder huge
Strong forts,' and with quick determination I removed the jewellery
And discarded the silks I wore and decided, that
With resolution strong, I would earn respect due to me,
By own merit and not because I was born a princess
And that I would stand against the male world of authority
And prove my strength as an individual like any male.
But then decided to retain but only bangles and the
Nose stud as they were symbols of auspiciousness, and
Changed into a simple white saree and wore flowers in my hair.
And, walked in easy strides but became aware that he who had
Won me was throwing stealthy glances at me and that
Filled me with pride and, again, suddenly, with a rush,
Waves of affection and love sprang with me coupled with
The satisfaction of having been won by a man virtuous and

That it mattered not whether he was rich, for he was, I knew
Brave and strong. As I walked, my soft, tender feet began to bleed
And the celibate Brahmin said:
'Lady, are you tired? I am sorry for you. I shouldn't
Have jumped into this task and married a princess. What
Has happened has baffled me too. We came looking for a kingly feast
And leaped on to this adventure. No, why this swayamvara?
Why win a contest? No, these are not for us. Ill-matched we are,
And all this is a game only of fate.'

Surprised I was by his talk and asked him not to
Prattle like children, but he continued: 'Who can
Come in the way of gods and who can stop the chariot of
Destiny? It is best if one accepts whatever happens.'
Listening to him I walked on and as I did so
I stumbled, and was about to fall. Then the long-armed
Handsome one bent and held me and spoke in words soft:
'Devi Krishne, except at the moment of wedding, when I held your
Hand, I have not touched you, for the wedding rituals we have to wait
Till we receive the blessings of mother. Do not get me wrong.
I depend on you. The citizens of Panchala must have suffered
Much for what has happened!' With those
Words we walked together and in a tone of seriousness he asked:

'If, by Krishna's blessings, the Pandavas survive and the middle
Pandava comes and asks for your hand would you wed him?'

'You are my husband and we walk the world together,' I said and
When talking this way, we reached Ekachakra Nagara, he tapped on
The door of their house and called out: 'Oh, mother,
See, we, the five brothers are back victorious' and the eldest
Said, 'With us we have brought a divine, invaluable fruit,
Open the door, you'll see what we have brought with us.'

I stood with my head bent and shy as I listened to the affectionate

Words of the eldest, then came from within the voice of the
Mother: 'Ah, children, happy I am to listen to your news.
And what divine fruit you have brought with you, lovingly
Share it equally, all of you, god will bless you!'

The eldest in consternation and anguish and confusion
Was struck dumb and the others in oppressive silence
Stayed still; I, caught in the fire of shame, pulled aside my veil,
And as the door opened the mother, an incarnation of
Love and compassion, looking like goddess Annapurna herself,
Stepped out and in great surprise and bewilderment, stood
And as I, reverently touched her feet, she, haltingly spoke:
'Ah, What did I say? Thinking they had brought the usual
Provision, I spoke. But now I see a princess who is a mine
of beauty!
What a miracle!'
'You have spoken the truth, mother,' said the eldest. She is no
Common woman. She is the fire-god's daughter and the
daughter of King Drupada;
And your third son, Partha won her at the swayamvara and
To get him wed with your blessings we have come here, but
Drupada
Does not know who we really are,' and these words mystified
her more and
She said to herself: 'Oh, god, pushed I am into a pit of deep grief;
I am helpless now but what if my words go false? Won't
I be untruthful! And if what I have said is not obeyed, they
Disobey *dharma*; if they obey, all the five will have to wed
The lady, and that would be more strange!

To uphold *dharma*.
Should the honour of Draupadi be sacrificed, and make her
Wedded life a hell? How could I ever push her into an
Inferno! Who, who will save me from this predicament?
Isn't death preferable to this torture?' As she in pain
Sat worrying, the eldest in transparent humility said:
'Mother! Our greatest ideal is to faithfully live by whatever you

Say and that for us is the ultimate *dharma*. That Draupadi
Should become the bride for all the five of us is an event most
Wondrous in the world and it can't be stalled!'
My husband in distress great went into silence,
But within me rose a spirit rebellious and asked myself
'Can life be quartered this way or is destiny a carry-on
Eating vulture or is it the fall of *dharma* itself and is there
None to ask for my opinion? Have I become a goat chosen
For a sacrifice? Or has the spring of culture in India
Gone dry? As per the rules of swayamvara, I put the garland
Around the neck of one who had won me, but then how do
I become the wife of five? Why accept them as husbands?
This is injustice and alien to the culture of Bharata.'
I looked at the face of the eldest and there was in his eyes
The burning desire of lust and I wondered, 'Is this the eldest
Who will not stand up against injustice?'
Who will feel, for fate?
Maybe mother, for maternal heart knows the feelings
of the heart.
Then arrived Vedavyasa and he spoke:

'I have known Krishne, the intelligent and discriminating one
Who knows the essence of Vedas and Upanishads and she is
The one who in difficulties great stands firm and wisely.
None can impose their decision on her, this is true.'
Listening, I wondered: How is it that Vyasa, whom I know in
my soul,
Has come here? What relation is he to the celibate Brahmins?
is he come to save me from this terrible dilemma or is he
Making me responsible to make the words of the mother
come, true?
Or is my wedding a golden sword meant to destroy my life?

Guessing the state of my confused mind, Vyasa remained silent
And the mother with reverence placed before him the situation
In which she had found herself: 'Revered Vyasa. Please, listen:
We are caught in perplexity and you have come as saviour.

These sons of mine did not, when they came, tell me that they
Had come with Draupadi and if they had, this would not have
Happened. Please see that I keep my word and that the virtue of
A woman remains unblemished.'

When she spoke this way, I got up in searing anger and
Said: 'Oh, mother! Why this play acting? Why say share equally
What the third has won? Why add to it the question of
breaking the word given?
Hardly there is any transparency here. And it is
Obvious there is some conspiracy, some hanky-panky. Seeing
My beauty, and to capture it, they have laid this trap. And
These five celibate Brahmins are no real Brahmins. Their
Mother has the looks of a queen, and in their eyes the
lustre of kingship.
And Vyasa, seer has also arrived! Who will clear this conundrum?'

Then spoke Vyasa: 'Have you forgotten the message I gave
That the five had come for swayamvara and that only the
Middle Pandava could pass this test of archery? In
Bharat, women are free to choose their spouses and now
This Himalayan problem can be solved by Panchali alone.
She is your conscience keeper. If you all stay together you
Will progress or all of you will be washed away in the deluge that
Will follow, and there won't be a road for escape!' Saying so
Vyasa disappeared, and all stood dumb struck.

To what should I sacrifice myself, and to whom? Is it to
Keep the promise of the mother? And how about my virtue?
Is it
Not unfair to push me into a sea of unfaithfulness?
I cried within myself, silently and then prayed:
'Govinda, I, as a friend, trusted you, surrendered
My life to you thinking you to be the wisest and the most
Compassionate. These five celibates with their mother
Are cunningly making me a sacrificed lamb. Now, where are
You?' Crying out, I stood at the door, and at that instant
Appeared near the door Krishna and Balarama and they both

Reverently touched the feet of Kunti, the mother of the five brothers,
And she, in great relief, said: 'Govinda, like a real
Friend and kinsman you have come to relieve us of this
Excruciatingly painful moment and we are grateful.'
Krishna innocently said: 'Why? Why are you worried and
What about?'. And, I stood facing him straight and spoke:
'Tell me, you were there on the day of swayamvara. The
Third of these brothers, won me, took me home
And the mother asks the sons to share the prize equally. Now
Do I obey her words or do I live in the path of accepted virtue?
And what has happened is against all familial norms,
And my right to freedom has been jeopardized. Tell me,
You, the all-knowing, what answer you want me to make
In total surrender to you, I ask this question.'

'Panchali, the five brave men are the five Pandavas, and
This lady is their mother, Kunti, and the man who won you
Is Arjuna in the form of a Brahmin and all the five are
Unequalled in bravery, and the five are really one and
The one is a conglomerate of the five! And, the words of
Kunti never have gone false, and do not forget that the
Duty of upholding of dharma is on Yudhisthira. If the five
Stay together, the violence and the injustice caused by Kauravas
Can be torn down and it will do the world immense good,
And this is the reason why Yudhisthira spoke the way he did,
Kunti's words are only a foretelling of the future,
You are the maker of a new epoch. Save the unity of the
Pandavas, you alone can do it. This is the truth.'
'The ultimate fiery test for me. I, who swam in an ocean of
Happiness because I wedded the bravest of the brave now
I hear I have to wed the brothers too! And, to keep them
United! And, for the cause, the cause of familial, national unity—
Am I to be sacrificed for an ideal? Does disunity spell
The destruction of *dharma*?' As the conflict raged within me
There arose a feeling, which said I was not to
Make the words of Kunti untrue. It is my duty too to

Preserve *dharma*, to achieve which I have to sacrifice myself.
What if it injures me? Protection of the nation, of its unity,
Is the greatest of my *karma* and I, sacrificing myself, shall
Be born again another Yagnaseni, and seek new meaning to
My life. To re-establish *dharma*, and to keep burning the fire
Of sacrificed fire, I shall offer myself the sacrifice and
See that the path of righteousness triumphs.

'I shall be wife to the five Pandavas, I shall bow to the dictates of
The law which upholds *dharma* and I shall accept the advice of
Krishna,' and when I said so, Kunti, in affection hugged me and
Said, 'Your stand all the world will praise, and as the
True wife of these five, you will be the light of the world!'

CANTO IX

YAGNASENI HAS CROSSED THE FRONTIER OF THE EPOCH

That night we spent sleeping in a hut of the Potters' Colony
And the mother rested on a bed of dry grass and the five
With their heads touching her feet spent the night and
I made their feet my pillow and it looked as if the five elements
In harmony with nature were present together, but then
the question rose:
Is this the *dharma* for the women of Dwapara yuga?

Kunti, aware that I spent the night sighing and weeping, said:
'Yes, I know. During the swayamvara, you, in a world of
sweet dreams.
Fed, on delicacies, but these are days different and they are painful.
And all this is but the irony of the play of time. You know
I wedded the Prince of Hastinavati, Pandu, but he, a prey to a
Curse, was not to be blessed with children, and what could I do?
I do not blame destiny but my desires were yet unfulfilled,
I patiently waited on him yet repined for there was
None to protect the empire. Managing some contentment I lived,
And derived some satisfaction by knowing that we were
The progeny of Vyasa, and later through the blessings of a
Sage I became a mother. Receiving a boon from Durvasa,
Dharmaraja and Bhima, of a wolf's waist, and Partha were
born to me; and
Madri was blessed with the birth of twins, Nakula and Sahadeva,
And Gandhari similarly became mother to a hundred and

One children, including Suyodhana and the birth of all, had the
Sanctions of our wedded spouses. All through my life
I have suffered much humiliation and injustice but myself
Did nothing wrong, and the situation you are caught in
I understand but *dharma* surely will protect and stand by
You. Please listen, the five sons are vastly different from
One another, and they go to extremes but in the history
Of Bharat they have to live together in this Dwapara yuga
And this unity they have to have. There is no alternative to it.
You alone can have them bound with the chain of unity,
Otherwise all will fight one another and the duty of preserving
Dharma will go unfulfilled, and to avoid which all the five
Will have to stay together and fight and keep the unity of the
Nation. You, Yagnaseni, you too will find fulfillment in aiding
Them although it forces you to transform yourself into a stone-
Hearted woman. Remember you are the one who is going to put
The Kuru dynasty on foundation firm and proper.'

When mother Kunti spoke this way, my soul went dry as dust,
And I understood their plan which forced me to accept all
The five as husbands and to give myself away to men other
than my husband
To only to breed men bold and courageous and
This custom of selling myself to others to preserve the cursed
Kuru dynasty
This is how I was to become a brazier, offering myself as oblation
to keep the five together for their own selfish ends?
Drupada was also surprised to hear that all night they discussed
The art of taming elephants and losses and of running a nation,
Of managing the fiscal policy—sure it made me think that these
Five were no celibate Brahmins but the Pandavas themselves.
The King, therefore, made all necessary preparations for a
Kshatriya wedding and
The five dressed in finest silk *dhotis* and wearing shining jewels,
And pleasantly perfumed came out and Kunti greeted them at the
Wedding dais and then asked the King to have ready five
Places for the wedding-ritual, and the King in shock asked:

'Has the third one chosen to marry four maidens? I know not
Where the other five are!' Kunti softly whispered in his ears
'The daughter has agreed to become the wedded wife of all
The five brothers, and in no contradiction to *dharma*.' Hearing it
Drupada was most surprised, and in bewilderment asked:
'What am I hearing? Did I hear it right? Did you see
It being said? This is preposterous shamelessness! And has
No approval of the world nor of the Shastras of the land.
If the Pandavas are people virtuous, would they really shame
The world of women?'
Unprovoked Dharmaraja said with composure:
'Not possessed by lust nor ruled by our crude senses and never
Transgressing what is *dharma*, on the word and wishes of our
great mother,
And responding to the challenges of our time and intent
on walking,
The road to unity and dharma we have allowed ourselves to
be united.
By the great goddess Durga herself, who is your daughter, and she
Thinking of the five of us as her wedded spouses, will help us
perform our duties, of protecting righteousness in this world.'

Drupada in confusion stood trembling and spoke stammeringly:
'The world has accepted the custom of one man marrying
many but
Five husbands marrying a single woman is unheard of! Oh!
Shiva! Shiva! Kunti you are a lady, tell me, would you accept
This which is against the accepted practice of our known world?
A wife with five husbands surely is against *dharma*, is it not?'
Then spoke Dharmaraya: 'Consider this: to obey the words
Of the elders is one's duty. Did not Parashuram behead his own
Mother because his father asked him to? We grew up without a
Father, and, to us, our mother is our goddess and to listen to
her words
Is *dharma* and for the five of us to wed Krishne is action righteous.'
Drushadyumna in much distress said: 'If what the elders say
Is unjust, it is unjust to obey it, it makes no logic;

And how can one justify what is against logic and *dharma*?'
Without losing his patience, Dharmaja spoke: 'Listen,
In the whole of Aryavarta, Kunti is the wisest and is well-versed
In *dharma* and therefore for the five to wed one is surely not
Adharmic, in our epoch, we have to go with it.' Then,
Krishna Dwaipavana
Aware of the complexities of *dharma* said: 'Oh, King, listen:
Can one without a thread make a garland of flowers or beads, and
Offer it the lord? If *dharma* is to be preserved, all the five
Pandavas, like the flowers or the beads, have to be together,
and this is unavoidable.
Your daughter is beautiful and is virtuous and
The way she can make garlands out of beads and flowers, she
Can make these five a single entity and this the epoch itself
Demands and do not try to say no to it.
Forget not the wondrous way in which the daughter of the
fire took birth
Here to make the pages of history glow and you desired to
Have Arjuna as your son-in-law to avenge the wrong done to
Drona and now to speak of what is right etcetera you will
Only weaken the movement of the chariot, of *dharma*:
Yagnaseni has crossed the frontier of the age.

The mountain of *dharma* melted and flowed and flooded
The world and I, as by becoming a piece of string, kept the
Pandavas bound
And who will listen to my cries, agonies, and heart searches?
The world has become blind and deaf, and helplessness has
descended on me
And one day under the direction of Sage Dhaumya I wedded
All the five, one after another, and became on my own
resolution free
The wife of the five brothers.

II. Movement

SHARING AND CARING

CANTO X

YOU ARE SUFFUSED WITH MOTHER-EARTH FEELING, YOU ARE

With sincerity in heart and speech, without feigning,
Three times I repeated the words the wedding priest chanted.
Yet within me arose waves of anxiety and doubt and these in turn,
Set in me a tumultuous storm of conflicting emotions and when
At first, sage Dhaumya, placed my hand in Yudhisthira's and said it was
Best I spend the first night with him, I, in devotion and respect
Surrendered myself to him who looked an incarnation of all that
Constituted maleness and honour and then I touched his feet with reverence.
He who was silent, then, in soft tones spoke:
'Worried are you? Have I hurt you? Pushing you into this
Marital trap, have aroused in you only disgust? Has your
Anger lessened now, I should like to know, speak to me.' Bending
My head in reverence, in low tones, I said: 'You are virtue itself;
You live in virtue and anyone who transgresses your order,
He would be guilty of unrighteous action. I shall not break my word'

Hearing it, innocent as a baby, Dharmaja spoke:
'Yagnaseni, listening to the story of your miraculous birth,
I became attracted. You are the protector of Kurudharma and
By becoming, in the presence of sacred fire, my wedded wife,
You have made me gratefully obliged to you. Since Arjuna won you at
The swayamvara, you should live with him alone; the rest of us,

For the sake of the nation, have acted the way we have.'
When he spoke so my humiliation burst through my anger
And I, as if stabbing him with red hot iron, spoke this way:
'Yes, yes, you *dharma* incarnate have spoken the truth and
This me, praising you all the time, will go to rot, get putrefied,
And I shall always be puzzled, by myself! Having accepted
You as my husband, how do I live with Partha alone? Won't the
World say I live an immoral life? Won't it brand me a criminal?
And won't I, living in guilt, spend my life cursing myself?'
Though these sharp words hit him hard, he sweetly, softly said.
'Who would not desire you? But listen, we are five and
Each one's nature is different and therefore how can we lead
Life together, no, it would be impossible. Understand:
If I ask you to go to the temple, Bhima would want you to
be in the kitchen and then Partha desires to go hunting! Then,
Nakula would want you to go horse-riding and Sahadeva,
Sitting, in the open, would, staring at the starry sky, think of
the future.
What will you do? I do not know what you would want
But my brothers will never disobey whatever I tell them.'

Confuse me it did and I wondered what my other husbands
And Kunti would make of this situation but silently
My anger flowed through me for he was the first one
To burden me with a heavy story, which strangely silenced me!
But he knows that changes cannot happen this
Instant, then why think wastefully, saying, so to myself
I said: 'I am yours and totally, this is my pledge,
I am the earth which sustains everything and I shall never
Deceive myself nor you, this is the truth.'
When, he touching my shoulder, said,

'Come, Yagnaseni, you are my better half, you are my
Inevitable the other self, you are the strength behind the great
Yagna of *dharma* we all have began,' said he.
The first night, I accepted my husband who was open-
heartedness itself,

And bowing to him I stood still and he continued softly:
'Queen, you are a wife beautiful and virtuous, and great you
Are. While I am busy playing with the dice, you sleep, and
Without knowing your mind how can I know your body?
How shall I sleep with you who my brother has won? This
Is but a political alliance, a ploy, a thread to keep the five
Pandavas together, in truth it is this and I cannot cut the thread
Nor can I use it right to thread the spilt beads and when our
Minds meet and you know our differing natures, you won't
be able to enter them.
Until then we stay outside of you but I do not
Know how this is going to wound your feelings.'
Spreading a bed of flowers sensitive and soft he, without
Trampling on my dream-world, made my night and I
Spent a night sweet and memorable and I was thrilled.
The next day, as night descended, the second one,
Vrikodara called me stretching his arms huge as the
Sahyadri mountains and stood there like an elephant
And I shivered in fear, but coming near, he, like the
Breeze carrying the fragrance of lotus flowers, whispered,
Without any inhibitions, with an open mind:
'Draupadi, irascible I am and without worrying who it is
I am quick to punish those who disregard their duty,
And sharp words I am used to and unacquainted I am with
Forgiveness and speak words as they come to me but the next
Moment I forget and gracefully pardon, and beg their pardon too.
Tell me, can you tolerate me, you who are virtuous and cultured,
And, like mother earth are full of kindness and forbearance?
When once forbearance is lost, the family bonds crumble, and
Fall apart, this is true, speak to me please.'

I perhaps exist only to stitch together the fabric of
Togetherness of the five Pandavas or else what place do I
Have in the lives of the five? This may be the inevitability of
The Age. The Kaurava through violent injustice has fractured
Peace and I have to keep together the unity of the Pandavas.
So that righteousness triumphs. The life behind the unity I

Have to be, and, therefore, have to bear the bitterness and
The burden and to do this job I am committed, for the fall of
The nation has to be stopped and that right there waited a
Miracle for me: the huge Bhima, the way a mother puts her
child to sleep,
Took my head in his lap and narrating stories of several
Adventures put me to sleep. Who knows what mellowness of spirit
Lies within hard, muscular bodies? Ah, now comes the third one!

Thinking that this should be my memorable night I had
Waited with high expectations, and with that feeling, climbed on to
The nuptial bed covered with thin guage like silk curtains. And,
Within was the brave Phalguna: the face handsome, the body
Perfumed and on the neck, down to the waist, a sweet
Smelling garland of white flowers. I looked and looked and the
More I looked the more I wanted to look but stopped by
natural feminine shyness,
Slowly I went and sat near him as the pendent in my
Emerald green chain reflected the face of the love-god, Eros!
There was in it a smile accompanied by a boyish prank and all this
Got mirrored in my bracelet and ring and the other jewels I
had worn,
Small beads of perspiration made his face more charming and
As I looked he sweetly called, in a soft voice, 'Krishne' and said:
'Why are you disturbed? What conflict is there in you? I know,
But without knowing you, how do I become one with you?
You know the way the Pandavas are and yet…' he
Stopped, and looked at my pale face and in choked voice said:
'Ah, dear, my climactic moment of happiness has vanished;
When I won you at the contest, that moment was sweet like nectar!
It was a prized moment of my life but, dear, do not lose heart,
Be brave and have courage, whose are you not? You are a jewel,
But I know not how I am going to make it mine own.
Blame you I can't for in the cause of righteousness we have
Tied you to the sacrificial post of *dharma*.'

In surprise I looked at him, without fear and without

Shyness, for what shall I say? All my sweet thoughts had been
Put out at the time of lighting itself! In the bud itself
It was destroyed. What are these rules and rituals of *dharma*?'
As waves rose and rose and dashed against the wall of the
Heart, the Adishesha swayed his hood, and then understanding me,
Dhananjaya held my hand raised me and put me on the
Couch of soft flowers, and then whispered what was in his heart:

'That day when I stepped out of the swayamvara stage,
Like twin birds we walked the rugged forest paths
In my mind there wasn't any other thought but the happy
Feeling that I was the most fortunate man in the world
Who had won you, my lady, but now look I have become
one with you
After three days, and strange it is of this epoch. For this
Union I had to wait for three days, and after the turn
Of Dharmaja and Vrikodara, it is my turn! And the next
Two nights you spend with Nakula and Sahadeva!
To be a silent spectator, and send one's wedded wife
To another, is it not most tragic? Why am I fated
For this kind of life?'

In sad, heavy tones I said:
'You won me, and then why did you agree to this?
Why, without protesting, did you keep quiet?
Why didn't you say "Krishne, is mine!" You committed
A crime unforgivable? You overlooked your duty of a husband
And because of your epocal blunder blame not others?
What use is it and what point is there in accusing others?'

In great distress Arjuna spoke:
'What could I do? Dharmaja and mother Kunti put me
In the prison house of *dharma* and I had to keep silent, but why
Were you silent, why didn't you speak? You did not ask for
Time to answer the question. What had put you, and in what
prison of *Dharma*?
What familial rule made you keep your silence?
The day you wed me at the swayamvara you had all the freedom,

And today, after having, given it all up, why shed tears?
The wheel of time has gone past, why waste words now?
To bring goodness and to keep *dharma* alive in this epoch
We have to give up our personal desires. May be it too
Is for our own good. Born we are for things great and how
Could we give importance to the passing moment? How
Could I ever be away from feelings fraternal? Repentence
Cannot be life's objective, Krishne, you, the wife of the five,
Are born to uphold and keep the *dharma* of our age. The
Wedding of you and me had been much awaited for, and
Krishna is my friend, and with you I write an epic of mutual love,
And I know Krishna, in the notes of his flute, had already played
And recorded our love
And therefore you have come to stay in my heart.'

Shyly I bowed my head but wondered whether Partha
Understood that his was but a reflection of Krishna's love
For me as I came to know that Krishna was in possession
Of the palm leaves on which were my love poems and if so
It had come into me via Krishna and Partha, and that
Night as the southern wind played Raaga Ananda Bhairavi
And sang the praise of Krishna, I spent with Partha.

Truly Nakula was the spitting image of the god of love, and
His face was bright like the flower that blossoms in moonlight
And on the fourth night, he, smiling, said:
'Ah, Panchali, did you see the horses? I have heard that
You, in your childhood, spent much time in sanctuaries
For birds and beasts and that you too know their language.
This also I have heard: elephants in heat which go berserk,
The moment they see you calm down for the affection you have
For them; this too I know that if birds do not eat the fruits,
You worry about them and fortunate I am to have found you
Through the wonderful play of Krishna. You, a rare jewel.'

Surprised I was by the enticing games of Govinda, and
Nakula was there admiring himself in a mirror and was
Busy, innocently, making his clothes look neat and I felt

Like taking in him in my arms and hugging him hard
For love had made that demand on me and yet controlling myself
I said:
'Yes, the horses look wonderful and so do you. In this
Ocean of handsomeness, like snow, I have melted, but tell
Me did you like me or was it the words of Kunti that have
Bound you?'
With a smile, he answered: 'Listen, they say that the beauty
Of the entire world is but a reflection of me, but I am yet to
See anyone more beautiful than you. You are the queen of beauty.'
I saw the waves of feeling playing in the heart of the
Young man and within me too sprang dreams of delicate
Emotions and as they did I got mentally ready for the next night.

Sahadeva, a man of few words, gentle, soft and skilled
And thinking within himself, would predict the future and as
He stepped into my apartment, he stood still for a while,
looked round,
And then gazed on me and I, mesmerized, forgot myself and
Silently shed tears and, he knowing my heart, held my hand
And said: "Krishne, here, on this earth, men dream within
Themselves too much of the future and hence suffer much,
Which is mindlessness really, and that is why animals are
Burdened not. The moment I saw I wanted you to be mine
And we are princes who have gone through fire and
I do not know what made Govinda bring up all together.
However, I shall remain your loving friend as I see in
You the feminine form which has found perfection.'
It was morning and I pondered over the five:
Dharmaja was righteousness itself; Bhima was energy personified;
Partha valour incarnate; Nakula, handsome and Sahadeva was
Wisdom itself. Each was different from another, in his own way.
Could I give myself equally to all the five, and how do I live
With them? A question which kept coming up and for which I
Had no answer. Whom do I trust? Who will give me succour
Till the end. Ah, Krishna, do you desire pleasure by making
Me dance to your wishes, all over the world!

CANTO XI

BE A WIFE UNTO EACH A YEAR

Limitless were the gifts brought by Krishna from
Dwaraka but among these were two exceptional ones:
One, a beautiful blue stone ring and another, a friend, Maye,
Gifting me with these he said:

'Oh, Krishne, it is with my
Blessings that I present you with this ring which was with me
A long time and if looked at intently it helps you solve
many problems;
And Maye, a friend from my boyhood days, is an achiever.
Most successful, strong and dispeller of all kinds of troubles;
If anyone bothers me, with resolution, she protects me and through
Understanding your need she works miracles, and without her help
Our knotted problems we cannot resolve and therefore here I
Brought her to be with you all the time. You need her.'

With concern for him I said, 'But how will you, without her
Take care of all the daily, routine and thorny problems?
Who will look after you if you send her here?'
Govinda, with more concern for me, spoke: 'Do not worry
About me. Ready yourself to go through life with five husbands
For it isn't easy. But I know you have taken on
Yourself to face challenges severe of this epoch and in this
Task Maye will help you. Otherwise how will you get out
Of this forest of problems? She will be your guide here.'

As he spoke he smiled, and that drove away all worry and

Doubt. But I also felt he was conscious of the fire into which
He had pushed me and therefore, had left, along with Nitambini,
The very shrewed and wise Maye as companion
Who stayed all my life with me as Govinda's great gift.

The next morning Drupada spoke to me:
'Dear daughter, listen. It is better you stay here in
Panchala till you get back your kingdom. It would also
Enhance the good fortune of ours. I can't leave you, my
Dear daughter, here with no place to go to.'

'How could I say "yes"? It hurts my honour and it is
Hard to stay with one's father once one gets wedded.
And to live with the brother, it is much worse. Is this
Kind of miserable life my permanent lot? And as days
Pass by the hard earned fame of my husbands fades away
And people will look down on them. My duty it is to
Guard their honour. What if they have lost their kingdom
And are homeless, the world admires them for their valour
And their characters and it is better one lives by one's own
Strength and on one's own merit. True, I am caught in a vortex of
Problems and yet to keep them happy and partaking of their
Happiness is the duty of the wife. But to wed one after
Another and still manage to preserve the sanctity of wedded life
And protect *dharma* too is difficult. I know who will ferry
Me across this ocean of a life, troubling and troubled.
There are in the dark sea whales and crocodiles and
I know not how, and from what direction they will attack us
To whose hunger we would be food? Like a dry leaf I am
Being tossed about by the fierce lashing winds,
And I have none to take care of me.'

My feet went heavy as lead and the humiliation heaped on
Me burst like lava in my veins and I sank down on the bed;
The fire of sorrow had turned me into a charred
Coconut shell and suddenly the story of the coming together of
Sage Parashara and Satyavati, in a flash, unraveled itself in my mind;

The river Yamuna was in floods, overflowing its banks;
Matsyagandhi's lusty youth was brimming over and the
Great Yogi Krishna Dwaipayana was born when Parasara made the
Smelly fisherwoman smell fragrant and united with her and so
was
The great Kuru dynasty born whose impotent progeny,
Vichitra Veerya
Became the cause of the exploitation of the helpless women and
The rape of women became common with the Kuru kings and,
The cry of the fisherwoman echoes and re-echoes even today;
No man gave ear to the sad cry, and so was born the
Tragic poetry of the human race. Re-calling the revered
Story of sage Parasara and Vedavyas I was all on fire
And yet he it was, who without any trace of shame, became
The great epic poet of Mahabharata and made the world
The recipient of the epic poetry of the whole of Dwapara epoch!

From Hastinavati proceeded a huge army to be
Present at the swayamvara of Ambe, Ambike and Ambalike;
The daughter of the King of Kashi; knowing that they would not
On their own, wed Vichitra Veerya, Bhishma led his
Army, and they, too afraid to resist, tamely gave in and
At Hastinapura, Ambe, who had given her heart, at the swayamvara,
To Salva would not wed Vichitra Veerya but wanted Bhishma
For her husband but he who had taken the vow of celibacy would
Not accept her, and Salva rejected her for she had been won
by Bhishma;

And so the birth of a girl child, in a male-word, was forever a crime,
And, therefore, how could the beastly heart of Salva heed the
Love-laden words of Ambe?

But in the Kuru clan the desire for sons was intense, and
Satyavati, with Ambike and Ambalike, spoke out her heart:
'Great riches are of what use? They are like trees which bear
No fruit, and so is the life a childless woman.
Puranas and sacred writings, I have heard, say that
If a husband is unable to gift his wife with a child, she, then

Through eight ways can bear a child, all sanctioned by sacred love.
Don't have doubts. To bear child through union with a sage
Has never been deemed improper; and sage Vyasa is no
Stranger; he is the eldest of our clan and to preserve
The rule of our dynasty, you, my dear daughter-in-law, agree.'

And, through this ambassodorial relationship, they gave birth to
Two children; one, Dhritharashtra, born blind and the other,
Pandu stricken with leprosy and disease; Satyavati
Again forced Ambike to sleep with Vyasa but she in disgust
Sent her maid instead who bore Vidhura and the wives repining
Over their barren state, in sorrow, passed away and left no heir.

There, Gandhari, issueless but through a boon from
Durvasa gave birth to Duryodhana, Dushyasana and Dusyala
And a hundred others. And, Kunti, on the pretext of a
Boon, through other men, became a mother of three and
Madri of twins, and recalling, this story of the
Kuru clan, I, in terrible distress wept to myself but I
Saw that the women of the Kuru clan had to loan away their
Bodies to others to keep the empire together, but should
Women's honour be squandered so without a thought about
Good and evil! This lopsided moral measuring is
An indication of the dominance of the male in their world.
When, I asked my companion, will this injustice end?
Vysa simply, silently smiled, laughed and stood
Like a pillar, unmoved, for to him life looks clear, like
Pellucid water, but he played blindfolded but I, with eyes open
I had to
Accept the burden of women, and live and conquer my
Five husbands, and win them over by responding to their wants.

But they have no notion of the sensitive, subtle feelings
Of womankind, and an overwhelming nothingness
In fact, swallowed everything and reduced it to total nothingness;
While I was thinking such thoughts, the eldest, Yamaja
Sent word to me. But Bhimasena who was in his apartment,
Looked distraught and waiting for consoling words from me;

But then came a maid conveying to me a message from
Partha! At the same moment Nakula wanted to have a serious
Discussion with me on some profound problem and so did Sahadeva,
He too sent for me to ponder over with him on knotty metaphysical
Questions and I did not know how to obey and whom; I did not
Know how I could be indifferent to any but as first priority
Was to be given to Dharmaja, I was about to go to his apartment,
At that instant appeared Maye, who stopped me and said:

'Ah, friend, which way are you going? Bhima has been waiting
For long and how will you handle his raging anger? You
First take care of him and then go to Yudhisthira fast.'
Hemmed in by confusion I collapsed, but then thinking it
Was right to obey the order of the eldest I proceeded
Although a cloud of anxiety had darkened my mind and as
I entered there he was ready to play dice, the dice-mat spread,
And smilingly he asked me to sit and watch him play the game
With Govinda and how he would defeat the clever Krishna!

What kind of a test is this? This is my husband and that
Is the veritable god I worship. How could I wish victory
To anyone? And therefore in intelligent modesty, I said,
'Forgive me. The game holds no interest for me and your
Brothers have sent word, I shall attend to them and be back.'

Govinda seeing through it all smiled and said:
'Dharmaja, this Panchali is no ordinary woman. She has
To keep together you and your brothers and has accepted the
five of you
As her spouses. She has to listen to your other brothers.
Let her go.'

At that moment arrived Narada who said it was not
Easy to reconcile fraternal wishes of brothers and then,
sagely spoke:
'Have you forgotten the incident about Sundopasundara,
The brothers, who sat on the same couch and ate from a single
Bowl and lived in fraternal affection but it didn't last:

Tilottama, the heavenly damsel, entered their lives and the two
Fought over her, and one killed the other in the end, and
their unity was destroyed.'
Listening to the story, my heart missed several beats;
Anxiety, foreboding future tragedy, struck me and Sri Krishna,
To add to it, nodded his head and said Narada was right;
The snake of fear ran through me, turning my face white:
But Narada continued: 'Know you all. There is, it is said,
In your birth-chart hid what is called the element
Of self-destruction. Bhima alone is enough to cause rifts in
The Kuru clan, and flaming anger and hatred will swallow you
All, and therefore, dear daughter, it is good if you among
Yourselves solve your problems. I can't be of any use as
Have moved away from the tangled web of familial questions.'
Krishna, the all-knowing alone can offer a solution clear
and acceptable.'
Govinda, with folded hands, but in affection said:
'Krishne, forgive me, I, for one, cannot offer a solution
To the tangled familial question. Whatever you think,
In the right answer, give it. It will be surely right.' But
The next instant he called Maye and whispered in her ears
And she turned to me and said:

'Friend, listen. To be a wife to
Five husbands and run the family is too hard; but there is,
However, one easy way out. Be a wife to each for a year, and
This is the way it can be solved.
Each year you are psychologically to prepare yourself
To be the wife of one and this way you can hold them in unity.'
All the five Pandavas said this was arrangement proper, but
Narada said there was another side to this ticklish question:
'If, while one is living with Draupadi, another enters their inner
Apartment, he, for four years, has to live the life of a celibate
And to atone for this transgression has to go on a pilgrimage
to some sacred place.'
All the brothers agreed to this condition and
In this way I was bailed out of my trying situation and

I walked towards the apartment of Yudhisthira and then for four
Years I lived, for the others, a life of sisterly and maternal love.
Bhima was staring at me and I wondered whether Arjuna
would say
Yes to this formula. Nakula and Sahadeva in patience natural
to them
Waited in silence.
To avert the onslaught of the male world, this alone was a road
Open to me and surrender I did with a clear mind,
To initiate a reconciliation made to protect the unity of the five.

CANTO XII

THE BURDEN OF KINGSHIP IS NOT EASY TO BEAR

One morning an invitation came from Bhishma and Dhritarashtra
Through Vidura who came with palanquins and chariots
In a grand style and the news which came with him
Said: mother Satyavati was eagerly expecting us all,
With this the rumour spread that the sons of Pandu were likely
To be bestowed with half of the kingdom of Kuru clan and this
Made everybody feel that from now on there would be peace and
Happiness everywhere.

Kunti herself felt that her daughter-in-law had brought with her
Good luck and congratulated her but all this was hard to
be believed;
Did the death-spelling, wicked cousins really wish happiness to
Their cousins? What has fate in store for them? Will the
Pandavas regain their kingdom? Is this really the beginning of
Good times? I trembled within myself and wondered:

Why this sudden generous gesture? And, why do the Pandavas
Desire an easy way of regaining their kingdom? Do they really
Want this kind of a compensation? And, although a comet
Suddenly appeared in the sky warning of possible danger,
Dharmaja, as if inviting happenings tragic, thought of living in
Palaces old; and I, agreeing with my father, was staying in
The city of Panchala as the doors of Hastinavati had been
closed for us.
Partha indicated his desire of going with Krishna to Dwaraka

And I wondered why he was leaving his newly wedded wife behind
And why he had become so hard-hearted. Helpless
I was but felt that it was but a vengeful act but the fire
Within him filled me with scalding tears of sorrow and his
Concealed violence lay within the desert of my mind.
Govinda in good humour spoke to Bhima:
'Are you contemplating on visiting Hidimbe? Any plans?'
Bhima in all seriousness replied: 'This is not the time to
while away,
The desire of the Kauravas to see us all is motivated by hate, and
Would I fall prey to the designs of Kauravas who want us
To fight over our love for our wife? If it happens, how
Can we stay together and how can we repel their attacks?
There isn't a single note of dissent among the hundred
Kauravas; there isn't one who will speak against Duryodhana.
The father and all his sons stand united.'

Guessing at the hidden meaning of Bhima, the veteran warrior
Partha said: 'It matters little who says what, for to me going
To Hastinapura is like swallowing poison. And, what do I do
There, what work waits for me? Dwaraka is best for me.
Krishne will wallow in pleasure as queen at Hastinapura
On the pretext of obeying mother's decision, and what would
she get
As my wife? In this tragic tale of Mahabharata, she alone
Stands to gain the greatest benefit. The world will admire her
Cleverness, she would be the wife of the epoch and she, through
Her peregrinations will change and rule over the world!'

The middle Pandava's anguish, like a volcano, spoke blindingly
And I could feel the torment he was undergoing and if I
Do not speak consolingly now, the disunity among the brothers
will be
Known and how would I fare in the house of the Kauravas, if
Arjuna is not with me there! It is now that I need help of
Sri Krishna, the pole star of our lives who can be a balm to
the pain Arjuna feels.

But I felt helpless. Right then to my aid came the discriminating
Maye who said:
'How can Arjuna go to Dwaraka leaving his soul-friend
Sri Krishna behind? He it is who is the life breath of the Pandavas.'
Krishna flashing a touching smile said: 'Yes, not for me to
Ignore the plea of my friend's wife's companion: What is
Dwaraka against Hastinapura!'
Within myself I admired the wonderful wisdom of
Maye and loved her, and was happy she was my trustworthy guide,
Who alone understood the seriousness of the situation.
Thinking to myself I said
'She is part of my life. And, true, I have not seen heaven but
In dreams I had seen it. Many a time, when Arjuna won me,
I had imagined visiting Hastinapura, a veritable heaven, which
Naturally overflowed with milk and honey and gold and jewels.'
Maye, and I were thrilled thinking of visiting Hastinapura,
Excited I was, and the excitement flowed through my veins.
Dressed in white, and wearing white flowers in my hair,
And adorned with eight kinds of ornaments, in pride
I sat in a chariot with Maye and Nitambini
And our chariot was preceded by chariots of
Govinda and Balarama, and the chariots of the five husbands
And behind theirs was Kunti's and as we all proceeded, there
Were red carpets spread on the roads, and from above a shower
Of rose petals!
Near the big portals was a crowd of Kauravas whose faces
Looked darkly frowning and yet the welcome was sweet and
wonderful!
However there was one who stared at me and his look
Pierced me as a sharp arrow does and then Maye whispered:

'That is Vasushena, brought up by Radhe and son of a
fisherman, by profession a charioteer.
He would have been victorious at your
Swayamvara but isn't each accountable for his own mean birth?'

Humiliation, helplessness, disappointment, the curse of the sage

And deep sadness visibly sat on his face and I asked myself:
'Is Karna a Kshatriya? Even if he isn't one, what does it matter?
Whether he weds me or not, why should people outcaste him?
Humiliation is more painful then defeat—this I saw when
I looked at him and if an opportunity arises I told myself,
I would ask his forgiveness. This is neither fair not acceptable,
Keeping away a competent, noble youth in this way.
In many other ways I rued within myself but the
Eyes of those gathered there were only on Krishna and
Balabhadra and great happiness on their faces was evident.
The hundred brothers showered flowers on us
And Vasushane was there with a bouquet of flowers
In his hand but did not know to whom it was to be given.

Then came Maye near me and whispered in my ears;
'Ah, friend, how did he know blue lotuses were dear to you!
He has brought them for you, go, accept it.'
'How did he know that I loved blue-coloured saree and
Blue-lotus flowers? Ah, I re-called on the day of swayamvara.
He sat gazing at the blue lotuses I held in my hand!
Among qualities
Of bravery, courage and handsomeness what is finest is the ability
To understand the feminine mind. None of my husbands know
That blue-lotus is dear to me; none of them knows my mind.
Karna was sensitive enough to intuitively know this and as I
Stood like a marble statue, a bouquet of flowers, like lighting fell at
My feet and I held it with my hand and Karna who was nearby said:
'I beg your forgiveness, Panchali. I got these flowers
To expiate the sin I had committed earlier, and also to honour
You. Please believe me. But the pain the body feels is much
Less when compared to the pain that hurt one's heart, and
For today's deed, I again beg your forgiveness.'
The festive mood and the rattle and clatter which went with it made
None notice the event and it was Maye alone, like the only true witness who

Observed it all and said softly in my ears alone:
'Karna, a person of great self-esteem, is most handsome and
Yet within him burns the fire of humiliation of having been
Branded low-caste by the world and if only
You had wed him then this getting married to five men
Would not have risen, and you wouldn't have been forced to
Live in the snare the five husbands have woven round you.
Your life is hard.'

Maye spoke the truth. Each second thousands of sharp
Arrows bore into my vitals, to add to which she weakened my mind.
My life is like a boat tossing over turbulent seas and
Without a compass: I called to my mind the sacred feet of
Krishna and yet the injustice of the world burst forth within
Me like flames of burning anger.

The next morning Yudhisthira walked into the court of Dhritarashtra,
Bowed to his grandfather and to the teachers, Kripa and Drona
And addressing the gathering of Kuru and Pandavas, said:
'It is better the empire is divided equally, we then can live with
Mutual respect and love and there won't be any bitterness in us'

To which Bhishma added his words and said: 'Yes, yes,
Between the cousins this is right for otherwise desire for the
Empire will poison them all and it would also stop people
from carrying tales to you.'
And as all agreed, the empire got divided:
West and north and south and east wise the line ran
And towns and cities and other regional divisions including
Indraprastha and Hastinavati and other places went equally to
The two sides as did elephants, horses, chariots and shining
Gold jewels. After which Bhishma spoke and counseled
Wise tolerance and at the auspicious hour sacred Arati
Was done and betel leaves and flowers exchanged and then the
Pandavas bowed at the feet of Kunti, Dhritarashtra and
Bhishma and
Vidura and other elders and then entered Indraprastha which
had been

Designed by the divine architect Viswakarma and there were in
The city grand palaces and magnificent apartments for all.

As if Indra was entering the heavenly capital, Amaravati,
Dharmaraja with Drupada, and with his other brothers entered
The city and people danced in happiness and offered presents
to him;
There was everywhere a flood of happiness, and Krishna joined
The Pandavas as did the great-grandfather Bhishma who
offered wise counsel:
'Dharmaja, listen. Truth has to be victorious and let not
Righteousness suffer in the desire for power and let not
The wicked harass the good and let you be sympathetic to
The poor and the needy. And may you have
adequate discrimination
And let there be no indulgence in the pleasures of hunting
And drinking. Do not be deceived by people's outward,
Hypocritical behaviour; be alert all the time of the day.

Take care of your people and make right rewards to deserving
People and to the army which protects the nation. Let
No internal dissension destroy the peace of the womenfolk
And others. You and your brothers should live in harmony
And at times of crisis do not hesitate to compromise and
In such a direction let your administration run.

In an enterprise, profit and loss could be equal but in
Another the loss is more and the work does not get done.
You have to, in such situations, think and act wisely;
Periodically hold consultation with ministers and officials;
Keep away the foolish and the lazy and be firm in your
Views; do not forget those who render useful service, and
Honour the deserving ones. Let not envy or jealously move the
Actions of your subordinates; give generously to needy. Punish
Theft, adultery, injustice, deceit, falsehood and deception—
Fraudulent ways; while dealing with women; with adversaries,
While eating and hunting and while on a picnic, be ever
Careful. If you stand firmly by truth, power would be yours.

The power of kings who are not aware of these truths will be
Like a lamp lit in a windy field.

The way bees collect honey from flowers without causing them
Injury, you collect taxes from your subjects and the tax
You collect should be used to better their lives.
Win over your citizens pleasantly and depute competent officials.
Bees, boars, king cobras, and monkeys and such like entities
Have to be kept at a distance.

Do not put your trust in riches and do not ever be proud.
Keep to the path of truth and virtue and do not get scared easily.
Do not go after other people's wives and be kind to servants,
Never ever believe in those who indulge in drinking, and
Debauchery, and be careful as clever and wicked may
Try to entice you with blandishments. Be alert all the time.
Take care of the poor and weak and keep a watchful eye
On granaries and the treasury and on reservoirs; with arms
Keep yourself ready if there is an aggression against you;
Whether it is life of the rural folk or of the rich, guard it well.
Let agriculture receive great attention as food is to be procured
And stored sensibly, and do not let the arrogant, careless ones guard
the palace.

Kingship is never easy to manage: it is like honey that is on
The sharp edge of a sword, or it is like the precious gem on the
Hood of a serpent, and, therefore, you have to be careful and skilled.
Let not the son be angry and abusive with the father and let
not the
Father run down his children and let there not be any
Litigious quarrels between cousins and other relatives.
He who is a minister has to be a master of all the four
Kinds of strategies and he has to master the craft of statesmanship.'
In this way the great-grandfather advised Dharmaraya.

CANTO XIII

PERENNIAL SPRING OF MATERNAL LOVE

Half of Hastinapura empire, Khandavaprastha, Dhritarashtra gave away
But there was not even a house with thatched roof, all but a
Thorny desert it was, starkly reminding the absence of the
Grand palaces of Hastinapura.

There was here, on the contrary,
The dark, thick forests of Khandavavana, teeming with
Poisonous snakes and insects and disease-causing flora and
Here, composing their minds, the Pandavas readied themselves to stay and live:
But as Krishna was with them, it did not take much time
For the Pandavas to settle down and in no time there
Arose in this forest-land, great mansions, around a huge big
City, newly created and with the magical touch of Maya,
The divine architect, another heavenly city, Indraprastha
Took shape and their lives lived here were pleasant and happy.

One day when I was sitting alone, Kunti came and said:
'Panchali, today I shall let you into a secret that has been
With me a long time. I have another son, and he is senior to
Dharmaja and is brave and handsome and virtuous.
But as the son of a charioteer and belonging to the caste of
Fishermen and brought up with love by Radhe, he lives!'
Thunderstruck, I stared into Kunti's face and wondered
How I could believe this story. Karna, her eldest son!
Guessing my state of mind, she said: 'Yes, yes. He

Is my eldest and right it is to view him as one of the Pandavas.
For him to have grown as the son of a charioteer in this
epoch is a great tragedy.
Of that there is no doubt. When I was still
Young, prodded by curiosity, I put to use a boon given to me
And then, in great confusing fear I had to abandon the son born to
Me and let him afloat on the Ganga and Athiratha who found
the baby,
Presented it to Radhe, his childless wife and made her happy.
She in great love brought him up but owing to doubting men his
Birth appeared tainted and through out his life he had to face the
Humiliating taunt of everyone and he had to live and grow and
Stand deprived of his natural inheritance and was branded
Low caste and had to suffer at every step from the day of his birth.'

Feminine compassion flowed through my veins and
With it maternal love in a flood. Respond I did to the
Motherly feelings of Kunti and understood the heart of
women.
My feelings of oneness with her grew and it enveloped me.
And I, a woman, listening to this exciting story felt that
Maternal affection was a sacred perennial spring, which could
never go dry.

At Indraprastha a Rajasuyayaga, a sacred imperial
Ritual was decided to be held, and kings and princes from
Several neighbouring provinces, and Krishna, with his five
white horses driven
Chariot arrived and with him came his wife Rukmini Devi.
And in other chariots Balarama, Satyaki, Ugrasena, Akrura,
Pradyumna and other Yadava heroes, and Bhisma
Stepped forward, embraced Sri Krishna and Balarama.
And then women with sacred water washed the feet of Krishna
And Rukmini and Kunti applied the auspicious tilaka on Krishna's
Forehead and Vidura put a garland of basil leaves around
Krishna's neck.

Dharmaraja and others, in respect stood up, and as the sages

Assembled touched in reverence the feet of Sri Krishna, the
King of Chedi was sitting with hurt feelings of prestige and as the
Prime place of honour was about to be accorded to Sri
Krishna, he sprang
From his seat, fiercely waved the mace in his hand and in a
booming voice
Shouted: 'Stop it, stop it right now! Crowned kings cannot tolerate
This humiliation.' In great rage and with flaming eyes, he thundered:
'Yudhisthira, you born of high-placed Kshatriya caste!
That you should
Insult and humiliate Kshatriyas is amazing. This wicked act
You have to stop, this shall not happen.
This shephered who grazes cows in the grass-field, tell me,
How is he worthy to be honoured first among all princes. No
This is ludicrous, I shall not accept it. Do stop this horse-play,
And right now!'

The burning jealousy that was within him from the day
Krishna won Rukmini at the swayamvara flowed in
torrents now
And he minced no words in declaring that Krishna was of
low caste;
Hearing these words of abuse Bhima took up his mace and Partha
Strung his bow and picked sharp, flaming arrows but Krishna
Paying no heed to these, slowly walked towards the sacred
Sacrificial fire and was about to drop the basil leaves into the fire
And while doing so through signs asked Bhima and Arjuna to be
Calm and silent, and sat in the throne that had been readied
for him:
'Is there none to stop him?' Shisupala shouted, menacingly and
waved his
Mace, and in a shrill and harsh voice cried loud: 'There are
here great heroes and brave kings and veterans of war, and
here, with all of us
Here, is prime honour to be conferred on this insufferable
duffer of a cowherd?
We see Bhishma, Dhritarashtra, Duryodhana, Saindhava and

Shakuni, chiefs of Panchala, Maghada sitting in this august assembly and besides
Them are venerable, great teachers like Drona, Kripa and Aswathama
And from amongst us all this dark-skinned, uncultured cowhered
Is chosen for the great honour! Does not this shame us all?
This coal-coloured Krishna, what attraction does he hold for you?
Did you not see this, fair-coloured heroic stature of Karna,
Sitting here with us?'

His anger spread like forest fire and darkened the skies and
Krishna stood up, like a cobra that had been stepped on, sprang
From his seat, and with his arm resting on his waist said:
'Ninety-nine times have I allowed you to abuse me without
Protest, for I had given my word to your mother that I wouldn't
Punish you till you crossed the limit of a hundred abusive words.
The next word of abuse crosses the line and therefore compose
Yourself and stop, for you have reached the end of the tether.
If not, your head this Sudarshana Chakra will sever from your body.
Beware, do not invite the ultimate disaster.'

But Shishupala paying no heed rushed towards Sri Krishna
Fast and bull-like, with arms raised and shouting abuses, then
I knew some terrible thing would happen and as I looked
The blue lotus-like face turned flaming red and the body
Became taut and straight and the peacock feather in the crown
Appeared to touch the skies and seeing it I felt the golden
Plank I was sitting on was melting in unbearable heat and
I felt I myself was growing to an enormous height and
Thought I saw Sri Krishna assuming a world-enveloping form
And in his hand was the circling Sri Sudarshana Chakra and from
Above a thunder-like voice from the firmament spoke and it made
All the assembled shudder and they heard the invisible voice
Saying: 'Shishupala, today you have committed the hundredth
Crime and now none, not even the four-faced creator, Brahma, can
Save you. Your arrogance of your Kshatriya blood has crossed
All boundaries, and be careful, your end has come.'

Staring at Shishupala, with the flaming Sudarshana Chakra

In his hand, he moved and seeing the fire-spewing sharp Chakra
And unable to face it, like a huge tree that gets toppled by
Fiery wind, he staggered and fell back and as a blazing blanket of fire flew at him,
He, like a deer, stood frightened, and the next moment
He madly tried to stop the discus with his bare hands and it
Cut his hand in two, and scared beyond his will he hid himself
Under a throne but as it chased him there too he, as a last
Resort, jumped into the Ishumati river and tried to swim away
But then, the next instant, only his bloody head became visible,
And the river turned red with his blood, and the sun set.

Then, however, the offering of prime honour to Krishna
Went without any hindrance
'What was Khandava forest is today the city of Indraprastha
And everywhere there was gaiety and the Pandavas were happy;
For the visitors and the invitees dining halls were made ready
And as Kauravas, Pandavas sat with Balarama and Krishna,
Kunti, in affection, had sent for Karna but discriminating as he was
He did not come for he knew he could come in the way of the
Cousins coming together. Kunti alone knew this and she
With her children and her cousins sat depressed.
And I with Maye and Nitambini took care of those invited,
Fed them to their hearts' content and all were praise for the
Rich and tasty food. Then, Dushyasana, held me by my hand
And I put up with it thinking it was a liberty, a brother-in-law
Could take, although I was aware of the base nature of men.

I did not want to upset the guests assembled but as I bent forward
To serve the sweet dishes, Jayadratha overstepping decency said:
'Ah, Panchali, the food you have prepared is so sweet and
How much more sweet you are we can guess, can't we?'
Dushyasana in obvious irony continued and said: 'How
Hot is the food you have served and it reminds me of the warmth
Which you made us feel the day we saw you at the
Wedding dias. The heat we felt on seeing you that day still turns us on!'

When I heard these words born of bad taste I felt
Infuriated but I controlled myself to honour the wedding guests
And pretended as if I had not heard him but Duryodhana
In naked animal hunger stared at me and in rising anger
I felt like throwing the scalding hot dish at his face but
Somehow I mastered my feelings, and saying that I was tired I made
A move to enter the inner apartments and Kunti, observant as ever,
Said, 'Dear Panchali, I admire your composure. Good you did not
React to the uncivil behaviour of the wicked. You have observed the duty
Of honouring the guests how so ill-behaved they are.
I am proud of you.'

With a face gone pale, I asked her: 'Oh, mother, you look
Worn out, and you have not eaten. How can I eat when
You have not?'
'How can I eat before serving food to our kinsfolk?'
'You look very tired and you have toiled much. Come,
We shall eat together. If we don't, it will be a day of fasting for us?'
Unable to hide her mind, she said, 'Without offering food to
The guest, you know, I don't even drink water. How can I eat?'
'No, mother, all the guests have been served. I don't think
I have neglected any.'
'Daughter, listen. Karna, the king of Anga is in the guest house,
And no one has served him food.'

Hurt I was and wondered whether she was fasting because
Of Karna, then, again she spoke:
'Do take care of Karna, to serve him food is our
Duty. You as the queen of Indraprastha take on yourself
This responsibility. Karna is not only our guest but
Your senior brother-in-law. Take Maye and Nitambini
With you and give him his lunch, and wait on him, quick.'
It disturbed me and yet saying, 'Your order I cannot disobey,
I am not against it but if he declines to have his food,
What do I do?'
I waited. But Kunti said, 'You are the wedded wife of

King Yudhisthira and you are his wedded spouse and caretaker
Of the house of Pandavas. The gods won't be pleased if you
Do not go and attend on Karna. If he stays hungry, how can
you eat?
You have to adhere to the *dharma* of the care of guests and if
You do not go, he will sleep on an empty stomach, this I know.'
Then I thought about it: whether Karna feels happy or
Not, Kunti surely would feel happy, and therefore I had better go.

The next moment I went with Nitambini and Maye and
Conveyed to him Kunti's message and he eagerly
Asked, 'What message? Did mother Kunti send you?'
We said we had brought the food on her orders and
An amazed Karna said: 'I intended to go to sleep without food.'
'No, you have to have something. Mother has sent dishes of
Your liking. And to keep up the tradition of waiting properly
On guests, Panchali has come. Please eat. Don't say no.'

Karna in a voice heavy with sadness said: 'No, no,
It is not proper for a queen to walk into the
Guest house, and certainly not at this hour of night.
Perhaps Kunti has gone blind with love and has forgotten
What is proper and what is not. No, I can't say yes.'

'You are the adopted son of the queen mother and you
Stay in an apartment assigned to you, and then how can
We overlook our tradition of taking care of our guests.
Draupadi has done the right thing,' said Maye.

Bowing to the rich generosity and love, he nodded his head
And drawn by some maternal longing he ate and I served
Him food to his heart's content and with the feeling of a
Newly-earned kinship I went back to Kunti and said:
'Mother, you pressed me to go and offer him food and he
In affection and with satisfaction ate the food I served.'
It was rather late when I returned to my bed chamber
And Phalguna had already slipped into deep sleep!

Disturbing thoughts, in waves, assailed me and sleep

I could not though it was past midnight and so I
Told myself I would go and stay a while in the
Balcony and when I went up the stairs there he was,
And the moon was smiling at me!

Looking at the sky and standing depressed I started
Counting the stars and then a huge
Shadow of a huge-built-man, I thought, passed me by
And in the darkness I wondered whose it could be;
But as it stood still, without any movement I stared at it and then
I knew it was none but Karna himself who stood
Like an image of deep frustration or rather like the
Icon of misfortune of the Dwapara epoch!
Soon another shadow also passed by and as I looked at it
I knew it was Kunti who was staring at the sky and
Sighing and sobbing. Ah, sad Kuru clan! Will the endless sighs
Of this unfortunate mother ever stop, I asked to myself.

From within came jubilant voices announcing the victory of
Yudhisthira at the game of dice; from within the heart of Karna
Came echoes of the wickedness caused by caste and clan, and
The sky was overcast and the beauty of the moon was
clouded and
As I stepped down, it was dawn.
Krishna who had returned from his early morning walk was
Groaning as blood flowed from his lotus petal-shaped toe and
Partha much disturbed asked, 'Krishna, what has happened?
You hurt yourself?'
'This is a wound caused by Sudarshana
Chakra to remind me that if life does not get bloodied
How can bloodiness of life be got over? How can I ever forget it?'
Amazed, I was. How small is this world compared to the vastness
Of his heart! His heart throbs in pain for the sake of the
Downtrodden and the deprived and the pain of this deprived world
haunts him.
The blood continued to flow and Arjuna, saying he would get
antidotes for

The wound, went in but I tore the end of my saree
and bandaged the foot
And the blood stopped and I was little comforted.

Maye came running and said: 'Oh, queen. What have you
Done? A most valuable saree and you have torn it? See, Partha
Is running back with ointment in his hand.'
'Oh, Maye, what are you saying? Each drop of Sri Krishna's
Blood is most precious as it is the blood of the ideal man and
You worry about this stupid saree!' And Krishna smiling
Spoke: 'Ah, dear friend, Draupadi, your magical touch has
Healed the wound. The bleeding has stopped.' Saying so
He pressed my hand against his heart and continued:
'The wish to repay my debt to Krishne stays deep within me;
Memories cascade in my heart and witnessing their encompassing
Design, you be happy' and with this blessing, Krishna returned
to Dwaraka.

CANTO XIV

TRULY, YOU ARE HIS SPRING OF INSPIRATION

In this way, as the cart of life rolled on, sometimes
Bhima, with his uncontrolled anger, caused unpleasantness;
Phalguna was busy with his practice of archery and the days
Went by, and as I, in my turn, was with Yudhisthira at night.
He said: 'Krishne, you really are the source of my life and
Well being. When you are with me things are so easy and I
Know it is not comfortable living with five brothers and yet
you have
Brought unanimity of feeling with all of us; this is a
Truth none can overlook or forget.'

As we sat talking, Phalguna, like a hurricane rushed
Into our bedroom, and with his head bent, eyes averted, he
Collected a few weapons and stormed out!

Dharmaja seeing it all said: 'Panchali, Phalguna is a
Great hero who fights for the poor, wipes the teary eyes
Of the exploited, and as long as he stands firm in his vow,
The whole world will remain safe'
When he went out he saw, in the outer courtyard,
Arjuna waiting there to meet him, and in the costume of a
Celibate Brahmin and anxiously he asked 'What is this?
Why this dress? Which way are you going?' And, Partha,
With folded hands said: 'Brother, permit me, please to go,
For I have to abide by what we have agreed on: when Krishne
Is alone with one of us in the bedroom and anyone who
intrudes one

Has to go on a pilgrimage for four years, and this is a vow
We all took in the presence of sage, Narada. And, I, now
Therefore, am going'

Shocked, I stood like a statue and in great distress Dharmaja said:
'Brother, what crime have you done? A Brahmin's cow was
being stolen
And you came in to collect your weapons, and that is no fault, really,'
Partha, in anger, straightening himself stiff, said: 'What are you
Saying? Vows cannot be broken, he who breaks the vow,
needs to be punished.
If he isn't, how can we protect righteousness?'

In a mood angry and hardened, he readied himself to go.
To see him off we followed, and I, to go with him, dressed myself
In a coarse saree and was about to join him when Maye came
and said:
'Oh, queen, how will you go with him into the forest? If you
go, your
Five husbands will also accompany you, don't take on this adventure,
You should not abandon the question of the safety of the nation.'

Partha came near me and spoke: 'Krishne, bid me goodbye,
After four years I shall return, do, not accompany me or restrain
Yourself, and live your life here.'
'But tell me why cannot I go with you? Who are you to
Question what I have decided? And the world without you
Around, is nothing to me.' He, with a show of deference, said
'I have accepted many of your decisions but this is a
Decision which cannot be accepted.'
'Is it not the tradition for the wife to follow her husband?
Did not Sita go with Ramachandra? Do not stop me. I shall
Go with you.'

'You have not one but five husbands; and, like Ramachandra,
I alone am not your husband. Why have you this illusion?'
Sharp as a sword, Arjuna's words stabbed me, and I felt like
Breaking down in sorrow but thinking it not proper, I with a sure

Mind replied: 'I did not accept five husbands, and you know
It, then why hurt me with raising the issue now?'

'See, Krishne, you are my wife and yet, you are so by turns,
And now you are Dharmaja's wife and therefore, you cannot come.
Be patient, if we do not protect *dharma*, who will? I shall
Involve myself in this great task, and let not, like a mirage, you bother
Me with ides of "me" and "mine". We move as life moves.'

Putting a tilak on is forehead, with a firm mind, I said:
'Go, Partha, let your pilgrimage be safe; you are to be celibate
For four years, may Krishna take care of you. Since protection of
Dharma is your duty, stay firm there. Let you peregrination be
Happy and strength giving! 'He in affection said to me:
'Krishne, you are wise; cause no pain to Dharmaja who, too is rigorously
Wedded to *dharma*; do not be angry with the sharp words of Bhima,
Do understand the innocence of Nakula and Sahadeva and, as far
Kunti, she has suffered too many humiliations in her life and for
Our sake; and, when your friend Krishna comes, do take care of him;
And do not worry about me. A true brave man learns to take
Adversities in life calmly. Otherwise how can we face the forthcoming
Huge war; your love and inspiration will see me through life; and
We, like sandalwood, spend ourselves and spread goodness and sweatness;
Our life is not ours, and you know it, and we have to reserve it
For the good of the people. The strength of our marital ties
Can win the world. Like Lord Shiva, you have to learn to swallow
The bitter poison and see that our sacrifice which has the goal of
Establishing *dharma* bears fruit, and to keep the chariot of *dharma*
In good stages you have to remain here as its charioteer.'
The words Partha spoke released in me a spring of
Hope and inspiration; bitter thought that had risen melted away
Like ice; but in my eyes was a pool of tears, my throat went

Dry and I could only nod my head to suggest my approval. Then
I, moving closer to him, said: 'I don't know whether others know,
But you have to tell me: did you enter my bedroom on
The pretext of collecting arms only to punish me? Weren't the
Weapons available elsewhere in the palace? And, to save a cow,
Did you need a heap of powerful weapons? Who, do you think,
Will buy your story? I am the fire-god's daughter and you
Want to blunt the instrument of knowledge that I possess
within me!
The sages in the forest are truthful souls and, if while entering
Their place, if you speak untruth, the fire of sacrifice and war
Will be doused out.'

Arjuna was shocked and, in the tone of a convict caught,
Cringed: 'Yes, I wanted to punish you, it was but the ego of
The male in me and you have found it out today. There is in
Me repentence and I beg your forgiveness. Don't you again
hurt me.'
Sorrow burst through me, my throat went dry, but the anger
In me was washed away and in love I sent away my Partha.
Early in the morning, bathed in the Yamuna, offered worship
To the sun-god and spent the day in japa and tapa and in the rest
Of the day household chores, taking care of Kunti and the Pandavas,
And in the evening listened to Sage Narada who narrated the holy
Stories of gods, and one day, seeing me dressed in the garb of
a sanyasini
Smilingly Narada said: 'Ah, dear daughter, you are living the
Life of a religious recluse but Partha is wallowing in pleasure.
Is there a limit to man's craving for endless desires? Don't be angry
With me. I shall tell you the story of your husband's life:

At the beginning he lived a rigorously religious life and once,
after the japa,
He got into the Ganga for a bath, and there he saw the nagakanye,
daughter of Naga king,
Ulupi, who grabbed him to her side saying, "You have not
taken a

Vow to live only with Draupadi, and if she can sleep with other husbands,
Why do you force yourself to be true to her alone?
Do not say 'no'.
In the forthcoming war you would need the help of the army of the Nagas,
Wed me, therefore, and strengthen the political relationship between
Our kingdoms; this is an accepted policy of all kingship and
Only matrimonial relationship can make countries stay with
Other ones. Come and build a great and strong Bharata.
Phalguna translated his pilgrimage into a campaign for an
Empire, saw big dreams and wedded Ulupi, and is now the father of a son!'
As Sage Narada detailed the political game of Arjuna,
I listened to it silently and became depressed, and speak, I could not.
But saw the wicked history of the masculine world unfolding before me,
And in it, each day, there was a new chapter!

'Walking in search of a sagely life he passed through many
Thick forests and centres of pilgrimage and hermitages of saints
And realized the wonders of a life of meditation and prayer and
As he did so he came across the princess of Kalinga and he became infatuated
When he saw her coming out of the temple dedicated herself to the sun-god.
She too looked at him and their eyes got entangled, and as he
Stood speechless she softly said, "You, sanyasi, what are you in
Search of? What are you looking for here?" and he in turn said
"Could I stay here for a short time? I am a sanyasi, is there any
Objection against my staying here?" and she said, "Our country,
Kalinga, is known for its kindness to pilgrims. You can stay here
For years together without a worry?" "Could I hope to receive
Every morning, from your hand, the temple prasadam?"
"That would be a great, fortunate privilege."
Then, the sanyasi, asked her eagerly,
"Young lady, I see a wonderful light within you. Are you still

Unwed? What kind of a husband would you want? Tell me, even
If it is Eshwara or Krishna or Karna or Duryodhana? Do let me
Know I shall try to fulfill your desire." And she said:
"I would like to have for my husband, the greatest of heroes. Known
In all the three world as Partha, he alone can be my husband."

Arjuna fell for her charms and got wedded to her and their
Life of happiness and mutual love lasted more than six months and
Then, Partha, stroking her chin said, 'Goddess, stay here, I shall
Come here every year. How can I ever forget the sweet
love you have
Fed me with, your Kalinga-love how can I ever forget!
Stay here, for the path I take now is thorny and hard, and
Your soft feet would get hurt. But the great love I have
Received from you shall forever stay with me green. Do
Allow me to go in your generosity for I have to tread along
the beaches and reach Manipura.
And there in Manipura he saw the crown princess,
Chitrangadadevi and falling in love with her
He wed her and the King Chitravahana celebrated their
wedding in a grand and befitting royal way.
This is his story of victorious love!'
As I listened to the narrative, the fire of jealousy
Flared up like the doomsday fire and burnt me. I felt that
My man, giving up asceticism, had fallen into the hands of other
Women; were Chitrangada and Ulupi more beautiful than me?
Did they offer better love than me? Burning questions of envy
Sizzled through me as Narada described in detail the
Amorous adventures of Arjuna but understanding my mind
The sage said: 'Krishne, political moves and designs are woven in
This way and since the cousins store in them, dislike and hatred,
Surely it will flare up causing a great war and at such times
Matrimonial relationships shrink enemies' grasps and strength,
And these widen ours.
The kingdom of Kalinga, Manipura, and Nagaland
Are huge and powerful and their support you will receive and
Therefore think of these relationships of Arjuna as strategic

Moves, and they in the interests of
Safeguarding our national integrity. This you remember.'

With interest I listened to Narada but I knew this made
No logic but only sophistry. Even granting them to be more
Beautiful than me, did the interest of the nation ever really
Touch him? How can one accept this made-up story and
How can anyone not see the influences of base desire and call of
The body? This great big drama of the deceitful
Behaviour of the male which had but one aim and that
Being the destruction of what is beautiful and natural to the
world of women.
How can I trust the story made up by men cunning in nature?
There is no one who will stand up for me—be it Father or
Partha—all, all are venomous creatures.

Then appeared my friend Maye and whispered in my ears:
'Oh, queen, Phalguna truly is a heartless man! A cheat he is,
Who in the guise of alliances savours not one but many
Women! When will women comprehend and cease to become
Preys of the stalking male! When will this age dawn?'
She tried to console me in many ways and to get over
Our sorrow, with our maids, both of us got into the cool
waters of the Yamuna.
The cool breeze was soothing and was a balm to our
Wounded feelings and we, unaware, swam too long a
Distance and then were swept away by the forceful current of the
River and no longer could we swim but had to allow the waters
To push us in whatever direction in which they rushed;
Down the floods took us fast, and a cosmic nothingness entered
Our minds and we closed our eyes giving up all hope; the waters
Moved swirling, my plaited hair was all undone and I simply floated
Down; at a distance suddenly I thought I saw an ascetic standing
Who after his bath was offering worship to the sun-god,

And before I could think of anything two strong arms took
hold of me

And drew me to the bank of the river and I heard a soft voice:
'Ah, surprised I am! The Queen of Indraprastha! Ah, you should
Not commit suicide. What deficiency is there in your life?
And, at this
Evening hour, should anybody jump into the flooded Yamuna?'
I wondered whose voice it was and who this handsome
powerfully built person was.
And as I looked I saw it was the valiant Karna,
The king of Anga and the next moment shyly I draped right
my wet saree
Which had got glued to my body but in a consoling voice, he said:
'Krishne, don't fear; this brave Karna will take you back safely
To Indraprastha. I was here on a hunting spree and I saw you
Drowning and I came and rescued you.'

'I was playing in the water but got caught in an eddy which
Almost killed me and you, god-like, came and saved me. How
do I thank you!'
Karna's wife Vaishali held my hand and led me to the chariot and
As the chariot moved, she said: 'My husband often spoke of you
Admiringly and I had always wanted to see you in person. True,
I am Karna's wife but truly you are the source of his inspiration.
And it is because of your presence that he has become a
Maharathi, a great warrior, I really am small before you.'
Lost in my own thoughts I recalled, in fact, I felt that
I had been less than fair to him, specially on the day of the
Swayamvara. If only Krishna and Drishtadymna had not raised
Objections, Karna would have been the right son-in-law to
Drupada! Can any man choose his birth? And, at every step,
He had been unjustly treated, and yet my respect for Karna
Went on increasing, and my mind like a wild horse went
Prancing in places wrong!

Shortly we reached Indraprastha and Karna, with folded hands
Bowed and said, 'Oh! Queen, we bid you goodbye now and
Happy we are, an opportunity came our way to save your life.'
And I said in gratitude everflowing: 'I am grateful to you,

And I shall speak of the help you were to us today to Kunti.'
Smiling he said,
'I have done only my duty. A charioteer's job is to protect
The womenfolk and see they reach home safe.' And I said,
'Although you are part of the enemy camp, you have saved me and
I shall never forget your kindness.'
But shaken I was and yet said to myself:
'From the drowning water I am saved
But would I now be pushed into a flaming fire'. This was however
A riddle which none could solve.

CANTO XV

A REARING SEA OF SELF-RESPECT

The news of the arrival of Krishna spread and with it
The fragrance of the freshly blossomed flowers swept
the city although
Krishna was yet to arrive! It was like fragrance preceding the
Blossoming of the flowers! What else can herald his coming?
I closed my eyes and with my inner eye I beheld his divine
Form, the sight of which thrilled my being, and I shuddered
In happiness!
Once I was about to be drowned and though I swam
For a while I got caught in a vortex and Karna saved me from
The jaws of death; I felt shattered when Partha left me and
Coming to know of his doings hurt me deep but on hearing the
News of Krishna's arrival I forgot all my sorrows and worries.
I wondered why he was here suddenly, was it because Partha was
Away from me? Has he brought any message from Partha?
All the same I made necessary arrangements for his welcome
and then came Maye who smilingly said:
'He knows that you feel lonely and
That is why he is here to lighten your worry, for who else is
fit to do it?
The whole world knows the brotherly relationship of the two
for he
Doesn't even inhale the fragrance of a flower before offering it to
Krishne: for ideal friendly affection the two are accepted icons.'

'Does Krishna want his devotees to walk the thorny path, does

He like it? And I have yet a long way to go. Again, although Partha
Has been away far long, Krishna has not thought of visiting
me here.'
With an inkling into my state of mind, Maye said: 'They say
Krishna has brought news 'that he is hale and healthy,
Staying, at Dwaraka,' hearing it I beamed in happiness and
I, with my head at his lotus-like feet, felt like a bird
Which flies high in the air, for it knows my dreams and
Desires are at the feet of Krishna, and Maye consolingly said:

'You know, the feet of Krishna and Arjuna are absolutely
Identical, so identical Rukmini and Satyabhama get confused. Ah,
Now, wake up and take care of Krishna.'
The next moment Krishna himself was there, saying,
'Panchali, are you well? Why do you look worried?'
'Don't you know my mind, Krishna? What kind of a friend
are you!' 'Are you lost in thinking about Partha?'
Understanding the irony, Krishna said:
'He thinks of you all the time, be assured,
For a year he will live the life of an ascetic in Dwaravati and
Then will come back to you. Do be unworried.' It puzzled me,
Why is Palguna staying for a year at Dwaravati, what is the
Reason? Krishna knowing my mind said, 'I have come to see
You without an invitation! Why direct your anger for Partha at
The small me! Today your responsibilities are great, and are of
Many kinds. You have to take care of the Pandavas, and you
Need now a campanion who would be with you all the while.'

'When I have you by my side why would I need a companion?'
Hearing me, he smilingly said: 'Oh, Maye, why is your friend
So dense! She it is who put people in trying situations. And, I
Am looking for the right kind of friend for her. And she
Will be with you!'
'I admire your concern and skill. You know
How to find a friend for me but already I have found friends
In Vaishali, Karna's wife and Haritha, wife of Drona.
True their husbands

Are opponents to each other but that does not affect us.
You are my witness I have spent the years alone, and without Partha, and I keep waiting.'
Sri Krishna carefully began: 'Panchali, don't I know how the sharp arrows
Of separation hurt you, and who else but me can understand you.'
Listening to Krishna, I turned my mind inward and thought of how
After the death of Kripe, Harita, took care of Aswathama as if he was
Her own son and he, in the love of the new mother, grew and became the apple of
Her eye and I was surprised by the affection she gave and went seeking for her
Friendship and some times she would, from her heart speak, of her
Husband's love for the Kauravas and that inspired me to serve
My five husbands submerging all my selfish thoughts.
Once Harita Devi told me, 'Krishne, you are the ideal wife in all of
Aryavarta. The world will bow its head seeing your patience, tolerance, self-respect
And you know Karna is in no sense inferior to
Arjuna and he is king, even without the help of Kauravas. True,
There is no end to the wickedness of Kauravas, and Arjuna is on a pilgrimage
To fulfill his vow.' These words moved me and I decided to sacrifice
All of me the moment he was back and now word came that
Abandoning, Ulupi and Chitrangada, Arjuna was back, and for me!
Hoping to meet Phalguna who had gone away from me
There in my heart sprang the desire for a sweet reunion.
And it burgeoned in me as in the heart of a newly-wed bride;
Separation which had rendered my being a desert, became
Suddenly a spring-fed land and a new world beckoned me with spread
Arms and as I got ready to welcome back my Phalguna, I saw
In the tray two freshly made big garlands and I wondered who
Else was coming with him, was it Krishna or Sri Rama?

Guessing my anxiety Maye said: 'Devi, forgive us for keeping
from you a secret, and do not be angry with us.
Now Sri Krishna's sister, Subhadre,
Comes, you greet her with a bouquet of flowers and take
her to her apartment.'
The grandeur of the newly-decorated bed-chamber hurt me
and the sea of
My sense of self-respect roared audibly but I in anger
Cursed and said to myself: 'Why has Phalguna behaved so?
And, defying Balarama how does he get wedded, and in Dwaraka!
How can Krishna be so heartless! What horrifying adventure is
this to bring
Subhadra into Indraprastha? Cheating me, is he? Why did I
not see that he alone
Was the real puppeteer who was staging this deceitful game?
Is it like the proverbial fence eating up the crops? Have I
Become a tool in his hands, and allowed myself to be deceived?'

Trembling in anger, I continued. 'Friend, you knew
Phalguna's tricks,
But why didn't you let me into it? I never thought you would
In this fashion play traitor to me? How come you became a
Part of this shameful game? Caught in this web of deceit,
I have failed. And, could he do this without the approval of
his brother,
Dharmaja? Like a rural idiot I have been swindled, and
That too in the game of the selfish male world! Indraprastha
Has become the land of my enemies. How could Dharmaja
Keep Phalguna's marriage a secret from me? Is it not real
Betrayal? Inexcusable sin it is to dally with several women
While observing for four years strict celibacy! It is wickedness!
Or did Dharmaja's devotion to truth get watered by his love for
His brother? That heroic Phalguna wed several princes is no
Act of heroism, it really is an act which should make
our head bow in shame.
Why do men romanticize this act? To gild such acts
With the lustre of bravery, surely is the male world's insolence!

Should I doubt Partha wedding Subhadra? No, this play of
Kidnapping surely is a trick of Sri Krishna. This I knew that
Krishna was black in colour but did not know his heart and
mind too were black!
I worshiped him thinking he was one of us but did
Did he, out of love for his own clan, become selfish?
Humiliation, shame and desperation sprang intensely within me
And I wondered how I was to fight all these, alone? Without
Going out to receive Arjuna and Subhadre, I sank into my bed.
In an ocean of tears freely flowing down I drowned myself
And then there was a knock on the door and when I opened
Sri Hari walked in, patted me softly on my shoulder and said:
'I heard you were not well. Are you all right now? What
illness ails you?'
With a heavy heart and in a note serious, I said
'Me, born of fire, what illness can enter me? Flames can
Burn our tongue but who can burn the tongue of flame?
How do I welcome Phalguna and Subhadre? How do I
Accept your sister as my husband's yet another wife?
The other day when you came you didn't tell me but
Since it has the approval of Dharmaja, whose approval is
Needed? Within the cultures of Dwaraka may be it is
acceptable
But in the culture of Panchala there is no room for it,
this, Krishna, you have to understand.'

Without waiting for a reply, I walked towards the main door,
Took the decorated trays the maids had got ready and waving the
Arati, I welcomed the couple, and, with tearful eyes, went back
Into my apartment.
Arjuna softly following me, walked, in saying:
'I come back after four long years, but in my dear girl's
Face there is no smile! And she returns without even looking
at me,
Why, what has happened?' In a voice sharp and full of anger
I said: 'Well, after sighting the lotus-faced Subhadre, my
Face, does it not look pale and colourless?'

'No, do not compare yourself with Subhadre. In wise discrimination,
Tolerance, courage of heart and mind, generosity and self-sacrifice,
And in beauty none of them, neither Ulupi, Chitrangade nor
Subhadre,
Can equal you and again, believe me, none of them can
Make me move away from you.'

'For heroes of the Kuru clan, women are the arrows in their
Quiver, and they do not ever think that the woman has a heart
And soul of her own or that she possesses an individuality of
her own!
Never has this light of awareness brightened the zone of your
Ambition. We are only your armoury and we, who do not
know that,
Are truly fools. But this you understand: it is a woman's curse
Which will raze your empire into dust.'
Krishna suddenly
Walked in, and spoke hurriedly: 'For three specific reasons,
I got the wedding of Arjuna and Subhadre done. Why do you
Blame him? My only intention was to make the Yadava army
Part of ours and the other was to get you a dear friend and
Again, the two knew each other from their young age and
their wedding
Was a foregone conclusion made by destiny itself, and how could this
be averted?'

With a sad, heavy voice, I said: 'In the interest of
Familial politics, do not get us trapped, and trampling on
flower-like
Minds, transform not Indrapastha into another Brindavan!'

Subhadre came running, fell on my feet, and washing them
With her tears said: 'Dear sister, I know I have no rights, and
I know
I am not worthy of being your sister, you always are the
Empress of the lunar race of the Pandava clan. Allow me only to
Remain your maid and I've wed Partha to make our lives meaningful.'
'No, you are the dear sister of Sri Krishna and Balarama and

You should not fall at my feet; I am moved by your
Affection,' saying so, I raised her, wiped her tear-filled
Eyes, and she, then, said, 'Now that I have seen you, I know
My decision was not right. Yes, Arjuna has not been fair to you,
But unfair it is not to me. From my young days, I have loved him!'
And saying, so she began to cry and shed tears in torrents.
What was her crime! An innocent girl she was!
Patting on her cheeks,
I said: 'No, be not afraid. You have room in my heart. Live like
A sister to me in Indraprastha, but do not trust the men here!
Your Arjuna and Krishna are both swindlers, but worry not.
Till today you were a dear sister to Sri Krishna and from today
You are a dear sister to Krishne, and therefore worry not
about the future.'
There blew a cool breeze, and no longer was there any sadness about
Receiving Subhadre as sister. My heart fluttered in happiness
and even
Decorating their bed-chamber was a task pleasant to me and
as I left her on
Partha's bed and returned, there a lotus of the lunar dynasty
had began blossoming!

III. Movement

PEREGRINATIONS

CANTO XVI

SHOULD YOU FALL, IN BROAD DAYLIGHT, INTO A WELL SEEN AT NIGHT!

One day, Vidura, counsellor to the Kuru clan
Arrived and, in an embarrassed tone, spoke with the king,
'Dharmaja, Duryodhana invites you for a game of dice and
If you say yes, I shall go back and convey your approval.'

The moment I heard these words, I shuddered in fear and I
Knew it was but a deceitful ploy and I immediately went to
Yudhisthira and said: 'There is much fraudulence here! Like a
Bad cat he is scheming and wants to muddy the clean
Waters of our lives and that is why he asks you to play a
Game dice. Please do not pay heed to the request,
and fall on easy prey.'
Yudhisthira said: 'Ah, Lady, I know the four vices which
Kings should keep away from: hunting, drinking, the game of
Dice and indulgence in sex, but when Duryodahan wishes
And the wish has the approval of Bhishma and the other elders,
How do I decline the invitation? Tell me, inevitable it looks.'

But without giving in I persisted: 'See, you are not
Skilled in the cunning game of dice and surely you will be
Defeated. Would you, in broad daylight, fall into a well, seen at night!'
'I know both war and the game of dice and knowing, that
I am not proficient at the game, Suyodhana sends an invitation!'
'Oh, you born to *dharma*, listen, the Kauravas do not
Tolerate our progress at Indraprastha; they lust after
Our kingdom, and that is the secret of this invitation;

They know they cannot equal us in riches or strength and
Therefore they have made Uncle Shakuni propose this
Deceitful design. I do not know what awaits us and don't you
Remember the words Vyasa spoke on the Rajasuyayaga day?

He foretold that for another thirteen years we would have to
Wade through fire. Do not be rash, and let not rashness
Bring ruin on us. If you want to fight, fight and meet death.
This won't make us sad or repentent but knowing full well
Why do you leap into the swirling waters of deceit?
Enquire with Vidura
And know from him why this invitation has been extended.'

Yudhisthira uneasily asked and even after learning that what
Was behind the invitation was the envy of Kauravas and Shakuni's
Wicked advice, he did not decline to play the game of dice.
I kept quiet for I knew they had no respect for our
Views, and convinced he was that dicing was right and proper
For Kshatriyas. 'What remedy will work with born fools?
Did he think dicing was easier than going to war with his cousins!
What shall I say of those who put their trust in destiny?
Why did he not respond to my words of discrimination?
Who can now save us? I know there would be in Hastinapura,
A great big shandy, and later we all would be pushed into a
fiery lake.
But still we went. Who knows what waits for us?
Since I was on my periods I was not to go to the
Council of kings nor was I supposed to see any man's face-
Some strange superstitious rule somebody had made!

I, like a fish thrown out of water, sat alone in a corner.
Caught in bodily and mental depression and there was within me
A foreboding of a terrible tempest which would uproot us all.
But there was Maye with me who stood plaiting my rich long
Hair and said: 'Friend, I knew princes would fall in love with
Your dark luxuriouis hair and therefore I had it covered with
Garlands of flowers.'
Because of uncleanness, I was wearing but a single dress and had

Left my hair free, unplaited and it was afternoon when
Maye came, sat near and said: 'Is it a fault if men lose
Their hearts when they see the rich glossy natural hair of women!
Why be upset with it? Truly it is, not strange that princes
Fell for your lovely head of hair.' The irony I saw and said:
'What is my crime? Is beauty a curse? But, think of what
Is happening there in the council, and what discussions?'
'But what use is our being anxious? We shall lose at the game of
Dice and return to Indraprastha with broken hearts.'
'No, why sit and prattle here. Go, and see what is happening there,
And come back quick and report to me the details of
Who won and who lost, and who says what.'
'All those princes who came for the swayamvara, I know,
Desire Dharmaja's defeat, but the reason eludes me. What
Could be their interest?'
'You would not know the tricks and stratagems of the envious;
I am disturbed, and my right eye-lid flutters and surely
It is an omen heralding disasters about to happen
Some black hooded cobra has entered the anthill!'

CANTO XVII

BE FECUND AT THE PALACE OF THE KURU KINGS

Vikarna's wife came running all the way and, gasping,
Told what had transpired at the council and how Duryodhana had
Sent for Vidura and said: 'Come, Vidura, go, call our
Slave, Draupadi, and ask her whether she would like to be a
Waiting-woman in the palace or stay at our seraglio.
Find out, know her mind and return with that woman here.'
In great anger Vidura spoke out: 'The queen of the Pandavas,
A housemaid? She is wife to one who hit the
Eye of the rotating fish and to another who fought and humbled
The Maghada Jaresandha and, do you think, this game of dice
You have won by trickery, will stand by you always?
Do you think Krishne would keep quiet? You will see not one
But a hundred women who with flowing hair will say the first lines
Of a song that is going to herald the end of the great
Mahabharata war.' Listening to the frightening prophecy of Vidura,
The king of the Kaurvas, in great anger, shouted:
'This Vidura is no use for anything, he is touched in the brain!
What use is assigning any work to him? Send Pratikami to
Fetch that woman.'
Here, while I was sitting surrounded by several maids
Who were proficient in the art of conversation, Pratikami,
Came running, prostrated and with great humbleness said:
'Oh, queen, listen, your master has lost at the game of dice,
And the Kuru king has won. He has lost his horses and elephants
And the royal treasury, but why detail it all: he has lost
His brothers four and with them you too, he has lost all,

And everything! Shiva, Shiva! How can I narrate the tragic tale?'
It was like a sudden, heavy snowfall on the blooming
Lotus flowers or like a heavy downpour on crops ready to be
Reaped! The faces of maids went pale with sadness and
I called Pratikami and asked him, 'Tell me, how did my
Husband lose the game? Did the Kauravas play a double-game?
What did he first bet? And what did he lose later? Oh, god!
Was cheating part of the game of dice?'
'Oh, queen, first he wagered all his property, then huge amounts
Of money, and then the elephants and the horses and his army,
Followed by the maids-in-waiting, then his brothers and then
Himself'; and as he paused I eagerly asked, 'Do not be
Afraid, tell me, did the king wage me after he had wagered
Himself, tell me that.' Pratikami said, 'Yes, Queen,
He first pledged himself, lost, and then he wagered you and lost.
Please, come with me, it's the king's orders, how can I defy?'
In great surprise I told him, 'It is unfair. Dharmaja
First sold himself and then how could be bet on me? Go, ask
The learned and the wise courtiers know their answer and if
It makes sense, I shall go with you.' Silently Pratikami left,
Went back to the assembly and in much fear submitted:
'Oh, King, this is what Panchali said: "If the king
Lost the game and himself first, how then could he wager on me?"
This is a sublte question of high ethics, let the elders answer
And then I shall come.'
The Kaurava king said: 'What! A question! Is not his
Wife his property? Why this quibbling?' Saying so
He called his broher Dusyasana and said: 'Oh, brother, you
Go and drag her to this place by her hair, and right now,
What arrogance for the wife of the five! She is our slave now.
What can anybody do? I speak right. Can the blowing wind
put out the fire?'
'Today, Yudhisthira's dear wife, the daughter-in-law of the
Bharata dynasty, dear friend to Sri Krishna, should she like a
Helpless woman, on periods, stand dressed in a single piece of
cloth? How will the

Five husbands face it? With this humiliation, can one
continue to live?
Is woman a man's merchandise? Or, an animal like a horse or
an elephant?
Am I a soul-less being? There is deep darkness everywhere!'
Dushyasana, with no touch of politeness, advanced like a
Conqueror and shouted: 'Hey, you, come, stand in the Council
Hall of the Kuru King; now, get off the couch and stand as
our serving maid there.'
I, with equanimity, said: 'Oh, brother to the king and my
brother-in-law,
Yes, Dharmaja has lost, all right; first answer my question;
It is not proper for a woman on her periods to enter the
royal council.'
The villain in more anger said: 'What absurd talk is this?
If you are on periods, here become pregnant at his residence!
Delay not, your wretched five husbands have lost and if you want,
Speak of the proper and improper at the council of the elders.'
Saying so the ruffian, drunk with self-praise, stretched out his
Hand, pulled at the rich hair which had been sprinkled with sacred
Water from sages and saints many, and said: 'Ah, you little dove,
Come, you are our wealth, you are ours from today! Forget your
Five husbands and forget too your high morality and
inhibitions ethical!
Come, we, who a hundred brothers, have become your owners now.
Why worry then?'
The entire assembly turned away its face and said to itself:
'Why have eyes to see such scenes of heartache!'
Seeing me, Bhimarjuna's blood boiled but with a sign of his
Eyebrow, Dharmaja silenced them: Partha controlled himself
Caught in the web of *dharma*; Silence became dark and heavy;
Hoping that Gandhari would protect my honour or Bhanumati and
Other sisters-in-law would come to my help I sped on but none
Responded, the doors of the heart of compassion had been sealed!
Mine was a cry in the wilderness, none heard it:
Rushing in like a wild bull, he, holding me by my hair,

Dragged me and I held on to the torn cloth that covered by
Breasts; my hair disheveled was spread on my back, and
I shuddered like a creeper hit by a tornado!
When he dragged and kicked me I fell, rolled on the
Floor, got up and with folded hands begged:
'I am on my periods and have but a single piece of clothing
on me.'
He villainously guffawing said: 'What does it matter to us,
The state in which you are? Be in a single piece of cloth or
Even without it, naked! For a slave woman, what honour,
what modesty?'
To overcome the humiliation I covered my face with my long
Tresses, and my breasts with my palms and in silence
Prayed to my dear friend Krishna as I knew that
He only could come to my help. My five husbands sat dumb,
And in their very presence their wife was being outraged!
Why won't Acharya Bhishma open his mouth, and does not
The blind father-in-law hear? What has happened to Kripa?
Are the citizens of this blind king also blind? Are all
Deaf? Dushyasana staring at me bellowed:
'Hey! Didn't the king pledge you in the game of dice? And,
He has sold you to us, what's the good of weeping now?
Be a part of the herd of menials at our palace, go!'
Witnessing this stressful scene, I could see, Karna's eyes
Become moist, and compassion flowed in a stream; there were
Of course good men in the assembly but none had the courage
To stand up to him. But within me rose a strange strength, and
Keeping aside questions of shame and humiliation, like an angry
Lioness I roared: 'What if the great Aryavarta possesses noble
Virtues, it has lost its gallant manliness! All the learned here
Are silent, and are scholars only learned but sexless eunuchs.'
Hearing, these words, Bhishmacharya rose up in fury and said:
'Stop this vile violence! Answer the virtuous wife. How really
Abominably you are behaving! Is this how you treat a person
Seeking refuge? Do not take the silence of the Pandavas
lightly: do not

Destroy truth and *dharma* and do not be unfair to the dignity of
A lady who belongs to our home.'
But the Kaurava paying no heed to these words said:
'Panchali, be guided by our just words. Would a serving maid
Need such expensive earrings and jewellery, tell me?'
When at this traumatic moment, the five husbands were of no help,
Something within me, some divine power, some divine
Force, the steadfast soul of great Bharat's women,
sprang from within me,
And surveying all the four directions, in the crowded assembly,
I stood with my head held high and spoke:
'Do not think I am a helpless woman; I am the empress of
The Kuru kingdom; you think you can burn me up with the fire
Of humiliation? No, you will be rendered deaf listening to the
Screams of thousand Kauravas whose heads I shall have quartered;
You surely will lose all the good that has come to you, for
You have destroyed *dharma* and I, like Janaki will disappear
Into the earth, and I shall rise like the fire which springs from
The explosion of atomic arsenal and then who will be able to
stop the unfurling of the flag of truth and *dharma*?
'Dharmaja, listen: you are not the soul of righteousness;
You are an icon of simple, clean, truthful man of culture;
Since they defeated you at the game by means unfair why did
You not stand up and protest? All that takes place here
Is immoral, stop it, why feel hesitant? You are a freeman.'
Kaurva with irony said: 'If you want liberty, ask me.
Why are you dependent on these helpless husbands of yours?
These, who follow not the path of righteous husbands,
and are eunuchs!
What use are those to you?'
Bhimasena could not tolerate any more and standing up he said:
'In all the history of mankind there isn't an instance of a
Man pledging his wife in a game of dice, and, although losing
All his wealth, he keeps quiet. But I forgive him not for
Wagering on his dear wife. Sahadeva, get me a torch, I shall
Burn the hands that pulled the saree of the daughter of

The fire-god!'
Duryodhana guffawed and said: 'Look at this slave of ours!
She is a mine of beauty! A fragrance-spouting lovely flower!
A parrot, really! She has been assaulted by the five Pandavas, look
At her eyes and you will see the hunger of unsatisfied desire!
And to
Quench her flame of desire, this Kaurava has enough honey
of love in him,
Ah! Place her in my lap, before the fire of desire burns the world.'
Saying so, he displayed his naked thigh and patted it in pride!
The elders and the teachers and the grandfather put their heads
Down in shame, and Bhimasena roared out in anger:
'You, wicked Duryodhana, the thigh you display in this august
Assembly, I swear, I shall smash it with my mace, I swear this
On my life! And, to teach all men a lesson they shall never
Forget, I shall make the rib of this shameless, creature a pen,
dip it in
His heart's blood, and create an epic which will demonstrate
the doom
That befalls on any who shows disrespect to revered
womanhood of this country.
True, we lost of the game of dice, but to drag,
Draupadi, clad in a single piece of cloth, is unheard of, despicable
Humiliation on womankind and I now swear, to avenge it all,
I shall, in the ensuing war, rip open the belly of Dyushasana,
Tie him up with his own innards and drink his blood and this
Duryodhana, proud of his thigh, I shall smash it and will hang it
Up as war-trophy!' But Kauravas called out his brother and said:
'Dyushasana, show this plague of a woman that the sons of the
Blind King are not blind, proclaim it to the world, and don't
Be afraid, and tarry not. Strip Panchali naked and place her
in my lap!'
Gandhari then stood up in fury and said: 'Don't behave like a
Wicked worm, be a human being, this is unacceptable, stop it!'
Lustily, like a flame, he advanced, held me by my arm,
And dragged me and I struggled to free myself, but

In the melee the flowers in my hair fall and he
Without minding stepped on them and then, with his foot
drew my saree down
And like a fly caught in fire I pleaded and begged and prayed:
'Don't you see the way they have treated the daughter-in-law of
King Pandu? Grandfather, wake up, where has your authority gone!
You, the final authority on questions of righteousness,
why have you
Gone deaf? Why do you sit with your head bent? It is the
Daughter-in-law of your family who is being stripped naked!
Is your silence an approval? Do acts of unrighteousness make
you happy?
Has your progency become eunuchs?' Beating my chest, I said:
'Oh, king of Anga, Karna, aren't you a devotee of the sun-god
whom
You worship every morning? Where has your strength gone? It
Is you who make the world bright but today is an
overwhelming eclipse
Everywhere. Why do you sit in silence?' Dushyasana roared:
'Ah, you slave-maid, who will stand up for you? No one
Will come to your help.'
As a creeper is pulled away from the tree it encircles, he
tugged at
My saree and said, 'These husbands of yours are truly eunuchs,
Call them wild animals if you like.' And then, like a lioness, I
Roared, 'You, the depraved, do not forget that woman-power
Is power co-extensive with Shiva's and that the end of the world
Is in her hands, and wait for the terrible end of the Kuru Clan.'
Turning to the councillors, I said: 'Oh, elders, teachers and
Revered Kripa and others, have you all become effiminate and
Therefore, are silent? But do wake up, protect your own honour,
And stop this stripping of your own sister. Aren't you men
Born of a woman's womb? Like a calf separated from the herd
I am begging for help. Tell me, has this land of Arya *dharma*
Become a desert, and you all eunuchs? Inquire, ask
Yourself and say whether it is proper for a man who gambled

And lost to pledge his wife? Answer me.' At that moment,
Like a mountain arising out waters, Vikarna stood up and
Said: 'Hey, Dyushasana, dare not touch her. This land
Has been made sacred by the feet of Devayani, Ganga, Satyavati
And many other belonging to the great tradition of great women,
Now you are stomping on the image of one like them. No, no
Husband can pledge his wife, this is common law
accepted everywhere,
And how can you do this injustice to a woman clad but in a single
Piece of cloth? Does this do honour to the manly tradition of
Aayu,
Nahusha, Yayati and Puru? This lady is the daughter-in-law
Of our house, and what you have done brings dishonour to us.'
Dushyasana hissed: 'Hey, Sukarna, what are you saying?
Is this woman who has given away her body to five men,
Is she pure? Is she equal to the women you mentioned?
A fool you are! The objection that has not been raised by
The Great Drona or Acharya Bhishma, why are you raising it?
Is *dharma* under your contract? Why poke your nose in this?
You are but a boy, keep quiet. In a way righteous, we have now
In our possession Draupadi and she is our maid-servant. And,
You, Draupadi, you have satisfied five husbands, would it be
Difficult for you to satisfy the sixth husband?
Vidura could not contain himself and addressing Dhritarastra said,
'Oh, King, by stripping Panchali we have broken all rules of ethics
And of *dharma*, and Kuru clan surely will pay terribly.
The reservoir of the patience of the earth goddess has burst.
Stop you wicked children
This awful game. This is truly high treason they have
Indulged in. Understand this: to save a house, sacrifice an
Individual; to save a village, sacrifice a family; to save a
Nation sacrifice a town and to save your soul sacrifice yourself.
This shall be the policy of nation building,' and Bhishma,
In much pain, spoke... 'Ah, what has befallen us! What
Infamy has come your way?' But Dushyasana continued to tug
at my

Dress and I, with tears, trickling down my cheeks, looked at the
Husbands who turned away their faces and sat in silence. I
Turned to the assembly and piteously begged: 'Should an innocent
Woman be dragged and stripped in such an august assembly!
Are all subjects of the King as blind as their King?
No, from here will spring a curse which surely will
Reduce to dust this epoch of unrighteous behaviour of men.'

CANTO XVIII

SAGA OF THE PEREGRINATIONS OF THE SACRED FLAMING TRESSES.

'Sri Krishna, I am being put through an ordeal, the foolish
Acts of your cousins are burning me up, save from these wicked
Ones who are stripping me of the cloth I am clad in! You alone can
Save me, the saviour of the helpless; If I lose my honour, can
I stay alive? You crossed the oceans and saved Janaki: When the earth goddess
Was kidnapped by demons, you dived into the sea to resurrect her;
Nine avatars you took to save the good people of the world;
You saved sixteen thousand maids from the cruel hands of Kamsa;
You saved Prahalada; you saved the sacred elephant, Gajendra,
From the jaws of the crocodile; you have saved the poor and the deprived;
Now, come, splitting apart the wide sky! Come, breaking open
The pillar, and destroy the demon; come, who else will save me!
My trust I have placed in you. Oh, do come and save.
How can you put up with the wickedness of the wickedest
Duryodhana? This is an age of barbaric darkness; the
Uncivilized may be naked but not heartless like these!
Sri Hari, come and save me, with my arm raised high,
I beseech you to come and protect me; my honour, is it
Not yours too? I, in devotion absolute, surrender myself to you.'
All of a sudden, as all the oceans in union if swelled and
Roared, there was deafening noise and accompanying it a
Fierce wind strong enough to uproot plants and trees, and

It looked as if the roof the palace would fall in pieces;
There was a strange sense of doom which held down the arms
About to divest me of my saree. Alongside, rose the sweet
Sound of the flute which had the strength of millions of
Musical instruments, and the next moment there was deafening silence!
The heart beat of the assembled stopped, it went dead;
Bright sunlight played on my body and it looked as if
Sri Krishna, the bue-hued, was there.
Would Dyushasana, like Shishupala,
Scream, and fall dead? As he tugged at my piece of cloth,
The assembly become dumb: as in a grass field one sees
Cows white and brown and black, there appeared streams of light
And one thought one saw sri sudarshana chakra wheeling in with
Fierce speed, and the grace of Sri Hari fell like leaves of the
Sacred basil plant and there was, from somewhere, a shower of
Flowers. The sordid man did not stop pulling at my saree,
But I felt many sarees had been stripped off me, and there
Was a hand unseen which spoke solace to me and from the
Four corners came the sound of the flute and with a
Thud Dyushasana fell and the assembled, were awestruck.
They simply sat mute. But the dirty hunger of the Kaurava had not
Had its fill and he making, lewed gestures and slapping his thighs,
Called me: 'Come, I am waiting, come and sit in my lap.'
Hearing it Bhima in a stentorian voice spoke which got
Echoed and re-echoed: 'I shall rip open his heart
And drink his blood; I shall smash Duryodhana's thighs
And feed the flesh to dogs and ghosts.' This roused me
And I swore: 'Until my rich hair is not dipped in the blood of
Dyushasana, I shall not have my tresses plaited.
The flaming tresses of this sacred head of hair will crush all
These into pulp. This I swear today.'
The same moment Vidura unable to restrain himself
Any more, said: 'Surely Bhimsena's vow will spell great
Disaster to the Kaurava clan. Draupadi's desire will be fulfilled and

Therefore quickly release her. Dharmaja pledging his wife out is
Patently unfair. This is the beginning of the terrible end!'
Dushyasana went back to his place, his face gone pale;
And I was lying in a heap of sarees and Bhishma came and said;
'Forgive us, such unjust treatment meted out to women is most
Unworthy'. And with that he came near me, patted me and
Took me near my husbands and Dhritarashtra, tembling in fear, said
'Krishne, you, a re-virtuous, are our daughter-in-law and you
passed the fiery test. Ask me for any boon, it shall be given.'
I looked at Dharmaja and said. 'Free the sons of Pandu,
And restore their weapons to them.' 'Yes, surely, ask for another
'Forgive me, I have already asked for two boons; one, the
Freedom of my husbands and two, the restoration of their arms,
Third boon, I don't need, for with their arms restored to them
They can, on their own strength, win all that is needed.'
The king said: 'No, ask for your own freedom, for my sake.'
Pain and humiliation tearing at my vitals, I spoke:
'My five husbands are great heroes, true, but without me with
Them they won't be effective. Would releasing me help any?
No, none has the right to pledge me, I am all free, and have
Liberty absolute. I am neither a thing nor a creature who can
Be bet upon; nor have, surrendered to anyone's authority;
I am not a subject of the Kuru empire; how can an empire
With the primacy of the male take away the freedom of women?
No, I shall fight all my life and win for the woman a victory!
I do need, in this, the help of the male and when
I possess freedom absolute, how can it be hijacked by anyone?
The question of granting, me freedom arises not;
This Truth of this epoch, the male has to learn.
None of the orders of the empire or by the Kings or of texts sacred
Like the Veda or the Upanishad can circumscribe women's freedom!
Beware, beware! The woman has crossed the frontier of the male!'
The assembly sat stunned as the voice of the woman echoed
from the sea of man's heart in a fiery blaze and spreading its
tongues of
Flame it danced a terrible primeval dance. Dhritarashtra
Shaken by fear, said: 'Oh, children, stop bickering, forget

Differences, and enemity with Yagnaseni give up right now.
Dear daughter, forgive this foolish old man who permitted
This game of dice to begin; I faulted there, I know; the
The Kuru clan is fortunate to have you as the daughter-in-law;
No, it is the result of the good deals of our ancestors;
Kauravas have been exposed and the Pandavas known to the world;
Dharmaja's righteousness, Bhima's bravery and the wisdom of
the twins,
Phalguna's self-restrain—all are now praised throughout the land.
Forget the humiliation you have suffered, comfort yourselves and
Since the lioness has been wounded please see that she does not
Become the epoch-destroying Durga of our times; make
peace with
The foolish Kauravas and douse the fire of imperial ambitions.'
Before leaving for home, I bid everyone goodbye and
Prostrated before the elders and said: 'Forgive me for I forgot
To greet you when I entered this hall this morning but I was
Possessed by sorrow and anxiety, and therefore the lapse.'
The next day again at the game of dice, Dharmaja lost and
As per the rules agreed, he was to live in the forests for twelve years
And to stay incognito for another year and I left in a happy mood
For I prepared for a free, independent life to living at somebody
Else's kindness and we all moved out, the Pandavas following me!
There was a fresh breeze greeting us and the fresh blowing air
Invited us as guests of a new world and a new life.

CANTO XIX

A PERPETUAL QUEST FOR THE NEW AGE

Like forest fire, the news of the banishment of Pandavas, spread far
And wide, and from Panchala came Drupada and Dristadyumna,
And in much affection invited Draupadi to stay with them but she
Declining the invitation said: 'Father, my duty let me perform;
Did not Janaki follow her husband and put up with sufferings many
In the forest? An opportunity like hers has come my way,
Persuade me not to accept an easier way of life
I am ready to face every kind of difficulty, a daughter of the
Fire-god, am I not? Return, I shall and make you proud of me.'
As I bowed to Sri Krishna in my heart, there he was, present!
'I bow to you. Kind you have been to us! How shall
I pay back for your affection!'
'Ah, friend, with words of praise do not distance yourself
From me. As a friend, what have I done for you? When Dharmaja
Was playing the game of dice, there I was fighting Salva.
Otherwise I would have stopped this folly.
The moment this sad news reached, I came here.
But I know not how you have managed the most
Humiliating situation but because of your grit and strength
Today you have restored self-confidence to woman-kind,
Truly, you are the daughter of the fire-god.'
Coming out of my reverie, I said, 'Krishna, what
You hope for, you achieve, otherwise who could have saved
Me from that humiliation? While I stood in a single piece of
Cloth, and on my periods, the wicked Dyushasana dragged me by

My hair. And I was the wife of the five Pandavas and sister
to Drishtadyumna
And daughter-in-law of the Kuru dynasty! At that testing
Moment I trusted you and you saved me and saved the
honour of
The women of this land. It is your nectar-like help, which
Helped me bear it all'. But the memory of it made me shed
Bitter tears copiously.
But after the humiliation I suffered at the palace of the
Kurus, I did not speak a word about it to the Pandavas.
And what good would it have done? It would have been like
Pouring water on a cold block of stone which never ever
Softens it! Krishna heard me and said, 'Why praise me
And make me feel guilty? That day when I had hurt my
Foot, you tore the saree you had worn and bathed me in
Your affection pure.' He wiped the tears that had welled up in
my eyes again and said,
'Krishne, do not think it is all over
Between us! I shall keep coming back to you to taste your
Love pure for me. Ah, my sister dear, between us there is not
Any question of buying and selling, pure is our love.' That
Very moment dark clouds of worry disappeared from me but
He, smiling intriguingly, said: 'Krishne, you are an avatar of
Sri Lakshmi. Without your affection fortune won't come our way.'
Hearing it I said: 'In the open hall I was insulted, and the insult
Blackened the face of Bharata, and if now you do not punish the
Culprits, the evil of disrobing women will increase, and therefore,
It has to be destroyed at the roots. You are everything to me,
why should I fear anything?
I have already sworn to wage a war against
Evil and injustice and I shall not plait my hair until I dip it in the
Blood of Dyushasana; empires will be reduced to dust when I,
with a
Flourish, spread and wave my unplaited hair; dynasties will perish;
Unjust rule and corrupt practices will be shattered by the
rocks of defiance

I shall let roll down and I shall not stop till a new breed of justice
Will spring and this is the solemn oath I take today; and my long
Rich hair, I shall not plait until thousands of wicked heads fall, and
The very grass root of evil and corruption I shall
eradicate completely;
Those who think of women as helpless and make them their
playthings of lust
Will be ruthlessly sacrificed at the altar of justice and until this
Happens the wheels of justice of Panchali will not become
stationary;
You be my charioteer, and I need no other help.' Admiring my
Anger filled words, Krishna said, 'The pledge you have made is fair,
And just. The wicked surely will be destroyed.
No, none can stop this
Spilling of the blood of the evil-minded ones.
But whatever happens,
The heavens could fall, the Himalayas could roll down, the sun and
The moon could disappear but the terrible vow you have
made will
Surely be fulfilled, and the remaining years of life I dedicate
To make your words come true.'
The moment of departure came and Kunti shed
Bitter tears, she who had lost her husband young and
Had been witness to the sufferings of her young children!
And widowed,
She had to bring up her children with much difficulty and
had to
Suffer many kinds of hardships, with my coming, there was
new hope
Springing in her but again had to see her children banished for
Thirteen long years! When would she see again her
grandchildren? Then I thought about it:
'Subhadre, my sister, would bring them up like
Her own children but even then Kunti alone knows the hard
truth of separation and alienation.' She, in pain, said,
'Dear Krishne,

You are an ornament to our family, your virtue a treasure, how
Do I now console you? But do take care of Nakula and
Sahadeva—they are young and innocent.
Pay particular attention to the meals of
Bhima who is ever hungry, Krishna took with him Subhadra
And the children and before leaving for Dwaraka said,
'I do not know how she is going to put up this long separation,'
But worry not, Krishne, I shall now and then see them and your
Affection for me is a source of inspiration.'
We left the palace and as we walked the streets, the town;
People in huge numbers came and sympathized with us. The
Pandavas who had gambled away their honour walked like
Fools, and I followed them, the fire of humiliation burning
me up!
The fire within made my face sprout dark fumes, and I saw:
Dharmaja who was being followed by Partha and the twin
brothers.
And Bhima was just behind me and the people who had
assembled said:
'Why are the brave and the honest punished? Is it destiny
Or is it the fradulant game of the Kauravas which has made
Them suffer so? Doesn't god have any kindness for them?'
Sahadeva consoled them all and asked his retinue to
Return all the horses and elephants, and the bullocks and carts,
And the treasury to the Kauravas as they had to live in the
forest now.
In violent injustice visible, the Kauravas had the Pandava
Insignias removed, and confiscated all that had belonged to their
Cousins. People standing on either side of the roads wept and
Asked themselves in overwhelming sorrow: 'Why did
Dharmaja play the game of dice!
How can we now suffer the unjust rule of the wicked?'
As they faced these questions within themselves, we moved
On, and our steps questing after a new epoch to dawn,
Thinking thoughts fresh and invigorating, we reached the
Kamyaka forests and there sprang within us fresh currents of

Thoughts, and bidding goodbye to narrow, self-centred interests
We stepped into a new wide world of fresh possibilities and
We knew we were in search of the good and the beautiful;
The eternal truth of the life of all mankind. Three days later
Walking along the Ganga, we reached the forests.

CANTO XX

THESE HUNTSMEN ARE NOT OUR ENEMIES

All around us were thick grown thickets of cane and grass,
And the green shoots appeared to invite us to the place!
Seeing me tired, Dharmaja said, 'See, here flows the daughter
Of the high hills, river Dandavati, who makes the lands fertile,
And offers relief to the thirsty. It is she who makes the lands green,
Even desert land turns fertile and if only men imitate the
Life of the rivers, they can make men's life full and meaningful.
The waters of the ocean allay not human thirst; it is the sweet,
Fresh water of the river that satiates human hunger and
Thirst. And, if our riches bring not comfort and happiness
To others, what use are they for anybody? None were
Born rich and none take with them the wealth they accumulate.
And since at both ends there is only a zero, why hate anyone
And why envy others, and be full of violence and wickedness?
Duryodhana has become King of Indraprastha but he does not
Care for the welfare of his people and he does not know that
Neither power nor riches stay with anyone for long.
Panchali, we, have been pushed into a twelve-year exile
And during this period we will try to learn all that will
Do good to all living creatures everywhere. See,
There are stars twinkling against the background of dark clouds,
They dance like divine damsels and these try to disturb
The meditative mood of the high mountains but they stay
Undisturbed! And look at the vast blue expanse of the sky, there
The birds fly high and freely as if searching for the hidden
truth of

Life! They are looking for a new world and are after it; see
These creepers which have wound round these trees,
signifying ever-present affection and love.
In these forests, there is no conflict, there,
It is only trust and goodness. The trees grow to their allowed
heights and do not squabble.
Man sees this, yet comes in the way of those
Who want to grow and reach the skies! And Kaurava is a
Symbol of and witness to those who stay stunted in their
growth, and ascent.'
Dharmaja went into a metaphysical mood but Arjuna
Stood enjoying the poetic beauty of the place; Bhimasena
revelled in
The new found feeling of freedom and Nakula forgot himself
watching the
Bounding spring and Sahadeva who was absorbed in tracing
the path of the stars broke his silence and said:
'Why should we not, on the banks of River Dandavati, raise
thatched huts and live in this peaceful region for twelve years?'
Dharmaja said: 'Is this place not good for us?
Surely it is as it is unhabited by ferocious barbarians? True, if
We live amiably with them, the place would be safe but do
you know a secret?
Way back, a boy from this hunting community went to
Drona to master the art of archery but Drona was, worried,
about the response of
The king, and did not accept him as a disciple but this boy,
Undaunted went back, made an image of Drona in clay, and
Practised and became a master of archery. Drona, afraid,
That he could be the cause of disturbance of in the family,
asked under guise of
Guru Dakshina, the ritual gift for the guru, Ekalavya,
The gift of his thumb which of course he received but it
made the
Entire hunting-community intensly hate the Brahmins and the
Kshatriyas, and they also vowed to exterminate these caste groups!'

Bhimasena stepped in, saying 'This too is well-known everywhere,
Phalguna and Yudhisthira pressed Drona hard, to accept
Ekalavya as a disciple: in this world all men are equal and
This young man, in no way, is inferior to men of either these groups
The right to have access to education, none can deny; it is to
Save his own job that Dronacharya cheated his disciple! We
Who believe in and practice the equality of all mankind, how could
We ever follow this policy of discrimination? Why has not
This been made clear to the hunter-tribe?'
Arjuna smiling said: 'This world forgets the thousand and one
Good deeds done but one unjust harm done will not be forgotten,
A scar it will remain in the minds of a whole race, and it
grows menacingly.
True, these huntsmen are not our enemies but they hate the
Kshatriyas, and since we are from this caste, they are afraid that
We would disturb the peace of their land. Doubts grow and
Therefore it is better we look for a place more friendly to us.'
In anger, Bhima thundered: 'Why go away from this so
Very beautiful a place? And, why fear the anger of the huntsman?
When Bhima is hero, why feel diffident? No, I shall not back out.'
Listening to him, Yudhisthira said: 'Understand this.
Violence and anger can cause only loss to both of us.
The wealth and kingdoms you acquire through violence
Do not last, and bring no peace. It is through
An alternate way, through harmonious relationship
That it can be achieved and this path of peaceful
Camaraderie Yagnaseni knows, and she can enlighten us here.'
Then I, hearing Yudhisthira, said: 'In Kamyakavana, there
Are diverse classes and groups and castes and, the injustice
We did to Ekalavya, and the wounds it caused, have to be
Healed right and we have to understand their psyche which
Is displeased with us, the Aryans, and we have to learn to
Make bridges between us. I have with me the Akshya
Vessel, the wish-fulfilling vessel, and with its help, if you all agree,
We can sit, eat together and this will create feelings of
Commonalty between us.'

Suddenly there was a terrible flash and frightening sound of
An explosion and Sahadeva looking in all directions four, said:
'Did you think it was a thunderbolt hurled? No, the community
Knows of our arrival and a leader, Kimmera, a bold, young man
Dying to kill and destroy the Kshatriyas and the Brahmins, has
Caused this explosion. There, hear, his terrifying war cry!'
Bhima, swinging his mace, moved towards the direction from
Where came the sound but I also could hear the sound of bugles
Signalling readiness to fight, and Yudhisthira became sad,
and serious and said:
No, not on the very day we enter the forest should the
land be
Turned red with blood, this should not happen, it has to be
Averted. Pursuing hatred does nobody any good. And if one
Tribal man is killed, a thousand others will appear and can
We face them all?
And, racial hatred will grow. No, between us a bridge of
Friendship has to be created, and Draupadi alone can do it,
An achiever, she is.'
In mad frenzy I rushed forward, stopped Bhima who
With his mace was about to smash the head of the young
man and
Begged him to desist, and said: 'No, stop, this is but an innocent
Boy, drop your mace, please,: but even before I had finished
Bhima had swung his mace and the boy had fallen
unconscious, and
I rushed and holding the boy in my arms I sprinkled water
And with the pallu of my saree fanned him and this act of love
Won him over and he, wiping his tears, spoke as my husbands
Stood stunned and watched, 'Oh, mother, who are you, Parvati
or Lakshmi!
To save this tribal boy, did you risk your life? How can I say
My grateful thanks, tell me, please.' 'Kimmera, think of me as your
Mother. Can't the wife of Pandavas become a mother to you?'
'Ah, mother, forgive me. We heard that someone was invading
Our territory and, therefore, in anger we came blowing our war

Horns. The ancient injustice done to Ekalavya made us angry but
The humiliation you went through at the Kaurava Palace in the
Presence of Drona, has made us your firm allies and we vow to
Destroy the Kauravas. You are well-wishers of us, the tribals,
And you can stay here for years in absolute safety.'
I said: 'We cannot live here if you think of us as enemies but
You are not our enemy nor are you inferior to us, we
All are equal as human beings. Why then should there be
Any conflict between us?' In affection Kimmera said: 'Mother,
From today we desire the friendship of Pandavas and there would be
No ill will between us, our friendship shall stay firm and the Aryans
Who stand by Drona we shall destroy, root and stock, this we swear on.'
Then, Vrikodara, in calm of mind, spoke:
'From the beginning there never was any difference between man
And man, they were created equals, and children of mother nature,
And each with a right inalienable to enjoy air and light and
The sun and the moon, and so too were they to man, accessible
Without discrimination. It is the selfish man-made civilization that has
Created artificial differences. If each works and gets rewarded
In accordance with his abilities, why have caste quarrels?
Let us all live together, give equal opportunity, a level field of
Education and jobs, and the obnoxious seed of casteism can be
Destroyed. Since we belong to one single human family, there are
No touchables and untouchables or inferior and superior beings amongst us,
Sri Rama ate fruits given by Shabari who had earlier tasted
Then, but did this affect his status or standing? He made friends
With fisher folk like Guha, did that affect him in any negative way?
Dear friend, Kimmeera, forgive us our wrongdoings and
Offer a hand of friendship, and then all sages and seers
Will come in groups to Kamyakavana and make this place
Of the aborigines, herald a new civilizational, cultural epoch.'

Thrilled Kimmera stood up and said, 'Fortunate we are,
With your arrival here, Kamyakavana has become a place holy;
There has come a new meaning to our lives and through our new
Friendship made, we shall struggle hard and see a righteous Kingdom
Is established. Only order us, tomorrow morning itself the army of
Our tribe will invade, and as the army of the vanars helped
Rama triumph over Lanka, history will repeat and we, subdue the
Kauravas and Hastinapura will be ours.' Yamaja then, with
Folded hands, appealed to him: 'No, friend, our purpose is not
To seize Hastinapura nor is it to destroy the Kauravas. We intend
To stay in the forest for thirteen years and return to re-claim
Indraprastha. And before that period is over, we will not do such a
Thing. To achieve selfish desires we shall not break the solemn
Word we have given but grateful we are for your friendship
And for wishing us well.' Seeing the puzzled boy, I said: 'See,
As long as we stay here, the Pandavas should not suffer for
Want of food, and from now on we shall sit and eat with you,
For there is not any difference between us and you.'

In the Kamyakavana, the hatred between the Aryans and
The non-Aryans disappeared and the sapling of fraternal love sprung up.
One day Bhima appeared wearing the costume of the tribals and I
Wore the dress of a huntress! With that we lost our pride that
We were of the Kuru dynasty and with that our imperial pride too!
A fond memory: One evening two of our tribal boys, Kambu and Chambu,
In fun, came to stab me with a childish spear. I played with them,
And fed them, and Kimmera's wife, Sri, began trusting us and our lives in
The forest became one of happiness, truth, and affection and the
Forest was transformed into elysian gardens, pure and simple, and innocent.

CANTO XXI

HUNGER SATED, GRATIFICATION FULL

This is the month of *Shravana* and today is Krishnajanmastami,
The day of the birth of Sri Krishna and with the help of
Akshayapatra, the wish-fulfilling vessel, I cooked varieties of dishes
And fed each to his heart's content, and immersed myself in thoughts
About Sri Krishna: Would he remember me on this happy day?
'Now and then I shall see you,' he had said. Has he forgotten or
Does he still think of us? As I went to sleep thinking of him, at
Night I heard the sweet, ear-filling sound of his flute and
he extending
Both his hands, stood near me, saying, 'Ah, friend, I am thirsty,
But water won't quench my thirst; it needs heavy rains and
Lightings and drenched whirlwind and there are in you
all these and
In Kamyakavana you have earned the name of the dispenser of
Nectar, and in your heart is the life-restoring spring of
affection, and on that
Day when the Ganga leapt down from the sky, Shiva caught her
In his matted hair but today who will be able to arrest the flow
Of love form your heart? Tell me, Sri Devi!'
There flowed into me a flood of happiness, and
Within me I thought I saw Yashode: And there was before
My eyes the wonderful image of Gopala, the little Krishna,
And in his face shone the light of the vast universe which
Reflected the dazzling brightness of Aaditya, Rudra and Maruta!
The whole moving and alive universe I saw, and the young god's
image

I saw, had a thousand eyes and a thousand feet and clad it was
In divinely beautiful clothes, and fragrant perfume emanated
Touching the earth and the sky and there he was present everywhere and this
Gopala, god omnipresent, was asking me for some milk! The same moment
Affection made milk gush from my breasts and I suckled him as one
Does an infant and with it flowed maternal affection in a flood!
I unconsciously murmured 'Krishna, Krishna, Kannaiah, my darling' and
Then Phalguna woke me up and asked: 'What did you dream? You
Know, how you have slept! I do not understand!'
'Yes, I was remembering my five children who in the form of
Sri Krishna came and begged for milk and I suckled them all to their
Heart's content!' The breast milk had made the saree wet and Arjuna,
Understanding my dream, said, 'A maternal heart overflowing with
Generosity, she suckles Sri Krishna, and in so doing feeds her
Five children, what is surprising here? The thought of this
World's hungry children constantly worries you, it in fact, has no
Limits at all, your affection that is.'
The night was pitch dark and it rained in buckets but then
Appeared Sri Krishna with a burning taper in his hand to reveal himself
To his devotees! The wonder-struck Partha in shock mumbled:
'Oh, my soul-friend! How, in this dark night, leaving Dwaraka, did
You come into this forest!' Krishna with a smile said:
'I who came from my mother's womb on a night terrible, is
There a time proper for me? All time, to me, is propitious.'
'How is Subhadre? And the children? Do they remember me? Are they are all right?'
'Yes, everyone is fine. I shall tell you the reason why
I came today. Today is the day of my birth and I thought about
The many tasty dishes Krishne surely has made for me; I also

Knew she would be waiting to see me and therefore without a
Thought about this terrible downpour, I came. Partha, are you
Blind, I am drenched in the milk of affection of Panchali!'
Arjuna with his shoulder cloth wiped him dry and I
Was struck dumb, watching this brotherly service rendered
to Krishna!
'What could I offer him at this hour of the night? The utensils
Were all washed and dried!' Worried, I thought to myself:
'From where can I got any food? He has came all the way
Eager to eat from my hands the dishes I have cooked. How do
I disappoint him? How will I pass this fiery test?'
Krishna dressed in the clothes of Arjuna looked famished:
'Ah, friend, I can't wait any more. I die of hunger.' These
Words made me more worried and I cursed myself I didn't save
Any food, not even a grain of rice. And, he continued, 'Why
Isn't there a grain of rice for me? Is it because I am but a
Poor cowherd, and therefore you show me this indifference?'
'Yes, I know, if guests go hungry from a home, they curse, and
Go away. All right, I accept, curse me, if you must; happily I shall
Accept it.' My friend smiled and said, 'Why think of curses,
Show me your palm, I shall tell you what awaits you
in future!'
I began to say something but Phalguna whispered in my ear,
'Once your friend holds your hand, he forgets his thirst and
Hunger and surely you would not be under a guest's curse!
Even if the lines on your palm point to a dreaded future, he, the
Great magician will straighten them, surely!' I, taking some courage
Said in fun, 'Beware! Today the number of such astrologers is
Large, and they are great cheats.'
Krishna, with care studied my palm, and as he did so he saw
A grain of rice sticking to the end of my middle finger, and
he, in
Great affection, ate what was left over in my palm after my
dinner and
The next moment his hunger was sated, and contentment complete
Appeared on his face, and he happily belched! Smiling he said,

'Oh, dear friend, even a grain of rice is dear to me. For a man
Hungry, a grain of rice is enough, with more he would have
indigestion!'
And then happily went to sleep.
The next morning became clear the miracle he had worked!
He had come in the middle of the night to save us from the
dreadful curse of sage Durvaasa.
The previous night the sage had been
hosted a
Sumptuous repast by the Kauravas who came to know that the
sage with a
Thousand followers would be visiting us. They so planned it
so that he came
Only after the akshaya patra had been used and this, he knew,
would make it
Impossible for us to feed the large entourage and that
Durvaasa in anger,
Would shower dire curses on us. Our friend Sri Krishna
came to have an
Inkling of it and therefore hurried and torpedoed their evil design!
The moment Krishna ate and belched, the hunger of the sages
had sated and
Bloated tummies, and happily went their way!
This episode of God's kindness became the talk of the world and
I with folded hands stood near him and he patting me said,
'Panchali, rise, tie up your hair and have a bath. Worry not,
The Kaurava dynasty will be reduced to dust and ashes. They have
Done themselves injustice. Do put up with the present problems
till the fourteen year banishment gets over.'
Listening to these consoling words
I said, 'Krishna! How does one go about doing one's hair?
How would you stop the peregrinations of my flaming tresses or
Would you help me carry it on, and make the tying up of the
Tresses a prelude to the bloody end of this epoch? The
Wheel of change will move without a stop and on its way it will
Crush many a creature, make the seven seas overflow and

The sky itself crack up. Which mysterious strength will achieve this?
The world knows your strength, and when will Dyushasana be
Killed and, when will I dip my hair in his blood, and then
I tie it up right.
You know, your soul knows it all, enough! But are
You not the puppeteer of this game of puppets? Once the
Wheels of my flaming tresses move then the wicked and the evil
Ones will be pulverized. Bhima and Partha will be victorious,
And a new age will dawn and I shall be the only cause of it.
I sing only the first lines of the song of this bloody war.'
Krishna, cheering me up, said 'Sister, rise up. You
Have suffered much but let the word you have given to the
Kaurava, the agreed fourteen-year banishment be over.
And through Bhima, the wind-god born, let good happen to you
I swear I shall see it happen, let the wheel of your flaming
Tresses keep moving, and none will be able to stop the chariot of
Victory. Let Saubhadre and the other royal consorts go to their
Parent's place and let the sons of the five Pandavas be taught
In Panchala. To the fire of the sorrow of the daughter of
Drupada, let the Kauravas become the sacrificial faggots.'
Krishna blessed us and left for Dwaraka.

CANTO XXII

EVEN BEFORE LIVING INCOGNITO ENDS, I SHALL COME

Once talking with Dharmaja in private, I said:
'If, when occasions demand, we do not demonstrate the
Valour of our Kshatriya race, all goes a waste.' He, in turn, said,
'Draupadi, if, as you say, demonstration of valour is our policy
Then there would be no peace, for anger is the root cause
of conflict.'
'This Yudhisthira cannot understand me, not that violence
ought to be
Part of us but if it never is brought out into the open, many
Misunderstandings will crop up.' When I explained my stance
Yudhisthira put forth his point, 'Anger does not quench anger;
It helps hatred spread and it will echo and re-echo from all the
Corners of the earth; the wound anger causes does not heal; the
Scar still remains and therefore our basic mantra has to be
Peace: this alone will unite the world. Otherwise it is
destruction of everyone.
One invasion causes another and there won't be room
For peace and tolerance anywhere. He who triumps over anger
Surely is a strong man and he who achieves this is the greatest
on this earth.'
'Not that I do not agree with your view but tolerance and
Forgiveness are to be exercised in relation to our times and if
there is universal tolerance of everything then those who are
caught in the

Vortex of the torture of the strong would become indifferent to us;
There has to be a limit in consonance with the realities of
our day;
If one is too polite, people laugh at us; if it is all violence,
people will rebel;
If restraint is exercised in the exercise of these virtues,
All would be happy. But you and your brothers do not see beyond
What you think of as *dharma*; Power came your way, wealth came
Your way but you did not become arrogant; and you always
held that
Dharma is the only great value for the sake of which you could
Give up your brothers, you could give up your dear wife, but think;
The *dharma* you stood by, has it stood by you? Has it
protected you?
No! Look at the pages of our history! It has brought so much
Misery and unhappiness in our lives.' He was silent but I asked
him again.
'Tell me, is there justice in this world? Are you truly a free man?
Is God kind? Look, all men have suffered and they suffer
because of
The deeds they have done; they believe that their *karma* alone
decides their happiness and sorrow.
They are the puppets in the hands of the
Puppeteer called *karma*! Men, like fallen dry leaves of a tree,
Get tossed around, and think everything is determined by it!
Some do good work, some bad, and although there is God in every
Human being yet he does everything to please the body alone, and
Who has seen the unseen God? He plays with our lives.'
When I put these questions to him, he said: 'Panchali,
What you say sounds true, and sweet. But are you not
advocating the view of the non-believers, of the atheists?'
'No, I could see in Dharmaja's words the disappearance of
The finer aspects of *dharma*: there was present superstition and
In his analysis there wasn't adequate sharpness or clarity of thought.
The meaning within the words I spoke, he did not understand.
He was not aware that I and my words presented a view of women

Who have suffered terrible, outrageous treatment at the hands
of men.
He has forgotten 'womanness' and has stayed with only 'manness';
Clouded he is with superstition religious and has turned his face
Away from the Real, and therefore, without understanding the
meaning behind
My words, he blabbers and tries to keep my mouth shut but he
Himself is slowly descending into the well of ignorance.'
Seeing that the situation was going beyond control,
Bhimasena came and joined our conversation; 'Brother, I have
Listened to Draupadi's views. Tell me who is responsible for
the sad
Events in her life? There are a million laughing at us and how
do we reclaim our kingdom we lost because of base strategies
except through open war?
As we continue to forgive our enemies because of
Our adherence to justice and truth, our moral strength is on the
Decline. We are strong, yes, but Dhritarashtra thinks we are the
Weakest, and ignores us. The fact is our reliance on values like
Dharma and artha ought to help us move toward achievement
of our just aims
But they have not, and our rigid, ritualistic adherence has
Made us weak and unmanly. This, you see, is the truth.'
'After living for twelve years in the forests and after spending
A year in incognito we get back our kingdom but if they spot us
Before the period of incognito-living, we have to undergo the
same trial!
Thus have we pledged our word, and we have to honour it!' True,
Yudhisthira was wedded to *Dharma* but he had enough statesmanship.
Knew the world and its ways, and, more then anything else he
had the
Blessings and approval of Sri Krishna! Every bit logical and nothing
Illogical! Had Kauravas come for a fight that day, would we have
Fought them? No, we would say their bowl of evil was not
yet full, and kept quiet!
Today Phalguna with his Gandiva was about to enter the

Forests to perform tapas! I could not bear the painful thought and
Said: 'Oh, dear, I have spent much time without you being
with me.
How many more years have I to suffer?' 'No, before the end
Of our living incognito, I shall return and I'll see them that my
Work is dedicated to preserve the righteousness of the Aryan race.'
He does not know my mind! And he with whom I want to
Stay close is moving away from me! And with whom can I share
The pain of my inner life? Then, Arjuna, consolingly said: 'Krishna,
Today I am on my way to perform a sacred rite, which
done would
Help me defeat the Kauravas which is not an easy thing and I have
To search and find the right means, if we are to re-enshrine *Dharma*
And don't ever think it is easy defeating Karna. I am yet to
Gain more skill and more discipline in the art of archery, or
Otherwise we are sure to be defeated.'
'Valorous Partha, how can I stop you! Last time, on your
pilgrimage you won many wives but now do not forget your
goal, do not fall
A prey to desires enticing; be firm of mind and with concentration
Undisturbed, move.' Holding my hands in his, Partha said:
'Krishne, do not doubt me, I shall stay true to the trust you have in
Me.' 'Dear husband, tell me, how can I let you go! If you
Are not with me, all wealth, all power means nothing to me, they
Hold no attraction for me. You have already lived away from
Me, how long more do you want me to live alone? No, please,
Do not go, stay back.'
Bhimasena held my hand and said: 'Panchali, why such
Weakness in you! If he stays here, holding on to the end of
your saree,
How will you ever fight unrighteousness? Small, sensual desires,
You have to give up. Or, are you going to halt the move of
The wheels of righteousness of this epoch? Would you want to
Weaken our commitment to what we have sworn to achieve?'
I felt as if my veins would burst, and blood would flow in
A stream from me; my tresses weighed heavy on me and then came

Back my vow to me, and with an effort controlling my thought,
I said to myself: 'True, what Bhima has said is the truth!
No, I should not come in the way of Parthas' resolution,
through discipline rigorous
He has to win and he has to protect the righteous in the world.'

CANTO XXIII

OUR TIME CALLS FOR UNIVERSAL FRIENDSHIP

All of us left on a long pilgrimage and with us was
Sage Lomasha, and while passing through Naimisha forest, we
saw the flooded Ganga;
And crossing the Ganga we went to Kashi and Prayaga
And from thereon moved west towards river Vipasha and
Went up and down a range of hills, circled Gandhamadana hills
And walked our way; I, tired and exhausted, with difficulty
Tried to walk further but a whirlwind rose, knocking me down.
And for a long while I was unconscious.
When I came to consciousness
I saw that my four husbands were sitting near my head and
There was a young boy sitting near my feet and pressing it softly.
I saw him and it instantly recalled to me my own children and
Wondered who it was and why he was showing this tender care.
He looked so cultured, so human and so full of selfless service!
As I looked, there sprang in me maternal affection and unable to
To control my feelings, I asked him: 'Young boy, who are you!
On seeing you there is much maternal affection in me, why?'
The boy sweetly smiling said: 'Because, I am yours, I belong to you.'
'Who are the fortunate ones who bore you? Bring them to me, I
Should like to congratulate them.' The boy looked at Bhima
And then affectionately smiled and said: 'I am son to
Hidambi, and I am Ghatotkacha!'
I hugged him, patted his cheeks and said:
'Young man, convey my regards to her, for I understand now
how great

And cultured she is; I know she reflects a culture that is great,
And now I know why, angry with me, Bhima went to your mother's
Place! Once our banishment is over, do come with us to Indraprastha,
Your mother I revere, she is senior to me, I have regards for her,
My affection for her you convey to her, right now.'
The boy listened and then he went his way and we leisurely
Continued our pilgrimage, reached Badarikashrama and took pleasure
In watching snow-clad mountain peaks and as we did, the sages
Prophesied that Partha would be back in another four years.
To assure
Him safe travel we, on many days, fasted and prayed and then
We along the banks of the river Mandakini walked; the sweet air
Almost made us forget the pain of separation and all of a sudden from
Northerly direction fell a shower of fragrant saugandhika flowers
And I called Bhimasena and told him of my wish to have them and
He walked towards the Kailash mountain, immediately!
More than half-a-day went by and yet there was no sign of
Him and in anxiety I rushed to Yudhisthira who listened and then sent
Sahadeva to inquire; who did so and returned with this tale;
Bhimasena went into the garden of Kubera, the Brindavan, and there started
Collecting, the saugandhika flowers, seeing which the guards fell on him
And then there was a battle going on between them.
Dharmaja soon went and spoke to Bhimasena:
'These flowers are from a garden which belongs to someone,
and without their permission how could you pluck the flowers!
True, women naturally are fascinated by fragrant flowers
But you should have thought well before attempting it.'
Bhimasena however,
Went on justifying himself: 'When, while living in the forests, did not
Sita desire the golden deer, and did not Sri Rama go, pursuing it? And,

How could I stop myself from fulfilling the desire of Yagnaseni, the
Wife of five of us?' Dharmaja then said: 'You know what resulted
When he pursued it; Janaki had to go through hell fire and how it
Became a lesson to the world. If I had not come, you would
have been in
Terrible danger. In a place unknown to us, it is unwise to rush into
Situations which could cause conflicts and battles. This kind of
Desires of women indiscriminate could be root cause of the
ruin of Kurus.'
For breaking the rule, Dharmaja, begged forgiveness of
Kubera who said: 'If only Bhimasena had spoken of his
wife's wishes
I would have brought not a thousand but all saugandhika flowers,
And would have presented them all to Devi Draupadi.'
Hearing it I said with much courtesy, 'We are bound by
Our *dharma* and now I shouldn't wear these golden
saugandhika flowers.
For a moment I forgot the vow we had made and therefore
Kindly excuse me. It is good Dharmaja woke me up to the
reality of our
Situation and showed us the path of righteousness. And, when
all my hair is unplaited, how can I wear any flower?
Even this I forgot!'
Kubera, in admiration, said: 'Devi, if you decline to accept
These flowers, it will hurt me and how can I show my face to
Sri Krishna?
He, if he hears this, will not forgive me, kindly accept the gift
of flowers.'
I saw in his words sincere affection and regard and I thought
the day,
For my dreams to come true had arrived and I spelled my hopes:
'Light has come into an area of darkness: listen, the
Time for peaceful co-existence between the Aryans and the
Non-Aryans has arrived and from now the motto is to fully
Eradicate ill-will between races and instill in every one
The idea of equality. So long as equality is not established

So long do conflicts continue, for hatred hastens the end of
The world. But friendship makes the impossible possible and
If we do not build bridges between our minds, how can new roads
Be built, new relationships, established? It is in unison of
Feelings that greatness is achieved? And, remember, this,
Sri Rama did not wage wars nor did he extend frontiers of
his kingdom,
But he went out to build gardens of love and affection and
Mutual regard among the Aryans and the non-Aryans and
Amongst the sages and the huntsmen and it is this which has made
Sri Rama immortal!
The wonderful Ramayana is vision made real, and, presented to
All of Bharat. Let matrimonial alliances happen and all races
Live in happiness and therefore distribute land to all those
Sages and huntsmen, the seers and the tribals and let universal
Peace descend and let all live a happy and contended life.'
Nakula said: 'Our Draupadi Devi, had to suffer much
Physical discomfort, crossing these forests and wild barren lands and
Therefore she has thought of building roads and bridges and rest
Houses which would be of help to all travellers.' Nakula smiled and
Half-in-fun said, 'And so, under the great guidance of Lomasha seer
Our life-partner, Draupadi Devi, lays the foundation stone
For the great mansion of cooperative building!' And Kubera,
Smiling said: 'Its massive pillar was erected in honour of
The wedding of Bhimasena and Hidimba, and it is the crest
Jewel of the mansion!'
We reached Badarikshrama and again waited for the return of
Arjuna and then suddenly, from behind the Gandhamadana
Peak there was a flash of light like lightning and Arjuna was coming
Riding the Airavata, Indra's divine elephant and looking at the
blinding aura
Surrounding, he smiled as he were handsomeness itself!
I, speechless, went into deep self-absorption bordering on yoga.
He came near, took out a pearl necklace and pushing it
towards me said:
'At the assembly, the Kauravas, inflicting much violence on

You, took away the jewels you wore and now I vow to cover
you from head
To toe with pearls rare, for which reason have I bought bags of
Pearls which, while entering Hastinapura, you will wear.'
Accepting the gift,
I gave it away to sage Romasha saying, 'True, Partha
Has brought these with love but breaking my vow, how do I
wear it?
I shall not bedeck myself; all this is to be used to find cordiality
Between us all.'
Arjuna admired his dear wife for her noble plans and
Stood in silence while Dharmaja said: 'The common
knowledge that
Draupadi's heart houses and emits only sparks of hatred is disproved!
She is full of the milk of human kindness, and values
benevolence, and
These, like the flow of Mandakini, are full of love and
kindness and compassion.'
Arjuna holding her hands said: 'Krishne, my job is complete as
This has behind it, buttressing it, qualities of concentration and
Selflessness. Through you, in me, has emerged the strength of the
Sun-god himself and it has, in turn, built bridges of love and
Affection between various tribes and communities and has now
Heralded a new age of change and development and everything
Looks, and is beautiful and true and full of auspiciousness. You
Have broken down the fort of lack of trust and made there sprout
Consciousness of the equality of all.'
The Pandavas enjoyed the rich luxuriance of Nature
surrounding them,
Bhima and Nakula revelled in hunting; Bhima once tried to
Catch a python and Dharmaja came running and saved him and
Then, Bhima happily relieved said: 'Brother, we have miraculous
Weapons, the whole of our tribal race is with us and so are
the Yadavas
Along with Krishna and Balarama. But the Kauravas, with help
from Karna,

Assume they can win a war against us easily and it seems he is
Into tapas which will help him acquire strange and powerful strength
And to add to it they are under the impression that we will, till
The period of banishment is over, return and I also hear that
Karna has vowed to kill Arjuna, and now, therefore, we have
to make haste and move.
We know. We are going to win and we should not miss
The opportunity that has come our way and even before the
enemy army
Is fully ready, in a full swoop, we should descend on them
And display our military skills. True, we break the word we
have given
But to this discussion of right and wrong we have to be indifferent.'
Dharmaja assuaging his feelings said: 'I know the vow Karna has
Made, and I know full how propitious it is for waging a war.
It is not out of fear
That I sit but we have pledged our word that we would
Remaining in the forest for thirteen years, and we are not to
break our word.
To declare war in arrogance, and in the name of peace
and harmony,
Will spell the death of millions of soldiers and leave behind them
Widows and orphaned children, and is it right to rule a nation while
Listening to their heartbreaking cries? Think, is it right to
Conquer kingdom out of a mad love for name or fame? No, wait,
This not merely spells the destruction of the Kauravas but of mankind!
Do dismiss the poisonous idea of warfare and, instead, think of
Founding peace permanent on this earth.'
'Why does Karna have vengefulness against Arjuna? Is it
Because he is a husband dear to me? Or, is it because he
Won me at the swayamvara, and made this a pretext to hate him?
No, there should be no ill-will between them.'
Arjuna came near me and said, 'Krishne, your depressing feelings
You drop! Be not afraid, I shall break the vow Karna has made.
I have acquired a weapon to silence him and I keep alive in me
The oath I've taken: kill him I will. Do not doubt my valour.'

With sadness written on my face, I spoke breaking my silence:
'Why did you make that vow without discussing it with me?'
'This I made a pretext to keep myself away from you
And also to rid me of the fascination I had for heavenly
Damsels. This, I thought, was the right path. This made it possible
For me to stay away from you. I know it caused you
Much pain but this too I know that, to achieve peace, we have
To cooperate with one another and wait for the coming great war.
The earth has sunk under the weight of the injustice of the
Kauravas and only through a righteous war we are going to
Wage, will men of the world see happiness and contentment.
Do not make me your Partha through an affectionate appropriation,
The times call for universal friendship and amity.'

CANTO XXIV

THE WIFE'S RIGHTEOUS DUTY IS TO IMBUE THE HUSBAND WITH COURAGE

Kamyakavana called us with open arms.
Jambukambu, Kumara, Kimmara, Kairatha and all the others of
The Shabara clan were happy with our arrival there.
One day friend Krishna along with Satyabhama came to
Enquire after us and I walked towards him and in familiarity, said:
'It is many years after you have come to see us and ask,
If Arjuna, your friend, is back? Ah, why this indifference?
Shouldn't you want to know whether we are alive or dead?'
Krishna was flustered by my words, and Partha, without
looking at me, said,
'Ah, friend, see how temperamental women can be! Did you
Forget to enquire after your aunt's children, their safety?'
'Abandoning the ease and luxury of Dwaraka, and away from
The company of wives, I worked hard thinking of the welfare
Of my friend's wife's safety, and what do I get in return?
Censure and harsh words as recompense! I remain
Unacceptable, everywhere!'
Arjuna smiled, and in a soft, endearing voice Krishna spoke to me:
'Dear friend every night, with eyes closed, have you not seen
The lotus-faced Partha, and felt joyous? Did you not, while
Walking the forest-tracks, seeing the shadow of Arjuna,
Imagine it was, but me? Tell me!'
'Dear friend, who let you in on this? How do you know
The secret none knows, and bring it into the open? Yes,
Every second Partha is with me but while wandering in the

World of illusions, forget the sadness I could, but not the
Feeling you were not with me. This I could not bear but
Who else like you will bear for me!'
Sri Krishna spoke his heart out: 'Many a time I tried to tell
You but I could not. As a last resort I sent along with
Swarna Saugandhika a letter, but it went unread!'
Listening to him Satyabhama Devi said, 'You write a letter
Of love to Yagnaseni but after sending away her friend
A long way away! Is this, your behaviour, right?'
Sri Krishna, floundering for an answer proper, said, 'Oh,
Bhama, do not read me wrong. It was but a letter of good wishes!'
'Would there be in your letter any room for good wishes? Do you
Think of writing anything but a love letter? Is there anyone
In the world who does not know of the first love letter
You sent Rukmini? You are the first in that category!
If it were a letter ordinary, why did you cover it with
Swarna Kamala flowers? What secret document was hidden there?'
'My dear, forgive me for the wrong things I did in the past;
Krishne, anyway, threw away, the letter, then why this
Confusing discussion, now?'
'Why are you upset? She only demonstrated that it was
A letter not worth reading, be silent now.'
Hearing to this lovers' quarrels, Arjuna said, 'I alone
Know what my dear friend told my dear wife but how do
I share it with others!'
Sri Krishna smiling said: 'Krishne would understand it, but
How can a woman like Satyabhame have any inkling of it? The
First love letter I wrote to dear Rukmini, she, forgetful, lost it!
Then what is there to say of Satyabhame?' Getting into
The conversation, she said: 'Then, you agree, that you did write
A love letter to Draupadi!' Arjuna intervening said:
'I do not know why you anxiously discuss a casual, normal
Happening like this!'
In the afternoon, after lunch, I rummaged through the flowers
Gone dry, and with intense curiousity, read the letter which
Had gone unnoticed, unread:

'Friend, the cause of creation is the sun, when he smiles in the
Sky, the lotus petals reflecting him, blossom, like his smiles!
The petals bloom with life and proclaim their fulfillment, their
Coming together. This you see, and those who see not this
will never ever see me.
When on that day you called me piteously, my heart instantly
Responded; The Kauravas plotted to have you cursed by
The angry Durvasa, I came in the middle of the night, and
protected you:
Whenever you have called me I have come with the speed of
thought!
I do not know how this happens:
With tiny little steps I followed the Gopis and teased them
and I was called worrisome!
When I responded to women in distress,
They with pejorative names called me, and ran me down!
Some ethereal bond has brought us together; it does not
matter what others say.
Do not fear; I shall stand by you, and protect you.
My life is dedicated to your welfare and whatever others might
Say I shall stay firm; your morning invocations to the sun are
My breakfast! Your evening prayers my music.'
I became a river and became one with the ocean
Of Krishna's love and generosity, and there I found fulfillment.

On each of the seven days of the week, Satyabhame capriciously
Wrangled with Krishna, and was she amazed to see me happily
living with
Five husbands! And did she feel terribly intrigued and grieved
within herself!
How ingeniously Bhima tore to pieces Dharmaja's arguments!
How well did he present his views! What felicity and what pleasant
Courteousness! And, all how beautiful!
Satyabhame wanted to see whether this bonding was natural or
artificial or was was all Illusion?
To get at the bottom of this, quite a
Few times she made attempts to ferret out the secret of

Our wedded lives;
One evening she came to me and asked:
Sister, tell me, how do you manage to keep five of your husbands
Happy all the time? At Dwaraka we are eight wives and yet
Are unable to hold Krishna with our threads of love. For us, the
Wives, it is not easy to understand him. We do not know where
He goes or what he does! Friend, I am sure you are in
Possession of some secret magical power or some herb or some
Garland of sacred beads. Tell me, how does one govern one's husband?'

I bit my lips hard and said: 'No, no, use not such
Expressions. It is only unwise women who think of mantra or tantra,
Or strange rituals to keep a hold on their husbands; I have
heard of them;
But this doing at oneself damage terrible, for such means make
Husbands victims of ill health, physical and psychological:
Often they lose their husbands. You are Sri Krishna's wife and
therefore, my sister
Do not take to ways sinister and wrong.'
'Yes, what you say is true but to keep familial bonds firm
In what way should I do?'
In reply,

I revealed to her the secret of keeping a wedded life in love.
'Give up excessive self-love; in truly giving yourself and your
Feminine affection to your partner, without expecting returns, you
Will own him. Move away from jealously and envy; and with
Composure, early in the morning, without taunting and with no
Petulance whatever, wish him well; when he returns from a
Long and tiring journey, receive him with love, greet him with
A smile, gift him with food and beverage and help him shed or
Share his anxieties and worries; do not bring in unwanted
Or undesirable topics for discussion; treat everyone at home,
All the time equally and enter not into a debate over some one's
Good and weak points and waste time; Get to know the mind and
The wants of each; desire nor other's wealth nor blame other women
Before him. Everyday with a bright and smiling face,
Share your happiness, and your anxieties, and try to fill

His mind with courage and steadfastness; this is the wife's
righteous duty!'
Listening to my words she said: 'Krishne, stop, enough!
The rigid and taxing life you live, and speak of, is too hard even
To listen! This I cannot bear. I just would want to live a wifely
Life, and that is all happiness to me!' I pulled Bhame to my side.
And spoke of proverbial wise maxims' Give up the desire, the pride
To make Hari yours; you have to truly become him! And, friend,
Then he will, forever, be caught in the net of your love; on
his own he will become yours, and forever.'
The talk made her swim in an ocean of familial love and
With a mind flooded with happiness said: 'Ah, friend, you have
Won the heart of the flute-playing Krishna so well!
I do not know my husband as well as you do him: seeking
Ways of pleasing him, the wives all tire themselves and made
Our lives dry and barren; and he without becoming anyone of
Us, remained himself! And separate! The lord of the world
Sri Krishna becomes yours and you became our teacher!'
Leaving for Dwaraka Sri Krishna bid us farewell and said:
'I shall send my other wives too to listen to the wise
Words of Panchali and then in the tug of war of love I shall
Win.' With this touching word of humour, he left and I
Stood watching the way he walked, yearned for things many!

CANTO XXV

LET NOT YOUR SHADOW FALL
ON ANOTHER'S WIFE

My husbands all left on a hunting expedition deep into
The forests of Kamyakavana, and me, alone, bored sat in the ashram,
Intoning to myself some song when I heard sounds of sweet
Music accompanying a wedding procession! Hearing me singing,
The bridegroom stopped, came near the door and offered me a
Red lotus, and in tones infatuated asked me: 'O, lovely woman,
Who are you? Do you belong to the world of heavenly damsels or
To the world of Yakshas and Gandharvas? In this world of green
Foliage you shine like a ball of fire or I would say like lightning
That appears against a background of dark-blue clouds!
Never have I
Seen a beauty like you! Your face is like a lovely lotus on
The waters of a lake! Your rich voice is like the sound of
Veena played by goddess Saraswati!
And Lo! I am, Jayadratha, King of
Sindhu region and am husband to Duryodhana's sister, Dushyale.
I am on my way to wed the daughter of King Salva but having
Seen you and your beauty how can I now proceed any further!
This sight of your heavenly beauty has made me blessed, really!'

Well, unhappy I was not to meet my regally-dressed brother-
in-law, and the Kauravas are not our enemies!
Dushyale was dear to me, a sister
Of the Pandavas and thinking so I greeted him and wished
Him happiness at his forthcoming happy welding ceremony.

'You are my eldest brother-in-law and yet you didn't recognize me!
Why behave like a stranger? We have met a couple of times,
I am your cousin's wife, Draupadi. How is your wife Dushyale?
Does she remember me? True, the brothers quarrelled that day
But our sisterly relationship stays strong. My husbands are gone
on a hunting spree,
Won't return before the sunset. When you come back with
your wife,
Do stay with us for a night at our humble home. Surely,
The Pandavas will be happy to meet you.' Gazing at me he said:
'How do I go to wed the daughter of King Salva, when there is
In front of me this mine of a beauty! Sister-in-law or the earth.
Goddess-it doesn't matter! I should love to have you as my queen,
You are Brahma's special creation of loveliness!
The Pandavas do not
Deserve to possess this jewel of a beauty.
And, should you live in such
Straightened circumstances? You have caught me in the strong web
Of your beauty, how do I escape? Tell me.'
Listening to his vulgar words reflecting, his low beastly desire, I
became a volcano of anger and said,
'Enough, not another word, you lustful man.
Thinking of you as kinsman I invited you but you cast evil
looks on me
And if you are caught by my husband sure it is death for you,'
How does a man gone blind with lust understand my words of
Morality? He grabbed me, and pulled me into his chariot and said:
'To me, your Pandavas are of no consequence; Duryodhana who
Hurled insults at you will make his sister your slave! In the
Backyard of my house there is a paradise lying waste and
With me, there, you can taste heavenly pleasures, come, have
All your desires fulfilled to your heart's content, come home.'
The chariot was moving in great swiftness and Jayadratha's
Horses as if they too knew their owners' mind for, without
Minding the terrain they ran and leapt and vaulted on and I
Then, suddenly, sprang from the seat, kicked the villain and
jumped out

Calling out loud 'Krishna, Krishna', lost consciousness, and when I came
To myself I felt that I was being lifted and placed on a soft bed,
And around me were my five husbands who had learnt of the
Abduction through sage Dhaumya, came soon and freed me and,
I unaware of all that had happened questioning silently looked at them.
Bhimasena consoling said, 'Panchali, do not worry. You are safe now,'
In great over powering anger I said, 'Place before me the carcass of that
Villain, quarter his body, toss the flesh as food for wolves, throw
His feet and head and hands in four directions as warning to those who lust
After women.' Listening, Dharmaja said, 'Yagnaseni, true it is
That Jayadratha is a villain, but why such cruel words?
The maximum punishment for evil doers on this earth is execution but if all of them are
Punished with such a sentence, who would really be able to be alive?
Men do become fascinated by feminine beauty, it is wrong, is unwise,
And yet he who insulted you is your kinswoman's husband, should
You make her a widow, an inauspicious woman. Would you
Approve of it?' I rose from my bed and hissed out:
'Dharmaja, you are kinder than Sri Rama who killed Ravana who
Had kidnapped his wife! You have forgotten your history!
To forgive him for being a brother-in-law is pure selfishness and
In your selfishness, in your partiality for your kinsman, you have
Abandoned *dharma*! A husband who does not get angry
When his wedded wife is humiliated, has he any masculinity in him?
Your blood not only not warm, but it has gone cold!
Don't you know the essence of the Vedas?
Those who kidnap women or usurp kingdoms
Are enemies of entire communities. Is this also forgotten by you,
Who are reduced to stupidity simple?'
Bhimasena came to my support; Partha, Nakula and Sahadeva
Took to silence and I, with tears in my eyes, said, 'Yes! Why

Punish innocent Dushyale who has done no wrong? True, but
Forcing a woman against her will, to kidnap and to rape her is
Clearly a criminal act and men are lasciviously drawn to it
And therefore this disregard to such heinous acts; is this like
The conquest of kingdoms, a habitual transgression? Do men take
Pride in becoming rapists? I do not know but sentencing
them to death is fair enough justice, I believe.'
Bhimasena moved by
My anger and sorrow, grabbed Jayadrath, had his head shaved
And made him stand in a single piece of cloth and he stood
Shamefaced and head bent and I told him: 'Let not your shadow
Fall on another's wife, go, and never ever resort to such acts of
Shameless criminality.' Jayadratha prostrated and then went his way,
And seeing him go Bhima and Arjuna laughed loudly.

As our stay at the forest continued, one day a
Huntsman came and said, 'Oh, mother, there is a handsome looking
Young man with bleeding wound and is lying helpless but has
A crown on his head and there is royal grace on his face, may be
He is bitten by a snake, the poison is moving up his body but
I know you have the miraculous power of extracting poison
Even from men on the verge of death. Please hurry and save him,
For he has many a time saved us from savage tigers.'
Listening to him I hurried out and, my god, what do I see!
It is Karna! Had his divine earrings and diamond-made breast plate
Failed to save him? Was he unable to save himself?
I felt great compassion but the next moment the thought came
That he was the one who was going to defeat Arjuna and I,
caught in a dilemma, stood there trembling, indecisive:
Had not the god-sent golden opportunity come on its own to
remove this thorn in my flesh?
To humble the arrogant Duryodhana, to make Indraprastha and
Hastinapura ours would be easy
And also war can be avoided and the anger of
Partha would be quenched forever. True, but the woman
Within me, and the maternal affection of Kunti,

Moved me to compassion towards the
Man lying on death's bed, and how could I lose my sensitive understanding of life?
No violence for me, if he is an enemy even; humanity
Should override all personal contrarieties, and destroying an enemy
Through deceit and cowardice is not for me. The strength to save
Is bigger than the strength to kill; and he saved me that day when
I was caught in the flooded river and I can't think of him as an enemy of my husbands!
No, I should not and the same instant I chanted
The serpent-mantra and the terrible hooded-snake came and sucked out
The poison and instantly vanished into the foliage of the forest-trees and
Signs of life appeared in Karna and the huntsmen cleaned the wound and
Applied native herbal ointments and the flow of blood stopped and Karna, as if
After a happy dream, woke up and I, the same moment, ran into my thatched cottage;
Satisfied I was, for I had saved a life and some strange power had worked
This miracle for me! Realize I did, that a mother alone could be truly
Forgiving. A little later I narrated it all in detail to Yudhisthira who
With care listened to what I was saying, and exclaimed immediately,
'Good. You have done the right thing. Our life is now truly blessed and you are its author.
We shall all be grateful to you.'

As days moved on, one evening, news came that Chitrasena,
King of the Gandharvas had captured Duryodhana who had come in
The way of their water-sport with their celestial wives and the Kauravas
Got into a fight with them, but were beaten as Karna was not with them and

They were now prisoners! King Chitrasena came, talked to his old friend
And Arjuna said, 'Ah, friend Chitrasena, on their behalf we beg your
Pardon but kindly release him, he is Dharmaja's cousin and so is he ours,
And the good name of our family should not suffer. Release him, remembering
Our friendship, and strengthen our mutual relationship.'
'How proper is it for you ask for his release? How do you put up with this traitor of a man?
To let him go free who that day humiliated
Draupadi, he would be a danger to all women. If we forgive him now,
A day will come when we may have to repent for this action of ours.'
'You have made him a prisoner and is there a bigger disgrace for a
Crowned king? Show him some kindness and generosity.'
The king of Gandharvas releasing Duryodhana said, 'Now, go and fall
At the feet of Dharmaja and ask forgiveness.' Duryodhana sunk
In humiliation self-inflicted went back to Hastinapura.

One day we wandered around a great deal in Dvaitavana
And became tired and exhausted and Dharmaja felt thirsty and sent
Nakula to fetch him some water but when he did not come back, Partha
Went looking for him and as neither was back Bhimasena went searching
For them and I waited for long with Dharmaja; he too became anxious and worried
And both of us, much depressed, walked towards the lake and shocked we
Were to see all the four stretched flat on the grass, and Dharmaja
Thinking within himself wondered how they could sleep when their elder brother
Was dying of thirst! But looking at the lifeless bodies, Dharmaja,
In great sorrow said, 'Yagnaseni, you are wise and you know that

Everyone has to die one day, but should young ones die in this way!'
And with that, his sorrow burst forth and he wept and I, seeing the
Death of my husbands, cried out loud, put my head near Arjuna's feet
But became unconscious and fell. Dharmaja to sprinkled some water
On my face, went near the lake and was about to dip his hand in the
Waters of the lake when a Yaksha who was standing nearby said,
'Yudhisthira, stop. Do not collect any water. See, the condition
In which your brothers are;
I am the guardian of this lake, unless you answer
The questions I have for you, you too, like your brothers, meet
The same fate, if you dare touch the water.' Amazed he was
And yet with patience answered all the questions of Yaksha
And the Yaksha admiring Dharmaja's fund of discriminating wisdom
Said, 'I shall bring back to life one of your brothers. You
Choose, and do not delay.' I was sitting holding the feet of Arjuna,
But Dharmaja without a second thought said, 'Nakula is the
Youngest of us. Revive him quick.' The Yaksha shocked much
Said, 'Bhima and Arjuna are your two arms, but then why
Do you seek the revival of the youngest of the sons of Madri?'
In generosity great, Dharmaja said 'I am the elder and I am
Son to Kunti and isn't it right that the eldest of the sons of
Madri should be alive.'
The Yaksha admiring the impartial mind of
Dharmaja happily restored all the four to life.

IV. Movement:

THE PROTECTOR OF THE WORLD

CANTO XXVI

HO! HOA! WHO IS THIS, A GODDESS OR A NYMPH?

The thirteenth year came and with it a fiery test for me.
Is it easy to live incognito? And, if spied, another thirteen
years of Banishment!
Terrible life it is to live away, again, from our Kingdom!
But he, Dharmaja, had said 'yes' to this condition, and Bhima
thinking of the future said:
'We have stepped into the thirteenth year but to
Live in disguise is not easy: it is like trying to hide the
Himalayas with a handful of grass!
People know us and how do we manage to escape their eyes?'
Thinking for a long time, we at last decided to take shelter
At Viratapura under assumed names, and slowly walked towards it.
Yudhisthira went under the name of Kankabhatta, an expert
In the game of dice; Bhima took the name of Valala, a chef of
Mythical repute; posing as a teacher of dance, Arjuna went with the
Name of Brihannale, an eunuch; Nakula took the name of
Granthika and became the chief of cavalry
And Sahadeva under the name of Tantripala
A caretaker of the cows; all took up jobs with King Virata and they
Wondered what Draupadi could become at the king's court
but she put a break on their thoughts and said,
'Worry not, I can take care of myself. I shall be
With the queen, Sudheshne, as her maid-in-waiting, under the
name of Sairandhri;
My virtue I can defend myself for none of you was any

Help when I was disrobed in the hall of the Kaurava and what protection can
You give me, deprived of power and wealth, you cannot safeguard me now! Why, waste words,
First, you take care of yourselves.'
They all met the king, introduced themselves, and each was
Appointed to the post he had sought and none had problems doing his job;
Virata with honour welcomed Kankabhatta and Bhimasena supervising the
Work in the kitchen was more than contented! Coming to know that
Brihannale was well acquainted with Draupadi, the queen and the crown princess
Were pleased to have Arjuna as their dance-teacher and Arjuna,
He, covering the scars made by arrows had them hid with flowery arm-bands;
Wore a nose ring and ear-rings and small jingling bells on his ankles, applied
Henna and collyrium and looking gorrgeous he taught Uttare dance-steps,
And I witnessed all this and I sorrowed within myself and cursed our fate
Which had done this to us! How sad he had to part from his manliness and even
Though it was only for a year, it gave me great pain, and caused much anguish;
But since this was inevitable, I made my heart a stone! Ah!
Nakula and Sahadeva to take care of cows and horses, what an irony!
The life of my five husbands looked harrowing to me!
As maid-in-waiting to queen Sudhesne I did my job well
And became close to her but she, seeing my beauty became rather
Suspicious of her aged husband; I could sense her anxiety and told her
'O, queen, I am married and I have five husbands who are Gandharvas;

But right now under a curse, and they therefore are away from me. Although I am
With you now, the moment my husbands return reprieved I will go back.
Don't you be worried, for my husbands are given to much anger and if anyone
Desires me they sure will see that he dies. And another thing, I shall
Not be ordered by anybody else and I do not eat any leftover
Food, and this is all that I thought I should tell you.'
Dharmaja was happy playing day and night the game of dice
With the king; Arjuna was happy with his dancing-classes and so was
Bhimasena in the kitchen; and I, in the company of Uttare the princess,
Overcame my sad feeling of separation from my own children for she
Was beautiful and spoke consolingly but cheerfully; and one day I said,
'If my son were a prince I should happily love to make you my
Daughter-in-law.' She, in innocence, said, 'You yourself are
So beautiful, how much more handsome he should be, I can imagine!
Surely he must be equally bold and courageous and I am dying to see him.'
I, at length, and with many details, described the
Soldierly skills and bravery of Abhimanyu, and she in rapt attention listened!
One day Keechaka, came to his sister's place, greeted her and
She, in much affection, held his hand and made him sit next to her on the couch
And for a long time conversed with him and then spotting me, who
To him appeared like the celestial Urvashi and he could not
Take his eyes off me, and for a second was lost, shot by the
God of love and within himself murmured, 'Ha, hoa, who is this here?

A goddess or a nymph? She surely is the sharp edge of the
Sword of the love-god!
Never have I seen such beauty! She is more beautiful
Than the Draupadi of the Pandavas. Oh, how she hurts my heart!
Like an arrow shot, she has lodged herself in my heart!'
Without any sense of shame, he became vocal and expressed
his desire,
And spoke to his sister, 'Sister, tell me, who is this beautiful doll?
She, like lighting, shines and dazzles; truly a mine of charm, a
stunner she is!'
'She is the wife of the Gandharvas, men celestial, and I take
care of her.
Do not speak lightly of her, she won't fall for you, you had
Better go home and forget her.'
But the god of love had hit hard and the arrow had made a
Deep gash in his heart: downcast and disturbed he went back to
His palace but the troubled mind would not allow him to rest
And the next morning he came back to his sister's place and
seeing me
Near the door, shooed away those who were with me and
behind me.
Rushed forward, stood near me and, I knowing his intent, like a
Deer frightened, stepped back but he with no niceties in a gruff
Voice stopped me, 'Oh, girl, do not move away like the peacock.
You have entered my heart and there I worship you, please,
Do not uproot my life-line which is attached to you!' And,
I boldly said, 'O, madman, do not invite misfortune, and do not
Vex me. Desire for another's wife is suicidal and my five Gandharva
Husbands will squeeze the life out of you. Go, get back to your
Palace; you will not win me and attempt not the impossible; the
World will then laugh at you.' But undaunted he went on:
'Hey, you waiting maid, stop! Like the love-god's sharp spears
You are hurting me and you alone can be the balm for my pain,
Listen to me, and please save my life,' with folded hands he stood
Before me. Forcefully remonstrating I said, 'Look, desire
For others' wives is sinful, and the goddess of wealth deserts him;

The fair name earned gets irrevocably dirtied, and in after
Life you will be pushed into hell; have you forgotten the story of
Ravana who was after Sita? Villain, go, don't you ever show
Your face to me.' But the wretched man said, 'Let heaven and
Good deeds go to hell; Let my kinsmen shun me and let all my
Wives desert me, let anything happen but you, without speaking harsh words,
Smile at me, spread the cool moonlight of your smile
Over me and ease this burning heart; sprinkle the milk of love
From your well-shaped pointed breasts and show kindness to me.'
Hearing these wicked words I closed my ears and remembering my five husbands
I sorrowed within myself. I said, 'Oh, Govinda, Oh, Hari,
Who will save me from this lustful scoundrel; please do protect me
The helpless one!' Then, in great anger, I spoke to him loud:
'You, wicked one, trying to commit a heinous crime you will set
Afire the root of your family tree. You, your wife and children
Will end their lives without a speck of comfort. Get away, you!'
But blinded by lust Keechaka said, 'Death is certain and
I am not afraid of dying. If I am to die, I shall die after I
Become one with you; I shall offer my body to the god of love,
Dear lady, save me, please, for without you I cannot live even
For a moment.'
'You, vile rougue, do not essay such wickedness; my Gandharva
Husbands will not tolerate this, go, back to your home, quick.'
'You do not know how brave I am! What can your husbands do?
I am strength itself and if I stand up and encounter them I shall
In no way be inferior to Pinaki, Lord Shiva himself.'
'I cannot kill you, and those who will kill you are elsewhere: and
They are my husbands who will sever your head from your body
And make all your queens widows sad. No, do not take the
Path that leads to your grave!' And, with these words I left
And Keechaka, burning in a fever of love, went to his sister.
Fell at her feet and spoke his innermost thoughts, 'Sister,
Your maid-in-waiting, her beauty, has made me her
Captive; without her, I cannot live; surely, I shall die heartbroken!'

'Alas! Has the fair name of our family all gone sullied: See,
Her five husbands are brave Gandharvas; and if angered, they will
Fight unto death; I am scared: no, do not meddle with her;
Whichever other woman you desire, I shall get her wedded to you.
Do not be obsessed with her, and go to rack and ruin.' But
Keechaka said, 'Sister, how can I forget this beauty which has
Looted my mind, please make her love me. I am wounded and
Cannot live without her; won't you fulfill your brother's desire?
Kindly help me, I am your brother, am I not?' With
These words he fell at her feet and seeing tears in his eyes
She too was moved said to herself:
'Ah! Are we inviting destruction!'
And then in affection raised him and said, 'All right,
Get up, tomorrow I shall send her to your place but
Beware, desiring other men's wives is unwise and dangerous.'
Dreaming sweet dreams Keechaka went home; the sun
Crossed the western hills and disappeared and with the moon
rising in the sky
It was cool all around; the rising moon looked like the sandal
Tilak on a lovely woman's forehead or rather like a mirror
held in hand
By the queen of Eros or more than that it was like burning red,
Live coal intent on setting afire the lover waiting for his beloved;
Each passing minute appeared an age to Keechaka and yet the
Sun arose in the east and Sudershne knowing her brother's
mind called her maid and said,
'Take this pitcher of wine to my brother's place.'
'O, queen, no, I cannot; he is wicked and my husbands are
mighty men.
It is better for your own self to send somebody else; I cannot,
for the life
Of me, think of doing injustice to you who have given me
refuge here.'
She burst out in anger, 'Come, for a maid-in-waiting you are too
Arrogant! Would our people suffer harm from yours? You do
not know.

My brother is a hero, admired all the world over, the bravest
man he is!'
'Alas, without any awareness, why is she assigning me this job?
Krishna! What fairness is this? The wicked man will meet his death,
You, killer of demons, you alone are our savior. The fear of being
Disrobed again is come to me, the Kauravas did it and you
saved me,
The fear has again stalked me, why repeatedly, shocks me!
Bestow discrimination on him.'
With such thoughts, and bowing, to Indra, Agni, Vayu and
Varuna and to the sun-god, slowly, walked towards Keechaka's place
And he, the villain, stood-up, and greeting me said: 'Ah! Girl, come,
Come, I have been waiting for you. Come sit on my couch, now
That you have come with love to me, why do I fear the god
of love!'
He came close and I shuddering said, 'Enough of your love talk!
Do not ruin yourself. The queen has asked me to give you this
Pitcher of wine. Take it, and do not jump into a blazing fire,
you evil-doer.'
'Ah, beautiful girl, lovely woman, come and do not spoil this
Sweet hour, do not tease me anymore,' saying so he rushed
Forward and held my hand; the pitcher fell on the floor; I trembling,
Ran into the royal court but he swiftly following me held me by
My hair and shouted, 'Where will you run? You are caught in the
Strong net of my love and here by my strong arms, where and
How will you free yourself? Ah, my dove, would I let you go?
Your five husbands have abandoned you, come and be with me;
I shall hugely satisfy you and drench your field gone dry.'
He tried to grab me and press me to his chest but I slipped out
And he in anger hit me hard, and blood flowed from a
gaping wound
And I fell; with difficulty I stood up, and fell down again; the
Guards who were around came to my help and caught him and
Beat him up and in the melee I ran home, dusting myself and
Wiping the blood stuck on my checks and chin. I turned to the
Assembly and stood all a-tremble and said, 'Alas, alas! To what

Ill luck have I come! None of mine came to rescue me!
The wicked Keechaka torments and harasses me,
The weak me has none to stand by me!'

CANTO XXVII

SHAMELESS HUSBANDS, SPINELESS TO LORD OVER THEIR WIFE?

I managed an opportunity to speak to Dharmaja
About the wickedness of Keechaka and he, listening, said:
'Arjuna has become effeminate, has lost his manhood; Bhima is
Without any weapons and, if informed, he will, in anger, reveal
us all
And we shall be caught; a war could right now happen, alas!'
I did not know how I could save myself with Yudhisthira bound
To principles of righteousness! In this trying moment, suicide was
One way open to me; my husbands were unable to protect me, and
Should I beg and save myself, my virtue? Earlier I had wept
Many a time but had also vowed that I would never weep again,
But would, swallowing my sorrow, keep silent. Now there was no
Other way but to confide in Bhima who alone was courage
unbounded;
The moment the news reached that lustful Keechaka had cast
his evil eyes on me,
He the very same moment, in fury unmatched would
Kill him, and this again would reveal our whereabouts!
Who but he can save me?
After food, Dharmaja was engaged is playing a game of dice
With Virata; Bhima was in the kitchen; Arjuna in the dance hall,
Nakula and Sahadeva in the stables and the cowshed; add to this,
Uttare and Sudheshne were watching Brihannale dance, ah what
A fate is ours! The other day at the swayamvara dance, he won

Me, winning me with his skill and prowess in archery and
Today to regale the womenfolk, he dances! What an irony!
What humiliation! Trying hard, I controlled myself from weeping
But Sudheshne gestured to me and I went and stood near her
And she said, 'Hey, Sairandhri, come, take this box of perfume and
Give it to Keechaka, and now itself this needs to be done.'
Much pained but summoning courage I said, 'O, queen,
I have already pleaded with you, on small errands I cannot
Go; it is not right to send me to a man who is drunk;
In fact, no woman is safe with him, do not push me into the carnal
Fire that is blazing within him, forgive me, please,' Till today
She had never treated me as her waiting maid, had, in fact, seen me
As her soul-mate but today with much harshness she said,
'You know what will happen if you flout my orders, take care.'
'Truly, she has connived, and wants me to satisfy her brother's sensual
Craving! We but need refuge here for a couple of months, yes,
But if anything goes wrong, thirteen years of suffering comes to
Nought! How can I allow this to happen Shiva, Shiva!'
Holding the casket in my hand and murmuring, Krishna's name,
I entered Keechaka's house, 'Spewing, fire within myself or like
Leaping into an ocean unfathomable or like entering a dark cave to
Satisfy the lust of an animal, I am going, but can I escape from
His lustful grasp; I have to help and save me myself; right now,
Am rather like a deer entering the cave of a hungry tiger;
O, friend,
My soul-mate, Sri Krishna it is your friend and soul-mate who
Begs you to save her honour; you did so in the packed hall
Of the Kauravas and today too you alone have to protect me.'
Keechaka who stood waiting for me, with outstretched arms
Rushed towards me but I leapt and pushed him away hard
And he fell like a huge tree uprooted and I, with heart palpitating,
Ran like a deer and entered the kings' dicing chamber but Keechaka
Drunk, followed me and, pulled at my flowing hair, made me
Fall to the ground, and raining abuses stamped with his foot
on my fallen body,
But as if nothing was happening Dharmaja, in silence continued

With his game, displaying no trace of pricked manliness on hearing
Me cry out Bhimasena came running, and seeing him Dharmaja
Loudly and harshly said, 'Hey, you cook, what work have you here?'
Bhima swallowed his anger and went back but I exploded in anger:
'Are all doors of courts offering justice to women in the
kingdom of Virata shut?
A drunken lout, in public, attempts to rudely
Outrage a woman's honour but you eunuchs, you sit doing
nothing! You sit on the throne,
hold the threads of administration in your hand, and
Yet are helpless to save a woman from being molested! What
Manliness is this? What justice? What fairness?'
Since the real power was all concentrated in the hands of Keechaka,
Virata was silent, but Dharmaja said, 'Sairandhri, without a
Knowledge of facts, what opinion can the king give? You now
Get back to your ladies' apartments, for issues related to
Women are to be resolved by yourselves and not at an open
Royal court. And without inquiry by the judges, how can we
Pronounce any judgment?' Saying so Dharmaja picked up the dice
And I, wiping my tear-filled eyes, thought to myself:
'What concern has the king? Moving each pawn, he is
absorbed in the game,
And is all smiles! Does he care about a woman
being outraged!
My husband, might by seeing my dead body, and the eldest
Perhaps does not even know the quandary I am in! The game of
Dicing has been my death.' While I was thinking so, Bhima bit his
Lips and is fiery anger, burning like live coal, he said, 'The
Wicked man who beat my girl, I shall not spare him; and I shall
Kill Virata and his kinsmen, no, I shall not put up with this
Beastly behaviour.' Dharmaja, surprised, said, 'At our time of
Difficulty, Virata has given us refuge, and what has he done to us?
We shall find a way to punish Keechaka. If it gets known that
We are the Pandavas, another thirteen years of banishment
is certain.
And, therefore, essay not such mindless adventures, and not

At this critical point of time.' Turning, towards me he said
'Oh, lady, you go back, we cannot punish the guilty, the
King will take care of it, not we. And, this is not the time to get
Angry. Yes. Your five husbands are not cowards, be bold and be
Courageous; virtuous you are, and forgiveness is its base, trust
This.' Refusing to concur with him I said, 'No, I shall not
Accept this. If the villain is not destroyed, injustice will have no
Limits. You men have become impotent and spineless; do not
Try to slip away cleverly; I shall pursue my vengeance.'
Replacing the pallu of my disheveled saree, in much
Anxiety, I walked in, reached the kitchen and searched for Bhima
Who was not to be seen anywhere, he, my sole protector! Then,
I saw him: on a heaped mass of kitchen utensils he was fast
Asleep, a rough blanket covered him, and unmindful of it all he
Was snoring, overworked and tired, he had deposited himself in a
Corner. Seeing him, compassion sprang in me; he who was
used to rich food
And rest and enviable royal living, had been reduced to this state!
If I wake him up, he will, like a whirlwind or like a volcano
burst forth;
I don't know if my visit is going to be a success or a failure; tossing
In confusion, willy nilly, I would say yes sometimes I would
say no within myself
But knowing that there was no alternative but to go to
This giant of strength I bent and softly said 'Bhimasena' and tugged
The sheet he had covered himself with, and he blinked and then
Slowly opened his eyes saying, 'Ah, wife! Why this anxiety
on your face, tell me.
And why come at this hour, and how did you
enter this Kitchen,
What has made you worried, tell me.'
'Oh, you, the wind-god born,
Yesterday, in broad daylight, the most wicked man Keechaka,
Tried to deprive me of virtue, held me by the hair of my head,
And drew me to him but I kicked him away and escaped and
All the others were mute spectators! Who will come to my rescue?

Tomorrow morning he will come and forcibly, violently he will take me.
And before that happens I want to commit suicide and to let
You know of this I have come to you.' Seized by mounting
Anger, he said, 'No, stop, do not speak such words. Already,
A blazing fire has got into my soul and it will reduce to ashes
The lustful villain and don't you do anything that would end
Our heroism and leave the Kaurava unharmed; let us keep the
Light of our terrible ambition alive.' 'Oh, dear husband, you alone
Know me; the other take their delight and disappear specially when
Questions on my dignity or honour are raised; you alone
Understand me, the others do not share my sorrow and, live in
Indignity I cannot. That is for certain. Send Keechaka to his
Death, push him into the kingdom of the dead, that you must.'
This good deed of yours will help me live.'
'Without my brother's permission, I cannot proceed.'
'To save the honour of a wife, do you need permission? You all profess
To live and observe high moral values and are famed heroes of the world,
And yet spineless eunuchs, you are! That day, in the open court
The heartless one disrobed me! And, today, in the presence of the King,
Keechaka kicked me. Is there any difference between that day's
Brutal molestation and today's disgraceful attempt at rape? You
Are all cowards, green-livered you are! Those who cannot protect their
Women folk, what use are they, living or dead?'
Listening to my harsh words,
Bhima said, 'Speak, speak as harshly as you wish!
I shall not complain.
The other day I swore that I would not rest till
I tore open his belly, and drink
His blood and smear it on your hair, and am waiting for that moment
To arrive. I do not want to be blamed for transgressing my brother's order.

You put pressure on him, make him agree; get the bold Arjuna
Into the war field and ask Nakula and Sahadeva to accompany him,
Don't you pick on me alone, there are the other four.'
Listening to the son of the wind-born god, my throat went dry;
Like a tender banana leaf held over a blazing fire I turned ashy
Pale, felt exhausted and was like a torn string, fallen on the
ground, and
Barely managed to whisper, 'Which young one did I harm in my
Previous life? Which sin did I commit? Let not sorrowing women
Like us ever be born; and let not husbands like Bhima too be
Born in the world. If there is not any to share my sorrows,
Why do I not die? Why does not death come to me?
Why do I live?'
Bhima's heart melted; his eyes shed tears; his anger, like
Fire, spread and his feelings were all shaken and troubled,
he bent,
Pressed me to his chest, wiped my tears with his shoulder-cloth,
Patted me on my head and my chin and sprinkling some
water on my
Swollen face, he spoke like the bold man that he always had been,
'O, queen, if he but stirs I shall now tear open his belly and
along with him
Will erase the entire family ofVirata. Ah, I am guilty of inexcusable
Crime: I have made you weep and suffer; forgive this shameless
Husband of yours. If my brother gets angry I shall ignore him,
And if Partha and the twin brothers try to stop, I shall, the way
A lion kills off fleas, I shall destroy them. No obstacle, even as huge
As the Himalayas, can come in my way. Forget your worry, I am
With you,' he said and after a second gnashing of his teeth continued,
'Call the villain,
Ask him to come to the dancing hall at night and I shall rip open
His heart and offer his blood as sacrifice to ghosts and gobblins.
The lion has now come out of the cage.
Nothing will stop it now; tomorrow's
Sunrise Keechaka won't be there to see.'
And I seeing his firm resolution,

Praised him and said that among the greatest of men he was truly
The greatest and that he was the fruit of all my good deeds and
Left the place.

CANTO XXVIII

DID THE GANDHARVAS APPEAR FROM NOWHERE AND KILL KEECHAKA?

Returning to the palace early in the morning, and about to
Enter the apartments of sister Sudheshne, I saw Keechaka loitering
Nearby and the moment he spied me, he drew near, gestured
and said:
'The last night looked an age to me! Be kind; the moon, like
the god of death
Tortured me all the time.' Sternly I replied: 'Yes, even the
Moon sometimes becomes the god of death, like nectar
turning into
Poison or the snow becoming scalding hot or like relatives
becoming enemies
In no time. Keechaka, listen, even the earth goddess can't bear
the burden
Of a wicked man who desires another's wife.' But even before
I had finished
His eyes burnt through me and said, 'No, I cannot listen to your
Moral sermons, I have lost all patience, be understanding, and dress
Me in the cooling cloth of your love, and cure the gashes your
Arrows of beauty have made.' With folded hands I begged him:
'No, keep away or my husbands will kill you; they wait for me at
The dancing hall every evening at sunset; and you, along with
the sun,
Will sink into the ocean of time; it is during dusk my
husbands come to see me;

If you have courage to meet them and vanquish them or it will be
The death knell for you. Think, do not invite death. Be wise, be careful and
Give up your unholy carnal desires; if you strike at the anthill,
The hooded cobra will spring at you and you would be a dead man,
Do not take the road that leads you to death.'
I indicated in so many ways the danger that waited for him.
But are not the infatuated blind and reckless? Building castles
In the air he went home and I went straight to the kitchen and
Spoke to Bhima, 'Listen, I have asked the smitten scoundrel to
Come to the dancing hall. Make him fall, trample on him and rise
Victorious. The world will be grateful to you.' Smiling, he got up,
Over a tightly-pleated costume of boxers he wore a saree, put a
Tilaka on his forehead and wore bangles on his wrists, and I sprinkled the
Auspicious coloured-rice over his head and in the dark he went to the dancing hall
Lay down on the precious-stone studded couch; from another
Door Keechaka, drunk on dreams of carnal pleasure, tiptoed
Heavily perfumed he was wearing fragrant smelling flowers in his hair.
And like a moron entering the gaping mouth of the god of death, he
Swaggered in and felt and groped, and imaging it was Sairandhri, said:
'Ah, lotus-faced beauty, the perfume is wonderful and the jasmine flowers
Are fragrant and your costume enticing. Truly there are not any who
Is equal to you even among the heavenly damsels! I have put strong
Men around the dancing hall to stop your Gandharvas from getting
In; hard it will be for them to enter, and if they do manage,
They will all be dead. Without a touch of worry you can now swim in

A pool of pleasure, of enjoyment, of voluptuousness. I swear on you,
A woman who takes pleasure with me would want to taste it again and again:
Is there anywhere a woman who will not fall for me?'
'Hey, Keechaka, none is as handsome as you and there is none equal
To me either and there is not a man who will not fall for me and we make a lovely pair;
I love you and you me, come enjoy this embrace firm
And hard as that of death.' Blind and deaf with lust, Keechaka in
Great happiness drew him close and felt him and not finding soft breasts,
He, in anger and fear, said, 'The chest is hard as stone, and where has the softness gone,
And where is your girlie body? What strangeness, what oddily?'
'Hey, you, listen, for those who desire other men's wives, nectar becomes
Bitter poison and softness hard as stone.' Saying so he held the
Forelocks of Keechaka and pulled but he thought it was
Sairandhri
And Bhima punched and battered his nose and face and
Keechaka in pain howled and cried:
'Ah, I am ruined! This is no woman but truly
Her husband, the Gandharva, what misreading I have done!'
Escaping from Bhima's hold, he ran but Bhima followed and fell on him and
Like two hillocks fighting one another they fought, and then Bhima
Bodily lifting him up high in the air, dashed him down on the hard floor.
Then with his clenched fist he hit him, and as if the forehead of an elephant
Had been ripped open, blood flowed and then Bhima wrenched out his
Intestines, and transformed him into a ball of lifeless meat!
In exceeding happiness and contentment, I drew him to me,
Held his hands, danced and kissed him all over his face and said

'Ah, you are dearest to me; you have saved my honour and I feel blessed.'

But then trooped in the brothers of Keechaka and along with his
Dead body, they bundled me in and began to transport me with
The dead man; I in great fear and sorrow stammered, 'Hey,
You evil ones, do not dare to touch me, and no rough
house neither.
Jaya, Vijaya, Jayarama, Jayasena, Vijayibhava, my
Gandharva husbands come, save me, these wicked ones want
To burn me with the body of their dead brother, come, soon'
Vrikodara in overpowering anger rushed out. Pulled a sturdy
Tree from its roots and with its thick stem chased
And beat them and they all died and then he reached
Home silently as I too did.

The next day the news was all over the place and people
Everywhere were talking about it and the king got worried:
'This woman is no woman, she is a fiend, a monster;
This Sairandhri should go away.'
The queen hearing this got frightened and she sent
For me and with folded hands said, 'Ah! Great lady, we fear you.
As long as you are here, we shall not be free of fear. Sairandhri,
Please go away. You have come to destroy us; Do not
Frighten us any more. And, there is not any who is equal to
you in beauty on
This earth, and men, fascinated, like moths, fall and get burnt in
The fire of your beauty; we do not want any more such sacrifices.'
'Oh, queen. Please remember I have sought refuge with you
for a great purpose
And only thirteen days are left for the period to be over
And then my five Gandharva husbands will come and take
me away.
And it would bring good fortune to the king. This is certain.'
'You can stay here for days or for months but do see to it
That my husband and children come to no harm, that onus is
on you.'
As the period of banishment was coming to a close, spies from

Four corners went and met the king of Kurus and submitted:
'Maharaja, the Pandavas are not to be found on this earth; we have
Every nook and corner searched and yet there is no trace of them,
You have truly triumphed and are unvanquishable.' The king,
Pleased and happy sent them away with rewards appropriate
but the same
Evening there was fresh information. 'Lord, last night
mysteriously, some
Five Gandharvas wrought havoc and killed the strong man of
Virata.'
'Say it, say it again. Are the strong men of Virata destroyed and
He is rendered helpless? Did Keechaka die?
And, did the five Gandharvas have, but a single wife?'
In reply, the spies, in detail, presented
Their news, 'Yes, my lord. A lady came, pleaded and managed
to get refuge,
And Keechaka fascinated by her beauty asked her to meet him
Secretly at the dancing hall and there, in the dark, the
Gandharvas, killed him in a wrestling bout.'
Kaurava, putting his index finger on his nose, spoke,
'Then, surely it is Draupadi! The killer of Keechaka is Bhima!
This is visual proof of the existence of the Pandavas.
The Gandharva heroes are none but the Pandavas themselves.'
Listening to the King, the counsellors said:
'It is the bee which knows best the ways of
The fragrant-blowing wind and you know best the ways of
your men! How would the ordinary ones know such secrets?'
Angry Duryodhana Said, 'What is very mysterious here?
Bhima, Balarama, Keechaka
And Shalya are known for their great valour and this
Has now become public! The Pandavas are living in the Matsya
Kingdom and are waiting for the period of banishment to be over.
There is no doubt of that. Now we have to expose them,
nail them,
And send them again into banishment for another twelve years!
Let the army move, ferret out the secret or otherwise

we shall be lost!'
Saindhava, Kripacharya, Karna, Aswathama were all sent for,
And at a meeting held, it was said, 'Truly, it is Bhima who has
killed Keechaka
No doubt of that. And wherever Dharmaja stays there will
be always
Prosperity absolute. Where the Pandavas live, there stays
halcyon days.'
Then, spoke Dronacharya who was all praise for the Pandavas;
'To the North,
The Himalayas and in the other three directions there
is drought and famine,
But only in the mid-lands there is plenty and happiness.
That truly is the region where the Pandavas live.' Gangeya added:
'Yes, if the Pandavas are spotted before the period of
banishment is over,
They have to, on terms agreed, go back into the forests for
Another thirteen years! But, Kaurava, listen. Do not jump into
Action precipitate: the Pandavas walk the path of truth and are
Not afraid of war. Do, therefore, after the period is over,
invite them
And return their kingdom. Walking unjust paths will destroy
The entire family.' Responding to it, Duryodhana, spoke his mind:
'Yes, right you are, but then should I cede the kingdom to
them? No,
This does not have my approval. Like fools we shall not enter
into a treaty
With them. This path we will not pursue. We shall
Now invade the Matsya Kingdom, catch all the cattle-wealth
and seeing this,
The Pandavas will come out in the open and then we can
Send them back into banishment for another thirteen years.'
The assembly broke up and the next day at an auspicious
Hour, the king, with Bhisma, Saindhava, Aswathamas, Karna
and Kripa,
Followed by a large army comprising of cavalry and foot soldiers,

And elephant-mounted veterans, left, and the dust raised by
the army
Clouded the sun and day-stars twinkled causing consternation.

CANTO XXIX

THE PROTECTOR OF THE WORLD BLEW THE WAR-HERALDING CONCH!

After the painful thirteen years of banishment came to an end
King Virata desired to offer his daughter Uttare to
Partha, and he, courteously declining said, 'I was teacher to
Uttare, and in kinship terms almost a father to her, and therefore,
My son Abhimanyu would be the suitable groom for her.'
And in much joy and pomp the wedding took place and
Subhadre, Balarama, Sri Krishna, their wives and the five children,
And Drupada, the father, and Dristadyumna, Draupadi's brother
All assembled; Vidura stayed home for he was unwell and
Kunti too; Subhadre, the would be mother-in-law, looking at
Uttare said, 'Draupadi, our daughter-in-law is a
Beauty unmatched; your choice is impeccable; but for the other
Children, I shall choose the brides.' Hearing her, I said, 'Ah,
I do not know what awaits my five children in the future;
Abandoning them, I walked the forests and, now how can
I call them "my sons?" You have the right to call them as your
Children.' 'I, of course, felt a pang, for the Kaurava had forgotten
To return our kingdoms to us. Again, war is inevitable,
How would Dharmaja get ready for it? As a last
Resort, he, to avoid internecine war, persuaded Sri Krishna
To go as their ambassador, and strangely, he agreed!
Speech true and powerful does not completely represent truth;
The whole is eternally whole, and truth eternally true;
It is many-faceted, ever plural, never ever a single,
Mono-faced entity; it has no end and can never be seen in

Its wholeness; like the story of Mahabharata, it is endless;
For if there is an end, it possesses not totality, and therefore
One has to make an effort to see it in its entirety.
This is what once I told Arjuna: 'Partha, don't you know
What is true and what is not? I am sure your heart knows and
The heart is true witness and whatever your heart says, you
Listen to it; hear what it says; the true story, the mind knows,
But it is not to be kept suppressed as a sly man does, and
Follows the wrong path. Do not think of me as one abandoned
And those, through sheer effrontery do things or act,
Do themselves harm, and land in a bottomless pit of evils;
The sun, the moon, the fire and the sky and the wind and
The earth and birth and death—all, all of this is fruit-born
Of man's truly better-half, of the wife it is all born and
She is a true friend who helps you move heavenward
and god-ward;
She is the source of all strength spiritual; she it is who
Helps elevate the soul of man; a life in which she is not,
Is life incomplete; if she is with you, life is full and fully
Realized; any indifference shown to her makes life
A graveyard; she is the one who protects love and happiness and
Makes for progress; do not wish such a one bad or mean
end, beware!'
Thinking on these lines, I went to Hari and said,
'Krishna, what will you do? To talk of peace is a wasted effort, tell
Me, would minds concur, think. Is it possible to forget the
Bitter happenings of the past? Every time you push the Pandavas
Into fresh whirlpools of trouble, but why? Why this hide and seek?
Is this playing with Gopis or a game of gambling? Are we the poor
Pawns of the game of chess? The Kauravas took advantage of
our weakness
And yanked away our kingdom, and how will you get it back
to us except through war?
This attempt at peace will make us all look
Ludicrous and Kaurava, as long as he is alive, will not through talks
Or treaties, return us our kingdom and therefore, do not shame

The valour of Bhima or the skills of archery of Arjuna. Keshava,
Tell me, without smashing the thighs of Duryodhana and
ripping open
The belly of Dushyasana and dipping my hair in his blood,
how can I plait my hair?
How else can the flame of my anger be doused?
How will you put out the fire that has been burning me up
through these thirteen years of banishment!
Arrows of sharp words wound me all the time.
Dharmaja, understanding the painful shame of others,
Will not do anything. He will be led by his own selfish and
Superstitious, religious ideas and even if ages and aeons pass away,
Or disappear he will wait till his theories triumph here!
He has lost his Kshatriya power to wage war against injustice
And has lost his authority and aura! Or, else how can he
Forget that I was hauled into the open court of Kauravas and that
The pallu of my saree was jerked away? Or has he, because
of such
Terrible happening gone stupid? Cannot he open his eyes and see?
Or has the world gone blind and deaf? What strangeness is this?
My eyes have gone dry, and from now on only blood can
trickle from my eyes.
Perhaps your consciousness you will regain when from my
Eyes hot drops of blood fall on you; I have lost faith in all
Familial bonds; I have lost faith in my five husbands who wed
Me. And you who are kind to such men and listen to sermons
On justice, for you, I have only contempt.
Flames of anger are bursting in me and like a
Volcano it is about to explode but, Krishna, there is within me
Still a green patch of love and before it dries up,
Wake up, rush forth and be the saviour of our epoch and
Be the spirit behind its spiritual awakening. Do not put to
Test again an innocent girl, let her not meet more humiliation;
Let the divine saying that he who protects *dharma* is protected by
Dharma go false; how can you, like a dumb spectator, simply
Watch the injustice being meted out to a woman; such

Humbling of women does no credit to an avatar like yours.'
Krishna who had listened in silence now spoke, 'Krishne,
Stop shedding tears and listen to the promise the lord of
Dwaraka makes now: you will witness the destruction of all your enemies;
The Pandavas will receive back the kingdom they have lost
Unjustly; their wealth too will return to them; there is no
Doubt and these conciliatory talks, I know, will
Not bear fruit, for these are to satisfy the demands of
Political conventions. I shall not do anything that distresses you.
I know there is among the Kauravas a tiger in the garb of a sheep,
I shall destroy it. Panchali, trust me, and think right. Open your
Eyes and see everything in its totality; I do not swim against
The current, I, on the contrary, like the sweeping wind move, and
In the righteous war you wage I shall be your charioteer and
Achieve world peace. These talks of peace are only a ploy and wait
Till the moment the curtain raises, and do not do anything desperate.'
The protector of the world blew the war-heralding conch;
I came again to Dharmaja and said, 'You are the best of men, the most righteous
And yet you are not able to protect *dharma*; and although
Disturbed because of your *dharma*, why did you invite this tragedy?
The worthiest have suffered injustice and the wickedest have accumulated
Ill-gained wealth, are happily enjoying it all unhindered?
Whom shall I blame for this?
How do I save the good and the virtuous?
Why do you choose the way righteous? Why call yourself King? No.
Rise, stand up and with a brave heart move forward; smash the
Boulder of tolerance and moderation and step forward, for
Dhritarastra, infatuated with love for his children, has come here to invade,
In anger and is fear-blinded! Can we forgive him? No, therefore,
You have to become the lions that you are. The moment of war,

To decide everything, is come. Thinking us weak, they show
Benign contempt for us. Shake off your inertia, and become
mercurial!'
'Dear, how do I break the word I have given? To fight is easy,
But to forgive is most hard. Tell me, is it a weakness to become
Peace-loving? No, do not run me down. Friendship, peaceful,
is better.'
'I am amazed! Don't you get angry with insolence mean? Does
Not the blood of Khsatriyas flow in your veins? Why does not your
Anger burst forth, and destroy the wrongdoers? Witnessing your
Wife's lamentable condition, why does not your heart weep? Why
This helplessness, why this passiveness, why this torpor and
sluggishness?
Have too many wars fought turned you into eunuchs? Or,
Have you become too tired and superstitions and totally dull?'
Unperturbed Dharmaja replied, 'How can I act in the hope of being
Rewarded? I do what I believe in, whether it rewards me or not.
From my duty I cannot turn away, for winning awards cannot
Be the aim of life. My dharma is knit into me, and how could
it be an obstacle to me?'
'Who can bring changes in his thinking wedded to his own idea
Of *dharma*? How can one change a man who thinks not of
the fruit of action?
It is right that we get back our kingdom through right means.
I have no quarrel with that but in politics, is there
Any room for theories of statesmanship? The Kauravas can be defeated
Only through adoption of their own strategies, tricks
and subterfuges.'
Then, as I was thinking these thoughts, Dharmaja called us all
and said:
'How can I unfurl the flag of *dharma* I have hoisted all the
While? This infatuation for the passing is not for me; history
Has thousands of pages which speak of forcing away the good
and the Gods!
In the annals of India there are several chapters recording
Such happenings; in the chronicle of Rama there is a story of

the banishment of Rama himself;
And this fact of Pandavas spending thirteen years
In the forests will become part of that ancient saga and will,
Transforming itself into a huge river, become part of the ocean
Of life itself, and there evident would be small men's small
envious acts!'
Sri Krishna arrived soon after and spoke to Dharmaja,
'Remember whatever you undertake, if done with demonstration
Of strength, you will succeed; do not ever show your weakness;
Enemies first look for these and then fall on us; do not take into
Confidence your servants and officers.
While going to sleep be awake,
And when the wicked arise open your eyes wide and take decisions
Brave: this is god's message. Let there be awakened restraint
in your eyes and ears and speech; know that the movements of
Your hands speak of your character, and therefore take care of
Your body-language; do not ever think your enemies are weak;
Remember that a sapling grows straight and reaches
the high skies.
The castor plant does not bear pomegranate fruits, and a
Single spark is enough to set on fire the entire world!
If you are careless and allow a baby-snake to grow, it will
grow and bite you first;
Whoever does you wrong, use the right means of
Punishment or conciliation or rewards, and hold him under
your thumb;
Know that in war all means are right, for your enemies,
Like milk-hedge grow to fantastically gigantic heights and
smother you;
Allow not beggars and atheists to grow in numbers; the atheists
Plant suspicion; even the trustworthy ones you keep, watch
them with care;
Ask spies to keep a watchful eye on public places like prayer
Halls, gambling and drinking dens; see that no one comes to
Know national secrets; truth now has become servant to riches;
The words of the well-to-do appear to be true and those
which emanate from

Seats of power have the garb of *dharma*; he, who like the
Farmer toils in the field and makes a sacrifice of himself,
Is a true symbol of patriotism; time alone decides man's
Station in life; he is a brave man who knows what time is proper
To perform which act; some have this ability and some are
without it,
If life is viewed dispassionately and if richness of mind is acquired,
Then everything looks beautiful and full of auspiciousness;
Bravery, steadfastness, efficiency and unlimited courage are the
Characteristics of Kshatriyas; do not ever neglect these qualities;
When the feminine and the masculine principles of strength get
Fused, and are put it action, then the epochal explosion is
Sure to take place.'

CANTO XXX

BEYOND THE LINE OF LIFE AND DEATH, CHIRANJEEVI, THE IMMORTAL

Although Sri Krishna said that the talks were only a ruse,
I was doubtful and to test, one night I got on to a chariot and
Reached Hastinavati. In the morning Kunti came to the banks
of the Ganga
And some pain, some anguish I could see had weighed her down;
Or in desperation did she want to end her life by drowning?
Who knows?
I followed her, made the chariot stop behind a huge tree
And waited:
She moved on and stopped where Karna sat alone,
reciting the Vedas;
In the early morning rays, his body shone like beaten gold and
Was I amazed! Forgetting that I was looking at one from the
enemy-camp,
I stood and he looked like a bundle of sunlight
and he, after
Offering prayer and obeisance to the sun-god, saw Kunti and
prostrated at her
Feet: 'Oh, mother, why come at this untimely time? What can
This son of Radheya do for you? Have you come to ask or
say something?'
'Oh, son. I am here to share a truth with you which will release
Me of the sorrow of my soul; you are not the son of Radhe,
the wife of low caste charioteer;
You spring from an unfortunate womb of the sun-god's

Chosen one; you are the eldest of the Pandavas, and of an
offspring of the bright sun-god himself;
And, you and, your brothers wage war among yourselves,
And kill each other! How can I, a mother, witness the carnage?
The universe itself desires the reconciliation of Arjuna and Karna
Which will forever remove the curse that dogs your parents;
Draupadi wedded the five Pandavas only to make my words
true to the world;
I have come to you, dear child, and with folded hands,
I beg you to listen and grant me my request.'
There in the sky, it looked as if, there was a sudden flash of
Bright light and the sunbeam looked as if alive and breathing!
'Yes, Karna, Kunti is your own mother, you are the son of the
god of light
Don't move away from path righteous.' The valiant Karna
stonily said:
'True, accept, I do; but if I listen to my mother, it would be
the end of
Dharma! Who will protect me when my own mother chooses
to be selfish?
How could I be disloyal to my country? Those who gave
birth to me
Were Athiratha and Radha and where is a choice here? Those
who care
And rear are the parents of the child. Tell me, the sun makes the
Day light up with light, and should his son live in with
dark secrets!
Where had you disappeared, without ever disclosing my birth?
Where were you hiding, and in silence? From my childhood,
I swam in a vale of tears,
And then where had your concerns and tears for me gone?
Who is responsible for this? Did your womb become a stone?
When, during the Swayamvara Drishtadyumna asked me about
my birth, where was the sun-god hiding?
Were there dark clouds covering him up? Was justice forgotten?
I looked at the sky and was speechless,
But did you then follow maternal dharma?

Bhimarjuna receive every kind of admiring attention, but me, am the unfortunate,
Son! None has shown any consideration, all were deaf to me and today
You make known the secret of my birth, but for what purpose?
What benefit? That I be disloyal to the king who has fed and cared
For me? Shall I set fire to my own funeral pyre! What
Intention is yours that you come to impart this to me, now!
Is Krishna behind this game? He is fond of political sport, isn't he?
He has abandoned his foster mother, Yashoda, and has forgotten the
Sufferings of cowherds; artfully maneuvering is his life's chosen path: more
Than kinship what fascinates him is amasing power in his hands;
He is no exception to the rule of selfish behaviour; we all are equal;
I do feel guilty for I was party to the dishonour heaped on
Your daughter-in-law but do not think of her as marketable
Commodity; do not present her before us and try to make us psychologically weak;
I shall not transgress the path of duty and loyalty, and I beg
Draupadi's forgiveness; let her not sighs harm me; let her live
A long and happy wedded life. I shall not renege, disloyal
I can't be.'
The mother, crying bitterly, pleaded, 'Oh, son, I feel your
Pain and it is natural but your war is against the Pandavas, and how can
Draupadi's auspicious sign of Kumkum be saved?' 'Oh, mother,
I know now why you are here; it is to squeeze out the little life that is left within me;
What remains is a dry log for the funeral pyre;
The valorous Karna is only a living corpse; a piece of sugar cane
Chewed and thrown out! What can be done now, alas, alas! Yes,
Defeated I am, and I promise I shall not kill any of your sons,
Except Arjuna; he is my equal in skill, and in enemity; and
Too often have I been humiliated, and my valour insulted
Either he gets killed by my arrow or me by his; for which

There is no other course open; Karna does not fear death,
And he needs no sympathy from anyone; at the very end
Of my life you have come and made my life large with a purpose
And I am grateful.' With that he bent, touched the feet of
His mother, and washed them with his tears; Kunti hugging
him said:
'Oh, son, an unfortunate mother I am and can blame none; be
More renowned, and am grateful for I have a son like you;
Waver not from your duty.' Karna smiled and spoke: 'Yes,
Bless you cannot me with victory or longevity; Shiva, Shiva!
With your motherly blessing I shall, in the battlefield, achieve
Death heroic and proper to a son of Kunti, the mother of Pandavas.'
With tearful eyes Kunti Devi bent down, gathered the
Sand which bore the foot-print of Karna and holding it in
her palms,
Fondled it saying, 'Dear son, to my tangled life you have
Given meaning and I am moved; you live a life eternal, beyond
The dividing line of life and death.' The next moment she
Collapsed and I ran towards her, and lifting her in my arms, I said:
'O, mother, it is dusk and you, the royal mother and daughter-
in-law of
The Kuru dynasty at this darkening hour, should not be here
Crying; come, mother, come, I shall take you home.'
She said: 'You at least felt my anguish as mother; my five sons
are men,
And know not the heart of a mother; nor have they the mind to
Set it right.' Sharing this long-hidden grief had lightened her heart.
'This it is which is the great war of Kurukshetra! The fever of
the world!
Justice to one and injustice to another; faith in god at one end
And at the other end arrogance, selfishness and friendship with the
Wicked! Karna is caught in this conflict, I know not why, he
He has aligned with the unjust. If only Karna becomes king of
Hastinapura, injustice and unrighteousness will disappear as if
by magic!
In the happiness of the many, there will sprout the peepal tree

Of the compassion of Karna, and this took root in my mind too.'

Early in the morning, as Kunti Devi was returning from
Shiva temple, I walked in her way and stopping her I asked,
'Why is this special pooja offered and for whom? What
exceptional day Is today?'
Hearing me she was touched, spoke her inner most thought:
'Today is Karna's birthday, and every year on this day I offer
Pooja at the temple, for at home I cannot celebrate this! My
Heart wants me to send word for Karna, make him sit with
his brothers,
And enjoy the dishes with them; this is a great sight I ardently
Wish to see, I do not know when that moment will arrive.'
'Mother, why delay it then? Send for Karna, he will come running,
And your heart's wish will be fulfilled, doubt it not.'
I sent word and hearing the heart's cry Karna came running
To Shiva temple and I stepped back and watched the happening:
A rare sight, I beheld; witnessed the nectar-like sweet
meeting between
The mother and the son, and my maternal instinct made me shed
Tears of joy; I felt like embracing and holding them both to
my chest.
The mother pressing the son to her heart said, 'On your birthday,
Every year, I come here, offer worship to Shiva and pray for you;
But I do not know if I shall be alive till the war ends; I see
Only nothingness all around me, blank is my mind and blank
My life; today I bless you from my heart and desire a little,
For a short while, some happiness. Son, come and be with me,
I call you.'
Kunti became silent, the pain within her burnt her heart,
And seeing the ill-fated life of Karna, she wept within herself
and he,
In silence took part of the god-offered prasada and then
putting his head
In her lap, silently lay there enjoying a pleasure rare; she
caressing and patting.
His cheeks said, 'Son, I know the crooked nature of the Kauravas

And I also know how you saved Krishne from the flooded
river, and
I also know how Panchali saved you from a deadly snake-bite,
It is, therefore, clear there is no enemity between you;
on the contrary,
There is hidden trust and affection between you which
Tells that you are truly one of us; it is friendship with the Kauravas
Which is a thorn in the flesh, and which again bars friendship
with Pandavas.'
'Mother, I ask forgiveness of Krishne. In our lives strange events;
Have happened, and both of us, in this world, are strangely
ill-fated.'
Lost in some thought Kunti for a while was silent, and then eagerly
Went over to Draupadi and said, 'Dear daughter, can you
Be my palliative! Something within me tells me that
You alone have the strength to stall this war. Will you
Fulfill this old woman's desire?' Seeing me standing confused,
She continued, 'You are my daughter-in-law; your honour,
Achievement are to me huge things! You know well I do not
Intend or wish to hinder the vow you made the other day but
That moment has gone now, and there is no room for ill-will now;
If you can retract, and plait your hair then will this
Disturbed and furious ocean of ill-will regain its composure;
Bhima too will relent and step back and the imminent awful
Destruction of us all will be averted; it is all in your hands;
The destruction of our times you can stop or else surely it will
Be the final doom of Kuru dynasty! Let Karna move away from
The war, stay neutral; he surely will listen to you, and his
heart will
Melt and all my children will be saved. This last desire of
Your aged mother, kindly fulfill it; I spread the pallu of my saree
Before you and I beg, surrendering myself to you, Devi.'
Karna in solemn tones said, 'Krishne, in the entire
Aryavarta is the one who is wise and intelligent and well-learned
In the Vedas and Upanishads and she knows! To run away from
The field of battle is cowardice; all our reasons are only

Pretexts to save our lives and this is most disgraceful, it is worse
Than death. The valiant Karna will never ever be a coward
And run away from battle, and he will, on the strength of his own
Arms, make Hastinapura his and rule; but never run away from war.'
Admiring Karna's dignity and strength of purpose I
Spoke to Kunti, 'Oh, mother, man's heroism truly is admirable,
Truly it is great but in honouring a mother's words there is greater
Heroism, greater virtue. After Partha won me and you asked me
To accept all the five brothers as my husbands, I readily agreed;
But how can I ever forgive the wicked Duryodhana and
Dushyasana and their tribe?
No, this is unthinkable, it cannot be done.'
On the one hand was Karna who had chosen to stay true to
The king who had fed him and on the other I, who had
Sworn to wage a righteous war and between us stood the troubled
Maternal heart of Kunti! Knowing that reconciliation was
beyond us,
Karna, hiding nothing, said, 'Panchali, you being the wife of my
Brothers are like a daughter to me, remain fortunate, with the
Auspicious mark of *kumkum* on your forehead; you, who saved me
From the poisonous serpent are to me a mother too and Karna,
The cursed son of Radheya, offers you his grateful thanks; although
I believe not in reincarnation, if ever I am born a brother to you
In my next life, I shall repay for all that you have done for me;
Forgive me, please.' With these words, Karna, teary eyed, left.
Affection, admiration and compassion all, came as in a
Flood, and I in a trembling voice said, 'Forgive me, for
The humiliation my brother Drustadhyumna caused you in
swayamvara hall; forgive your sister-in-law, please;
Perhaps this is our last meeting in this life. For no crime of
Yours, you have been punished horribly and, I, as daughter-in-law
Of the Kuru dynasty, again beg forgiveness.
Looking at Kunti, Karna said, 'Mother, today you have
Made your son free of the curse under which he was born; I feel
Happy and grateful; like Panchali and me, all of us are ill-fated and
Cursed. What can anyone do? The wheels of this tragic age are

On the move and cannot be stopped.'
Without looking back, Karna sped away on his chariot.
I stood waching till he disappeared from the horizon of
My sight, and tears flowed down my cheeks. Suddenly I
Felt there was born a shaft of bright light and the next moment
It went out, leaving me in utter darkness.
In the west, the sun slowly descended, and then, plop
He fell into the dark oceans; and there was no sign of light
Ever returning back to any of us.

CANTO XXXI

TO YOU, I GIFT AWAY THE WHOLE WORLD

After thirteen years of banishment and a year in disguise
The Pandavas should have got back Indraprastha but the limitless, selfish,
Obstinacy of the Kauravas gave room to war alone, the world of;
Dreams, of peace got shattered, and there was future only for death
And bloodshed and bereavement everywhere, irrespective of the way in
Which victory favoured either, for on both sides there would be nothing but death.
Dharmaja's goal was not to win the war; but to see peace
Rule, everywhere, with no hindrance; but those who went to
Negotiate terms of peace returned disappointed, and with a dire warning by
The Kauravas that not an inch of land would be given to the Pandavas!
'Should we go back, again, into the forests and live there? But
That would be against the Kshatriya dharma, and reluctance
To return even five villages to us is wickedness, for which
Who is responsible? Would war bring us happiness; would the
Death of our kinsmen make anyone of us happy? For
Whom is victory and for whom this throne? All that makes
Life happy, all that lends value to life will be destroyed,
And forever. If war is inescapable, we need not have chosen
To live in the forest for thirteen long years. How absurd!'
Seeing Dharmaja sad and weighted down by worry,
Bhimasena said, 'Brother, have you forgotten the injustice

The wicked Kaurava has done us? Is it possible to overlook
The humiliation heaped on Draupadi! Can we put in
memory's cold storage
their attempt to burn us alive in the wax house? And,
They laid waste the land of ours and caused a terrible famine,
Can that be disregarded? How can you ever forgive the
Kaurava clan which is the very image of unrighteousness?
The blind Dhritarashtra
Is personification of enemity and jealousy. From sheer desire of
Power, did he not send Pandu into wilderness? Did he not
Die alone there, with none to take care of him, like a beggar?
Did not our mother, like one abandoned, live at Vidura's palace?
For how long have we to put up with the vicious, wicked
doings of theirs?
Now we cannot, and Draupadi's vengeance has been on the
boil, and will explode.
Should we continue to live helpless, unmanly lives, no,
My patience is at an end and I do not care what others will
do but
I and my anger, like the doomsday flood-water, will wash away
everything!
Feelings of kinship are dead in me and I shall, alone, wage this
Battle. Do not stop me, and do not preach mantras of peace; the
Sound of the war-bugle echoes and re-echoes in my heart and
It will burst soon, for it cannot be stilled!' The prudent Partha
Stepped in, 'Brother, to become too emotional is unwise.
We need,
Our well-wisher;
The world's wisest, Sri Krishna, to decide our future
Course of action.' Listening to our talk, Sri Krishna, said,
'The ending of all conflict and war is truly in the interest of
The Kuru dynasty; conciliatory talks have happened but unless
Both sides are firmly for peace, peace won't happen. I see
No signs of this, and, therefore, there is no alternative to
waging a war;
This also I know; this is not a family squabble nor a fight

Between individuals; it is a war between good and evil, and between
The righteous and the unrighteous, and it is to establish
lasting peace
For the welfare of all mankind. True, there will be death and
destruction. But can the duty of Kshatriyas be abandoned?
When the unity of the whole of Aryavarta is in danger,
Can we remain mute spectators? If we do, dark evil triumphs.
Not merely the Kauravas and Pandavas, but the entire, innocent
Mankind itself will face obliteration. No, our aim, sole aim
Is to protect the unity of the country and the righteous,
dharmic way of life!
If war is inevitable, who can stop it or escape it? The world is
Stunned and staggers for the unholy defilers of *dharma* are eating
All up; their bowl of evil is full, and the great war awaits us!'
All nodded their heads, in full agreement, and I, from the
Beginning wanted war as the unrighteous ones needed to
be punished; or, otherwise, how could many races be free of
age-long oppression?
An end was necessary to rape and humiliation of
women everywhere;
But how will all this end? I have with me the Pandavas
and Krishna,
My friend; and I have strength to protect myself; but what
Will the helpless, ordinary men and women do? How about
they living their
Daily, normal lives? How will simple, normal human beings
manage their lives?
The Pandavas were happy to buy peace with the offering of five
Little villages, but the Kauravas wanted it not! The evil-minded
Duryodhana wanted no reconciliation, and again, in the
open assembly humiliated Sri Krishna!
The news of the ensuing great war spread like wild fire
and although
Righteousness was sure to win, where is the one who would
keep account
Of the millions who would die, horribly, and present a gory,
and heart

Devastating scene? Krishna spoke to Dhritarastra but the Kaurava's
Selfishness and arrogance had made him deaf, and the blind king
Infatuated with power and indiscriminate love for children would
Not listen; if only he had heard, the war could have been averted;
But a death-wish unknown to himself had him strongly strangled!
Krishna, before returning, saw Kunti who was staying with Vidura
And her hope, that after the period of banishment was over, peace
Would return had been dashed and her health affected; when
We went to see her, the news of the war had broken her down!
At about that time, Sri Krishna met Karna and said:
'Vasushena, true, before Kunti got wedded, you were born, to the
Sun-god and were the eldest of her sons but fear of society made her
Float you down the Ganga; yet with every heartbeat, remember
That you are Kaunteya, a son of Kunti and I tell you this before
The war begins for if I do not a feeling guilt will haunt me.
I am your brother-in-law in kinship terms. I know you think of the
Pandavas as your enemies; I also know you will continue to think so and
Desire to fight them but, think, of your mother's affection for you;
Should you not remember it and join forces with them? Isn't that your Duty, too?
You pursued enemity with Partha and became a silent partner
To the public outrage of the honour of Draupadi, did you not?'

Karna perplexed, sank into deep confusion, and said:
'I…am I Kunti's son? Was I born to the sun-god?
From my childhood
I faced, but humiliating discrimination, thinking I was born a low caste man
And at every step met contempt, was scorned and on every
Occasion I worried about my identity. Poor and ill-fed. I was
Sad because I felt alone and abandoned and none came to
My rescue or support; it was then that I needed consoling words;
I was branded the son of a low caste charioteer and from daily
Inflicted pain, my blood froze, and never have I been my real self;

Today I have gained courage and can stand up, holding my
Head high; why are you letting me into the old secret now:
Is it to
Sprinkle salt on a wound about to heal? No, do not cause me
Pain, let me live my life and, do not disturb the lives of others,
The way you have disturbed mine.'
Seeing how he had wounded the feelings of the son of the
Sun-god, Krishna spoke softly, 'O son of Kunti, think. It is not
Late even now. Join heads with the Pandavas.
Why decline the Mother's loving and auspicious invitation?
If only you are with the Pandavas,
The whole world will be there at your feets and adoring you!
The dark clouds of yesteryears will all be blown away
And you could be the strongest of the strong, and rule the world.'
Krishna, spinning a magnetic web, in tones affection, spoke
'On one side certainty of death and on the other kingly authority;
On one side touching affection of Suyodhana and on the
other maternal
Affection of one's own mother! Shall I part ways and bid goodbye
To the trusting Kaurava, but how do I renege on my vow?
Draupadi is my brother's wife and yet I humiliated her;
I shall ask her forgiveness but part from the Kauravas I cannot.'

Caught in a mesh of thoughts contrary, Karna, bent and
With folded hands, said, 'Pardon me, go back, I cannot on my
Vow publicly made; a traitor I cannot become; death to me is
Preferable; for having offended my brother's wife, I shall beg
Her forgiveness; no, I do not see any other course open to me, Krishna.'

'Karna, none there is who can equal your generosity; surely
Panchali, understanding your predicament, will forgive you; but
O, son of Kunti, I shall gift you the whole of this world, for, you
Are the eldest of the Pandavas, and to wipe off the injustice the
Kuru dynasty has caused you, the best way is to be with us.
Bid goodbye to your feelings of self-importance and hollow self
Admiration, join us: if you become king, both factious will rejoice
And the Kurus will give up the path of destruction they have

Chosen; a new horizon there will be, and the entire world will
Move in the path of peace and prosperity and security.'
Karna, embracing Krishna, said, 'Truly, you are the most
Incredible of men! Yes, once, a long time back, I had sought your
Friendship. In eagerness to pursue enemity with the Pandavas,
I had suppressed it! It is true, I went deeper and deeper into
The pit of evil; I do not know who can ever lift me out of it;
I have gifted away my life to the Kauravas, and the promise
I have made I will not break; wedded I am to it, forgive me;
If I am victorious in this great war, I shall certainly seek your
Friendship; if not, I shall meet death on the field of battle;
After I meet with death soldierly, request Dharmaja to offer
Me oblation, and ask Kunti to call me "son"; and let her keep
My head in her lap and shed a few tears; let Panchali call me
"Brother-in-law" and let the four other brothers carry my bier
To the cemetery! This shall be my end, my satisfaction total;
What else can I say? What else can I do? Believed, I have
Never in the role of fate; the tragic story of my life is in
It self hard, and stony, and likewise my words are hard and story!'
'In silence, as Karna walked away, Kunti too walked,
Wading through a vale of tears. Before the war begins, I have
To return to the Pandavas and on their foreheads put a tilaka
And wish them success.
Wave I shall before them the auspicious aarati and send them
To the field of war, with a smile on my face.
War is inevitable, bloodshed is inevitable, and death of the
Kshatriya race too is inevitable!
Will Karna, in this great destruction, survive? How can you
Now stop this tragic war of Bharat! How ironical!
For peace, war is waged; and through war there is the arrival of
Peace! If Krishna's hand of friendship is rejected what can
Anybody do? What can anybody else do?

V. Movement:

VISIONS OF A DWAPARA PILGRIM

CANTO XXXII

TO KEEP THE HEART CLEAN HAVE AN OPEN MIND

The battlefield, Kurukshetra, was, from one end to another,
Sixty-three thousand feet long, and it lay on the banks of the river
Hiranyavati and on its banks had gathered the armies of the
Kauravas and Pandavas; though the wind blew fiercely, silence heavy
Had made the land its home; dark, anxious clouds watched the
night enveloping everything.
Once the night ends, in dreadful Kurukshestra, there will
Spring the blinding and horrifying fire of the war of the Kurus.
Dristadyumna, the commander-in-chief of the Pandavas on one side
And Bhismacharya on the side of the Kauravas—all stood ready;
For another eighteen days, everyday, me, the wedded wife of
the Pandavas
Have to put the victory marks, the tilak, on their foreheads and
Send them into the battlefield, wishing them a great victory;
Everyday I move round carrying the message of the goddess
Of good fortune; sad, but who can stop the goddess of time who
Will not stay still; some times I saw a cool and green patch of
Trees and there I would, for a while, rest and think that to be the
The finest gift of nature, in one's life, and would stay mesmerized;
Once caught I was, in such a mood by Sri Krishna who said,
'Friend, since last evening I have observed, your being is
Shot through with the light of hope and courage, and there
Is not the slightest sign of fear or anxiety, surprised I am!'
Hearing him speak in amazement greatly, I said,
'Yagnaseni, I am; and it is the Kshatriya blood which flows in

My veins and my face like red blood, is blood-red, and within
Me there is the unquenched fire of anger burning and I
Wait to jump into the fire of the battle ensuing and therefore, in
Me there is room for fear or anxiety; neither is there
Any love or compassion; there is only the flame of
vengeance burning
Bright and hard, and the secret of victory is hope and confidence;
They are my mantra and whichever way the dice is thrown, there
Sure will be excitement of battle, and so am, waiting to enjoy it.'
Krishna called all the Pandavas and spoke to them,
'Tomorrow is the war inevitable; do not hesitate, and doubts you
Drive away. I hold the reins of Partha's chariot, and, therefore,
Have no fear. There are with us thousands and thousands of
Soldiers absolutely dedicated, and we have the divinely inspired
And bound by her own sworn-words, the great Panchali, who will
Bring the auspicious moment of restoration of *dharma*, eternal,
And surely victory will be ours.'
Dharmaja bent his head and with folded hands submitted,
'Sri Krishna tell me, why have we called for the bloody
sacrifice of millions of lives?
This question haunts me? Why possess kingdoms, why hold on
To treasures of wealth, and for what end and for what purpose?'
Listening to Dharmaja's question, his friend, Krishna said:
'What is your fault or crime in this, where does is it lie?
To eliminate the unjust is dharma;
Without achieving this I cannot return
To Dwaraka, nor can I rest the divine Sudharshana disc.'
'Vasudeva, what game are you playing? Why this invitation for a
Terrible blood bath?'
Sri Krishna silently gestured to me and Maye, grasping it,
Laughed loud and it looked as if it reverberated from all the
ten corners!
There appeared hidden some mysterious silence in the loud
Laugh, and Krishna gravely said, 'This is war for righteousness!
And before we embark on it we have keep our hearts clean and
Our minds open. I shall be Partha's charioteer if only you agree,

Otherwise not.'
Bhima slightly annoyed with his brother said, 'Oh, king,
enough of discussion.
It is small business, why waste words discussing it. I
Shall speak first.' But then intervened Krishna, 'No, we begin
With the eldest.' Yudhisthira again with his head bent said,
'I desire peace, not this war. Since I shun all war and
Quarrels, I reasoned with the wife I had pledged and left to live
In the forests; or, otherwise, the war would have happened the same
Day. I know war is natural to Kshatriyas, and yet I prefer
Peace and it has been my basic mantra.'
Then in a loud voice, proclaimed Bhima,
'A lover I am of food, and easily provoked to anger!
While angry, can't think of anyone and this caused me much
unhappiness.'
Arjuna, respectfully bending his head, said, 'For my mother's
Sake I gave up my wished-for-thing and agreed to share Panchali,
But the feeling that it was I who had won her was rooted in my
Mind, and this I own is a weakness of mind.'
Nakula shyly came forward saying: 'Krishne is charmingly
Beautiful and more intelligent than me and therefore I am
Envious and wish I had beaten her in handsomeness and quickness!'
With heavy sadness Sahadeva spoke, 'My weakness is to
Think of Kunti as my mother and not Madri, for Kunti it is who
Took care of us when were rendered orphans in the world; Kunti
Is, naturally, everything to us.'
Listening to each with attention Krishna said, 'Well,
Without hiding anything you have spoken the truth and your face,
Therefore, shines like polished mirror and pleased I am with your
Mind which is open and clean and upright.'
'When you are charioteer to Nara, what doubt could be there?'
Hearing Dharmaja, Sri Hari said, 'What, and how shall I say it!
Your wife Draupadi is silent and without knowing her mind
I cannot be charioteer to Arjuna.'
Looking at my husbands, I spoke, 'Weaknesses there
Are many with me and of these the chief is the unknown,

Unnameable feeling that binds me with Krishna, his very
Name evokes in me inexpressible bonds of sentiment with him;
I know not why there are such spontaneous congeries of
feelings which rise in me with the mention of his name;
And the second infirmity is Kunti Devi.
Her worry is the twin brothers, they cause her much concern and
I, sharing her sorrow, am lost in sorrow and never can I
Live away from her. The third that holds me back morally is
Arjuna of several names; the burden of all the Pandavas is
On his shoulders and he to obtain arms divine suffered too much
And I worry why the others cannot share a part of his load;
Such thoughts eat, into me, and I am here only to keep the
Pandavas together.'
Understanding my mind, Krishna said, 'Ah, sister,
Krishne, a thousand grateful thanks to you, who like the
thousand-hooded
Adishesha bear the burden of the world! You are the
Saviour of the world and you are the light of the war at Kurukshethra.
I now know your mind, and its intricacies all.' Sri Krishna
Within himself smiled and, I unable to restrain my laughter, said,
'Why this magical weaving, Krishna? Why listen to the story of
The infirmities of Pandavas? But without sharing these,
Won't the chariot move! All right, we lay our hearts and minds
before him.'
Bhimasena clapped his hands and spoke, 'Only
Krishne can make Krishna break his silence and he has to
Tell us what weakness troubles him.' Caught in an
Unenviable situation, Krishna managed to say:
'My weakness encompasses the universe: whoever
Loves me deeply, such ones I harass and trouble; and
I dedicate myself to those clean souls who keep calling me all
the time;
Whatever I erect, I destroy it too and it is in such
Endeavours of conflict, I take pleasure.'
Some strange inexplicable aura of bright light
Enveloped the sky and the earth, and the heavens shone in

Dazzling hues, and anxieties and infirmities disappeared
And like a preface to a great epic, the sun rose in the East, shedding light soft and brightening!

CANTO XXXIII

THE EPOCH WILL SPRING BACK, AND BE ITSELF AGAIN

That day I heard Arjuna, in Kurukshetra, was much depressed,
Had lost interest in wars and battles, and so sunk in despair
that he had, on that
Decisive day, plunged into deep melancholy, but Krishna drove
the chariot
Towards the field of battle, and halted for a while.

Arjuna, with difficulty coming to his senses, rose and with folded
Hands, spoke reverently, 'Sri Krishna, how can I handle the bow
And the arrows on this field of battle? My being has lost its
spirit, exhausted
I am; my hands tremble and I see strange happenings before
my eyes!
The Kuru dynasty, broken and splintered, is falling apart and
it seems
As if a thousand of coloured moths are falling into a blazing
divine flame!
The great tree of the culture of Bharat, as if cut at the roots,
Is falling off of bough by bouh, and its rites and religions and
its truths
Too look as if they are about to enter the womb of dark primeval time;

Justice is fled; wickedness is rampant; dark clouds shedding black
Evil have made everything, all things disappear as if by witches;
No, Krishna, I cannot see anything. Take the chariot to the middle
Of the war field and let me try and see with whom I am to fight.'

On either side I see brothers, sons of my teachers, and my own
Revered acharyas and grandfather and by his side my nephews,
Uncles and brother's-in-law—all, all my own kith and kin!
Seeing them my throat goes dry, I swear, I am all a-tremble,
My bow, Gaandiva, has slipped from my hand and I see wherever
I look, omens dark and forbidding and frightening in the extreme;
By killing them whose good am I achieving, and whose well being?
No, my desire for victory has dried up: my longing for power,
For trappings of power are all fled from me; one, for whose sake
I wanted these things are all here ready to fight till death; no,
Not even if I am offered the sovereignty of all the three worlds,
I will not kill them and make them lie on the bare earth;

Tell me,
Should I fight for lands and kingdoms or for the sake of
waging war?
If all Kauravas are killed, what comfort would it bring me?
There would only be greater accumulation of evil, and wickedness;
Why should innocent people be killed and what would it do
For them in any sense?
I see everywhere men innocent, guiltless and totally helpless!
Should I not at least now step back from this sinful internecine war?'

The all-knowing, wise Krishna, of course, knew it all; he had
Heard the sound of the conch heralding the end of the epoch;
The land on which he stood shook, about to explode into
smithereens;
Sensing the catastrophe Arjuna said:

'Sri Krishna, this great Kurukshetra war will push the Kuru
Dynasty into an eternal hell; values societal as well as
Familial and national will all collapse, destroying lives in towns and
Villages and pull down with them the entire race; war, surely is
Wicked enterprise, diminishes men, and is unalloyed evil;
How does one support a war which kills friends and relatives
And aims at conquest, through tricks and deceit and stratagems;
Let Dhritarashtra kill us all, and let him live; let the armies stand
Still, causing no damage; let all problems of all assail only us!'

In great anguish, with mind gone numb, Partha threw away
His bow and arrows and sat covering his face with both his palms;

Then, Krishna spoke, 'The wise will say why has this weakness, which will deprive the
Pandavas of immortal life, crept into them? How could it affect Partha, too!
Why this effiminacy in a hero who makes his enemies tremble in
Fear? No, do not give room to such thoughts; spring out of this
Despondency; this is unholy for Kshatriyas, and without abandoning your
Dharma, rise, wake up, and be victorious.'

'Ah, you, the kind one, tell me, how do I enter into battle? See,
The worshipful Acharya, Bhisma, and Drona, my revered teacher
Are there: how could I aim my arrows at them? No, no, even
I am reduced to beggary, and have to roam the streets for a fistful of food, I shall not kill them:
The desire for conquest has left me;
Why wade through blood to indulge in living a life of luxury?
I do not know what is right and what is wrong, but kill them, I will not.
Krishna, be kind, save me, free me from this predicament; you
Are the preserver of all and yet you ask me to be destroyer of all!
No, I am helpless; strength of wise discrimination I have lost;
I surrender to you; I have wandered into a forest huge and
Dark and have lost my way, kindly show me light; even if
I am offered the lordship of a nation where there are no enemies,
No, fight I cannot; kindly be my succor, and help me.'

Standing in the middle of the divided war-field,
Krishna recalled the events of his life over ages several;
Events caused by the history of mankind. The blue-hued Krishna saw before
His closed eyes: Kamsa, his uncle, who had with love taken care of
His sister and had her married to the heroic Vasudeva; how he had joyfully celebrated the wedding

And since he had no children of his own, looked
Forward to finding a successor to the throne from the couple; but saw soon
In a dream that the eighth child would kill him, and the dread of losing
His life filled him with terror and he, stopped the celebration midway and
Had both the bride and bridegroom imprisoned.

Sri Krishna, through his mind's eye, saw the picture of Kamsa
Killing one child after another as soon as it was born, and remembrances
Such as these flitted through his memory and time looked endless.

But managing to come out of it, Sri Hari spoke,
'You cry for those for whom you should not cry; knowing as you
Do the history of mankind, and being wise yourself, you should not and
I can only laugh at your words.
Does one weep for those dying or for those already dead?
In a man's life, childhood, youth and old age succeed one another.
Don't you ever imagine that the world's beginning and end depend
On you? Why has this ignorance descended on you? The wise do not get flustered like you.
See, cold and heat and touch and sorrow and happiness
Are transient; they are guests who have no permanent houses to live in;
Give up this vacillation; stay poised; the secret of ages and ages
Is poise and self-possession.

The primal cause of life is Nature whose energy never gets
Destroyed; this is true; and from performing a task good, never comes
Out any evil; this you have to know and once you know, doubts
Will forever disappear from your mind.'

Krishna's magically sweet and charming smile created
Waves of happiness and Arjuna swam on these and as he

Moved on, there appeared in the middle a river of light and
Beside it many-coloured water-fountains and these, from
within him,
Struck some divine veena which made spring in him
the discriminating
Intelligence of yoga, which in turn threw on him the enveloping

Light of wisdom:
'Arjuna, why are you caught in the useless debate
Of defeat and victory? Look, in the eastern horizon rises the sun,
The sole witness of all that happens is here on earth; understand
That yoga is skill in work chosen and that alone is, to the
Sadhaka, the novice, is yoga, full and complete, and it lifts him to
planes high.'

As Sri Krishna stretched out his long arms and hugged Arjuna;
The rays of the sun, in colours light and beautiful, danced
And there was on the earth everywhere sounds sweet, and hues
Variegated, and Partha's being was flooded with divine swirls
Of melody! Each movement had in it a cadence and a
Song and each had in it a strange sacred energy that flowed into
Each cell of his being; it flowed like the pure torrent of the
Powerful Ganga and the age itself appeared bathed in the light
Of celestial poise.

Arjuna's soul, charged with this hallowed energy, touched
Each cell in his body and there was a rare coming together
of love, devotion and power;
It appeared as if there was a benign
Explosion of fire-carrying atom which planted in him strength
enough
To carry with him entire races to sacred heighs of the soul—
Power; action and thought had coalesced and burst forth in blissful
Ecstasy; and the moment for gods had arrived!

'Partha, the wise ones, taking to the plough to till the land, and
Obtain release from bonds everlasting; and obtain without
Much learning knowledge of Brahma; some are learned and

Have listened to enlightening talk and yet get confounded with
Doubts but once they see the bright flash of truth eternal,
There will be, as in you now, soul-knowledge which drives away
All doubts, and the soul-knowledge arising in its perfect form
Makes the epoch itself take a fresh birth in a form new and firm.'

CANTO XXXIV

ABANDON ALL CREEDS AND SURRENDER TO ME ALONE

The cadences of the lord's song, the Bhagavad Gita,
Flowed through each and every vein of Partha, and light itself
Becoming clean, broke into rainbow colours, bright and dazzling and
In that strange context of feelings varied, he felt as if every
Single creature was reborn and sojourned with him through
The tunnel of Krishna's music, and it was as if the earth itself
Was drenched in the life-giving music of his friend;

Arjuna savouring the nectarine words of Sri Krishna was lost in them and
Sri Krishna, pressing Partha to his bosom spoke in answer to the
Manifold questions raised by Arjuna in wonder and amazement,
'When the soul conjoint with the mind moves, then, effortlessly
You feel free and become one with Yoga Brahma; but why are you
Now confused? To possess absolute self-possession in this world
Right knowledge, right mind and right discrimination are to be
Earned, and thereafter no sorrow ever deflects you from your thought-out resolution;
A yogi of this nature undisturbed by sorrow of all kinds
Will feel one with Brahman; it is then that the body and the
Mind will feel spiritually clean and will see me everywhere;
And I shall be with him all the time; I move with him,
And with everyone else and when this happens it is possible
To see everyone and everything with equanimity absolute!'

Phalguna, still in a confused state of mind, asked:
'To be able to see everyone alike is most hard; the mind is a
Monkey which moves the way it wants to and cannot be easily
Controlled, for it falls easy prey to whatever it desires; how does
One control it? I know not the art, enlighten me, kindly.'

'This is the power of yoga and it is not easily acquired but this
Is the instrument which helps one attain the best of
Everything in life;
There is not a bigger tapas or penance superior to it; today
I tell you the secret of achieving it:

A clean mind without any fear; restraint; knowledge; faithfulness
To experienced truth; performing yagna and study of the Vedas;
Learning; simplicity; not causing violence to others; discriminating
Intelligence; compassion in all living beings; lack of arrogance;
To be rid of envy and jealousy and pride and avarice and selfishness.
Those who are acquisitive and have hatred for others and take
Pleasure in the destruction of their enemies, and are intent on
Amassing wealth and take pride in their caste and creed and
Say they belong to castes high and pure and have sacrifices,
yagas and yagnas performed are fools, pure and simple;
They are caught in their own stupidity but cause pain to others
Through malice, courteousness and cupidity—these I forever abhor!'

Listening to Sri Krishna's views, Partha said,
'Sri Krishna, how about people who are ignorant of Shastras,
Of rites and rituals but often worship with faith alone,
To them what course is open? How do changes affect human
Behaviour, what effect do they have on their lives? Instruct me, please.'

'Men are known by their behavioural faith and each, accordingly,
Is a satvika or rajasa or tamasa, which is that man has in excess
Either piety or militancy or malignancy in his
Psychological make-up; their thoughts reflect their samskara, their
Bringing up; There are those who are moved by intense sensual
Pleasure and others who lack discrimination and cause
violence to others and,

The third kind take to yagna, dana and compassion; there
Are the three kinds of tastes:
Food which is fresh and tasty and that which adds to longevity
And energy and health is preferred by the satvika people; very hot,
Very spicy, very sour and very pungent is liked by Rajasa men;
Unhygenic, and food gone bad and that cooked the previous
night and
That which is leftover and not easily digestible is liked by men of
Tamasa temperament;
Knowing this, one has to live life with care; the ritual
Sacrifices made because ordained by scripture and with no
Expectation of any return or fruit of action performed is
Yagna done by Satvikas; that ritual sacrifice performed with
Expectations is Yagna by Rajasik men; and those rituals done
Without any discipline and where food is not offered to
the deserving and
Where the intention is to cause damage and harm to other is Yagna
By men who possess a temperament which is Tamasa
temperament.
Again, studying Vedas and acting according to Vedas without
Causing injury to others and causing only good to everyone
in practice
That is Satvik; penances observed for small benefits and profits
Are Rajasa in nature; and those rites and practices done with
A view to cause harm to others are Tamasic in nature;
Gift made to the deserving to the right and proper is Satvika Dana;
Gifts offered with the intention of high returns is Dana,
Rajasa; and
Gifts made to the underserving and at times improper are Tamasa in nature.

Arjuna, listening to this, spoke with eagerness: 'Sri Krishna.
Enlighten me please on what constitutes right Sanyasa dharma.
The practices of the renunciate.'
'Dhananjaya, listen. To renounce expectations or returns from
Action performed constitutes the *dharma* of a sanyasi; he who gives
Up desire for fruits of action is a tyagi, a man who renounces life;
One should not give up performance of yagna, dana and tapas;

But one should have no expectation of returns from
duty performed;
Giving up these from skewed knowledge is Tamasik;
Expecting no reward
For duty performed is Satvik knowledge; Partha do not forget these;
For whom are you sad? For whom are you crying?
You are shedding
Tears for those for whom you should not. Action you shall not
Give up nor shall you look for fruits of your actions.
Death cannot touch the soul; nor does it have any birth;
Arms cannot hurt it nor can fire destroy it; water cannot
Make it wet; none can kill it; it is small and rarefied and subtle;
Sorrow not, therefore; the soul is beyond the cycles of birth and
Death; it is part of nature eternal and therefore, do not feel
Sad; birth and death are beyond your powers, and beyond
your control;
Just know that you are a Kshatriya, and waging war in your *dharma*;
It has come to you unasked; and the doors of heaven are open
for you;
You, the Kshatriyas are privileged, and do not spurn it and invite
Ill fame; the *dharma* you are born to, live it boldly; let you
Not become a coward and bring a bad name to your clan; do not
Become the villain of your long and much admired history.
If you turn your back on battle and run away, the age and the
World will ridicule you, and there isn't a bigger humiliation than
This. If you die, the heaven is yours; if you live, imperial
Privileges are yours; resolve to fight, and rise and wake up.
Accept happiness and unhappiness, profit and loss, with equanimity
And ready yourself for the great battle and ill-fame will never
be your lot;
The nature of the soul I have taught you; now I tell you how
You are to be free of the consequences of action; understand with
Care and with trust in *dharma* realize the true nature of the soul;
Do not fall prey to sweet and flowery words or theories
philosophical;
Cross these and see the true form of god which not many will see;

Fools run after pleasures, hanker after unreal things and these
Get caught in the vicious circle of birth and death and forever
Swim in the vortex of passing pleasure and voluptuousness and
Never manage to get out of samsara of tamo guna, life of dark
And haunting despondency; move ahead see the great, final
truth beyond this.
All rewards mentioned in the Vedas will surely belong to a
Brahmajnani, the one who has realized the truth of all truths;
but do not enter action looking for rewards; let all of your
mind move
Towards disinterested action. Arjuna, once you give up desires and
Attain to contentmentfull, then you will become a Sthitapragna, a
Man, undisturbed in all circumstances in possession of poise complete.

Do not be unhappy when sadness happens to you and do not
Be exhilatred when happy things come your way; he who
stays composed
Is a Stithapragna, a man of serenity absolute;

Like the tortoise which
Withdraws its sensory organs within its shell, the man of
equanimity should be;
Again, listen: It is desire which kindles passions and passions
Make you go after what you desire and if unable to have
your desire
Satisfied, you get angry; and anger destroys your discrimination and
The loss of discrimination destroys your mind and the loss of
one's mind
Is the root cause all evil doings.

When the mind is undisturbed and calm, sorrows stay away
from one;
Peace and happiness come into one's being and it would be
easy to be with the God for you are without 'you' and 'me'.
Stay happy with whatever comes your way and in the end
You will reach a state of absolute happiness, ananda.

Partha listened to Krishna intently and then said,

'Sri Krishna, you say knowledge is superior to action and yet
You are pushing me into action, kindly tell me the reason, for
With your alluring talk, you have made me your captive.'

'Arjuna, I presented two states of mind to you: But, know,
Even he who has attained the highest knowledge cannot dissociate
Himself from action. And release from action alone will not help
You achieve deliverance; you have to hold the action-performing
Sensory organs in checks all the time, and abjure sensual desires.
This also you have to know: it is from anna, from food, that beings
Take birth; from rains, there is food, and food is the source of all
Action; and the cycle of life itself is dependent on the will of god
And the basis of everything is anna, food.

Whatever the high and the noble do, the others too will
follow, and pursue;
If you, in this fashion, sit enervated and reject action, you will
Be responsible for the decay and destruction of the world. See, all
Oblations teems with Brahma; all that is offered as oblation teems
With Brahma; agni teems with Brahma; the one who offers
Oblation is himself Brahma; the one which is offered as
sacrifice is full of Brahma;
All, everything is in itself full of Brahma!
Some think of worship as Yagna; some think
Control of the senses as oblation; some offer oblation
Through the fire of the senses themselves; some through prayer,
Penance and the study of the Vedas offer their oblation; some
Through pranayama, control of breath, and through Astanga Yoga
Eight ways of yoga, and others, through eating, very little
offer oblations.
Some of those who know how to performs yagna desire
Through the yagna performed new knowledge and think of it as
Mukti, liberation; but knowledge merely good is not here, for it has
Gone beyond vignana and there are new worlds of knowledge;
The wise ones speak of a universe which is inaccessible to the
World of senses, and of wonderful spaces unknown to many;
And, these are not to be forgotten, for exploration unceasing

Reveals new areas, and every seer unfolds before us new
Horizons of knowledge and wisdom; and devoted and continuous
Exploration will allow us to know a little of these;
Arjuna, distance yourself from your illusions, and with the help
Of divine light burning within your own being, see; then you
Will see that there is this divine light within everyone of
Us and this will destroy all *karma*, action performed, and
Knowledge pure, unalloyed and clear will be yours, and so will
Be the concentration of mind of yours; and staying here
through knowledge gained,
You arrive at liberation final and eternal.

Arjuna now shall I narrate the magnificent extraordinariness of
Brahma, God, immanent in all beings; there can be no end to
the description!
I am the inner being in all creatures living; I am the middle and
The end and the beginning of all things that exist.
Among the Aadityas I am Vishnu; among things luminant, I am
The sun; among the Marutaas I am Marichi, among the stars I
am the
Moon, among the Vedas I am Saama Veda, among the
sense organs,
I am the mind and among all things living, I am the spirit
Within them; among Rudras I am Shankara,
Among Yakshas I am Kubera, among Vasus I am fire,
Among mountains I am the Meru Mountain;
Among revered purohits I am Brihaspati,
Among commanders of armies I am Skanda,
Among lakes I am the ocean,
Among seers I am Brighu, among words I am the Omkara;
in Yagnas I am japa;
Among immovable mountains I am the Himalayas;
Among trees I am the peepul, Aswatha,
Among the immortal seers I am Narada;
Among Gandharvas I am Chitraratha, among Siddhas Kapila
Among horses the Ucchaishravas, among elephants the Airavata,
Among men, the king, among weapons the Vajrayudha,

Among the Cows I am Kamadhenu, among serpents Vasuki,
Among water creatures I am Varuna,
Among Pitru Devatas I am Aryaman; among legislators I am Yama,
Among demons Prahlada, among the destroyers of time, I am
the god of time; among birds the eagle; in speed, I am Vayu,
the wind god himself; among the wielders of the bow, I am
Sri Ramachandra, among rivers I am the Ganga;
In all creations I am the beginning and the middle and the end;
Among vidyas I am Advaita; among the alphabets I am A and
I am the creator of time without beginning or end; I am
The devourer of all and am death itself; among women
I am beauty; all wealth, intelligence, steadfastness,
Tolerance—all these I am; in music I am the great saama;
Among months marga shirsha, among seasons I am spring,
Among the deceitful I am the gambler, in Yadu dynasty
I am Krishna and among the Pandavas Arjuna and
Among rishis Vyasa, among poets Shukracharya; in
Secrecy, I am silence and I am the seed, the life-breath of
All living and non-living beings.
In all the world there is not anything in which I am not the
In-dwelling spirit and there is no end to the web of Maya
I create and weave; I am the energy within all creation.'

In great excitement, Arjuna stood up and with folded hands spoke:
'Sri Krishna, today I feel blessed for I have received
The nectar of all spiritual and metaphysical thought, and you
Have remove the ignorance that had got into me. The
Cycle of life and death, of the nature of maya, of illusion
You have made me understand but now there is a deep
Desire in me to see your viswarupa, your global, universal form.'
In a benign voice, the lord of Ramaa, Sri Krishna, responded:
'Arjuna, who else but you in this world can see my viswarupa!
See, now millions of forms, see Aaditya, Vasu, Rudra, Aswinikumars,
And Marutas! But you will not be able to see with you earthly,
Human eyes. Look, I now bestow on you divine seeing power
See, all the great, extraordinariness of Viswarupa!'

Saying so Krishna waived away illusion ordinary and
Spun on him divine maya and displayed his universal form:
Faces innumerable, numberless, and countless hands and
Feet, and brightness of millions of suns shone in him:
Whichever way he looked there were groups of Vasus, Rudras
And Maruts and everywhere the colours of the endless sky
And jewels dazzling which were outshone by thousands and thousands of
Planets and stars, and glorious heavenly bodies numberless and all
Together presenting an image of inspiring opining grandeur!

In amazement, Arjuna submitted,
'Sri Krishna, in this your body, I see gods and beings alive
And inert and creation itself in various forms and everything
An image of yourself and all moving according to your wishes.
You are Achyuta, Anantha and the base and superstructure of this
Universe. I see neither the beginning nor the end. Holding the
Conch and the divine disc in your hands you shine like the
Sun and you are the primeval energy and the supreme truth
And I bow at your feet again and again.'

Watching Partha, Sri Krishna said, 'Look, I am
Time itself and I have set out to destroy the world. What if
You do not kill the enemies, the death and destruction of all is certain.
Rise up, do not be afraid; fight, be victorious and live happily in
The kingdom won.
All these are already dead, you are only a pretext. Bhishma
Drona, Karna, Saindhava have all been already killed by me. Since they
Are already dead, surely you can kill them in the battle.'

Partha bent his head down and said, 'Lord, I am a foolish
Man who does not know your greatness. Thinking you were only a friend,
I made fun of you like an idiot. Forgive my sins.
Please hide your Viswarupa and come before me as my friend,
As you did earlier. That is the form I love and admire.'

'Arjuna, listen. You are fortunate for you have seen the
Universe in all its forms. This great war is your duty and
Kshatriya dharmas is yours. Through me perform all action, and
You will be rid of all blame. I shall free you of all
Actions and make you access divine peace and enlightenment.
Renounce all faiths and surrender to me alone and
You shall be freed of all sins and worries and anxieties.
I have instructed you on the secret of the most secret
And sacred of knowledge and wisdom.

Gathering courage, Arjuna bent down, lifted the Gandiva and
Prostrated at the sacred feet of Narayana and said,
'Your Gitopadesha, your teaching has cleared my mind.
Infatuation and doubts have all disappeared, and from now on
I shall act as per the words you have spoken: Krishna
You are the Yogeshwara, the lord of yogis, and I am blessed.'
Wherever there is Yogisha there is the bow-wielding Arjuna
And there will stay forever wealth and happiness and victory.

CANTO XXXV

DREAMS AND VISIONS OF DRAUPADI: A DWAPARA PILGRIM

'Who are the rightful claimants of Kuru dynasty? And, who the
Proper descendents? There is only one and he, the son of Ganga,
Whose stature is high and pure as the Himalayas.
It is his renunciation, his sacrifice that will echo and re-echo
From one end of the world to another, he, the last link of the Kurus!
Desiring not to fight or face a eunuch, in battle threw away his
Weapons, and then was lying on a bed of arrows for ten days!
Dhritarastra, Pandu and Vidura are brothers and their father
Was Vedavyasa;
The Pandavas are not sons of Pandu; the Kauravas are sons
Only to Dhritarastra, and do not belong to the Kuru clan; but
There is none bold enough to reveal this truth!
The children born to Kunti and Madri were children
Born through the boon of Durvasa, a seer-rishi!
Not merely these five, there is another, who, caught in the
Hands of fate, has become invisible!
Pandu through a victory won the empire but today
It is Dhritarastra who rules over it and the ensuing war
Will it decisively take the conflict to a resolution full
And complete? Will it find an answer to problems many faceted?
In the war there is bound to be bloody fights and horrible deaths.
And surely it will sow seeds of fear in the heart of men
And destroy all human feelings and relationships between
Nations and could end the foundation of the entire culture itself!
Hopes and desires of generations of human beings which

Wished to see a vrindavan of happiness and fulfillment will
Disappear, and over it dark clouds of confusion will dance!
Why has Krishna planted this seed of war in the heart-fields
Of Kauravas and Pandavas, and become the terrible cause of the
Death of millions and millions of soldiers? Who will ask him?
The poison of hatred within, could have been forced and
Palliatives found out, but he made the fire of destruction flare up
And consume the world! Did Krishna not try to douse the fire
Of war?
What is the aim of my life? Is it to have slaughtered
Duryodhana and Dushyasana and avenge my humiliation?
Did he plan this chain of evil happenings in order to create a new
Empire of *dharma*?
He, the Preserver, why has he taken to the path of destruction
complete?
How strange and what contrariety, in this war to end every war?
Why did not Krishna on his own realize the truth of this
Terrible undertaking? Why try to prove the truth he knows to
The world outside? Is not thirst for knowledge to be
Quenched with cool water for one's own consumption?
And, the path
Of liberation, once shown, will be followed and there will be
Found truth absolute. And, it is from light within that one
Has to find one's way, and that in itself is liberation.

When communities are lost in self praise and in selfishness
Then they are pursued by death and destruction and
Moments such as these will arrive only with the poisonous
flame of war!
This is why, I lighted the fire of conflict for human race
Which is to be given a fresh lease of life!
In my ears, through the conch of Sri Krishna I heard this
message
And it looked as if it was a preface to the about-to-happen-the
Great deluge—and it was Krishna who was calling and waking
up the human race,
And it looked as if it called loudly to Partha!

When Abimanyu was still young, I taught him:
'Abhimanyu, do not neglect an enemy who looks weak,
For a single spark is enough to set on fire and destroy a whole
Forest; if heedlessly you spare a baby snake, it will soon
Become a fearful cobra, and with its hood spread wide will bite
You; this is but the natural way of the world; a dwarfish—
Looking foe could well cause the tragic fall of a huge empire;
Therefore, do not be taken in by men who shed crocodile tears;
This world is deceitful; be alert, and employing any means
Have your enemy destroyed; that would keep you safe;
Allow not the plant of hatred to take roots; have it pulled
Out by its roots, for it has the strength to grow in any
Kind of land; do not show anger on your face even if it is
Burning you up inside; put on a face of pleasing civility.
Before you launch an attack, be full of confidence and
Have faith that you will be victorious.'
Listening to such morals, this young boy grew and
Forcing his way into Chakravyuha, the maze of armed heroes,
He fought defying description of heroism: the wicked
Saindhava spun a web of arrows, had him bound, and standing
Behind, slashed with his sword but undeterred Abhimanyu
broke the heads of enemies the way one breaks easily rows of
mud pots;
The teacher, Drona himself, then leapt forward and slabbed the
Littles boy in the chest and the clean, clear, freshly blossomed
Flowers of the minds of the good, fell, and intoned the swan song!

Discussing the happening on the war field every night
And planning the next day's battle-strategies, and benefitting
From suggestions from leaders and elders, everything was moving
Towards the success anticipated, and this largely through the light
Shed by Vasudeva; true Dharmaja's foolishness thwarted us a little!
Human life is strange, moves in circles of ups and downs,
Acquisition, enjoyment, living in truth and untruth, choosing
Between good and bad, but these two twin banks of the river of life
Last forever!
In front of god's desire to destroy evil, both factious of the

Pandavas and Kauravas stand equal: the burning of the
Khandava forest, the killing of Jarasandha and of Shishupala.
Projecting Panchali to distract Karna from the Kaurava
Camp, to pull down Bhishma from his chariot, the
Strategies Arjuna employed,
And to make Drona lose courage, the way they spread the
Rumour of his son's death—all these are moves political
And presented as gifts given away to Krishna!
Hit by the arrows of Partha, Karna fell down and then
Krishna said, 'Arya! You Kunti-born, you the eldest of Pandavas!
You belong to the Vrishhi clan of your mother, come, I shall
Have you coronated; Draupadi will be yours and she will sit
With you on the throne; Dharmaja will be yours and he will sit
With you on the throne; Dharmaja will be the crown-prince and
You will be emperor of the three worlds! Doubt this not!'

Refusing to be swayed by Krishna's sweet, tempting offer
Karna remained pure as beaten gold, and although in a corner
of the mind.
Attraction for Krishne stayed, there was no desire to take the
road erroneous!

Moved by Duryodhana's genuine gifting of the Kingdom of Anga,
And by maternal love for Kunti—virtues unparalled but
These could not wipe away the stain of the mark of low-caste!
Seeing Karna sunk in a pool of mud and blood, Krishna walked
There and said, 'Son of Kunti, tell me, what is your last wish!'
With tearful eyes Karna said, 'Krishna, listen, my last wish
I shall tell you: have me cremated in land totally barren, and
I shall die comforted.' Unable to understand Karna, he stood
In silence, then the eldest of the Pandavas murmured:
'If I am cremated in a barren land, the sorrows and longings
of my heart
Won't be able to be re-born, and let them all be interred there,
So that there won't be another birth for me for ever;
Arrest forever the cycle of birth and re-birth! This, I pray.'
His voice was getting feeble, and as Krishna looked at him, he,

Scanning Hari's face, mumbled: 'Y…Dru…Moth…er…;' who
knows what he wanted to say?
Was he thinking of Vyshali, Draupadi or Kunti?
His eyes gazing at the sun offered oblations through tears and
it seemed
As if he was reciting the sacred Gayatri shloka, his lips went dry,
And his breathing became still.
In the sky there was a sudden flash of brilliant light, and Karna's
Soul became one with the sun god.
The sinking sun looked red as if in anger, and reluctant to see
The injustice meted to his son, he sank into the western ocean!
There was heavy darkness everywhere and the earth goddess felt
Lonely and there was all around only disturbing silence.

In the camp of the Pandavas, it was a night dreadful!
When Sri Krishna entered Arjuna's tent, Kunti, unable to bear her
Sorrow sank to the floor, and then Krishna, the demon-destroyer,
said, 'Mother, take courage, one of your sons is dead;
I shall take you
At the middle of the night to the war field; do not make known
The secret you have kept a well-guarded secret all these years.'
Then, consoling her,
He took her to the place where was lying the lifeless body of Karna,
And she like a creeper struck down by a fierce storm, went down
On her feet which were stuck in the blood and mire of the battle.
She slowly pulled aside the cloth covering Karna's face and stared:
He looked as if he was in happy, deep sleep, and the body itself
Appeared as if it was flooded with light! Like a baby fallen
Asleep on the banks of a river, Karna had gone into a deep
slumber, irreversible!
'Ah, my dear child of love, what has happened to you!
None, none of
My relatives came to see you, and you died the death of a sacrificial
Lamb in this world of deceit. You were of help to everyone
but to your help, none came:
The abandoned child, the crest jewel of the
Kuru race, you were thrown out like a dead orphan body!

Did you become a pawn in the hateful game of dice
between cousins!'
The flowing tears bathed the body of the son and Krishna held
Her in his arms, as if he were to the world an image of a god who
Stands by those who have been deserted by all!

Happy at the demise of Karna, Partha in happiness
In the evening walked towards his camp and washed the blood
signs with warm water.
For the Pandavas it was a night of victory
And celebration but on the ground lay thousands and thousands of
Dead bodies of soldiers and of horses and elephants in
mountainous heaps!

Karna's body was placed on the back of his favourite
Horse, Vayujit, the fast-as-the-wind horse, and taken to the cremation
Ground by Sri Krishna and as the bier was about to be
lighted, a lady wearing a white saree came,
Went round the body thrice, and stood:
Who was it? It was Vaishali and even before Krishna stretched his
Arm to stop her, she had jumped into the funeral pyre and within
Seconds was burnt to ashes!
My mind too was burnt, and the sacrifice had but left me
only a dry log!
Soundless lamentation alone remained a witness to the
end of an epoch!
Without his knowledge I followed Krishna back to the camp
of the Pandavas,
And he, in the light of torches, led the Pandavas five to the site
Of cremation and seeing that Karna had become one with the five
Elements, they silently bowed and prostrated, and wept
While alive the fire of enemity, and in death the fire of the funeral pyre!

Enduring seventeen days of tormenting war, we took rest in
The camp and at night I heard jackals howling, and yet in
love with sleep
I continued to lie down with eyes closed: the mind caught
Between sleep and wakefulness swayed and moved through

Hastinavati, Dwarakavati, Panchala; recalled my working as a
Maid-in-waiting, as Sairandhri; the capture of cows by
the Kauravas;
Another stint of living at Indraprastha, and images like these raced
Through; at the middle of the night, I dreamt I had plaited
My hair and the auspicious moment had finally arrived, the
Moment of the plaiting of the flaming tresses that at last come!
While I happily spent that night in the camp,
Shatanika, Prativindya, Shrutasoma, Shrutakarma, Shrutakirti,
The five children too were in sound sleep and then came
The son of Drona, Aswathama, and in cruelty unmatched
slaughtered all the five,
While they were deep in slumber, and how do I
Narrate the blood-stained story of Kuru dynasty?
To avenge the father's death, he killed Dristadyumna when he
Was fast asleep; to destroy in the womb itself the child of
Uttare he through incantation magical directed his weapons, but
Krishna saved the child, and such news was brought to me by the
Five brothers but I could not bear to listen to Dharmaja's
banal words of consolation,
'Ah, dear, do not cry! Understand that the death
Of sons and brothers occurred during a fair and just war, and
Therefore wipe away your tears.' What strange condolence offered!
The veteran of dharma and kshama, his achievement is this!

With stringing irony I said, 'Thank you much. And I offer
My best wishes to the emperor of Hastinapura! Living in the
Kshatriya tradition and offering as sacrifice sons, and wallowing
With equanimity in an ocean of happiness, offering solace and
Advising poise of mind—who, who would not praise a king
Like you!
The death of my children, of my brother-all caused by the son of
Our teacher burns me up and you think only of your
meaningless victory! 'Before my anger explodes with me and
before it consumes me,
I shall kill that wicked son of our teacher, Drona. On this

I swear and before the empire is made ours I shall have him
Quartered and his flesh thrown to dogs and jackals. Let not such
A rat be born again!
I turned towards Bhima and said, 'You have
Many times saved me from perils seen and unseen; you are the
One who has gratified all wishes of mine and you are the one who
Is most dear to me. Go, look for, Aswathama, catch him and
Like Rudra who massacred his enemies, rush at him and kill
Him and douse the fire of my anger and pain.'
Seeing me weep Bhima rushed out in great fury and he
Was followed by Dharmaraja and his other brothers and Sri
Krishna and once Aswathama was caught
Krishna told them not to kill as he was punishable
But not deserving of death; but to assuage their anger Krishna
Despoiled Aswathama of the priceless jewel he had on his head
And cursed him to eternally roam the world!

Bhima came back to me and said, 'Krishne, look, here
Is the crest jewel of the guru's son who killed our children.
Do you remember what you said while they sent
Krishna as ambassador to Hastinavati?
"Govinda, I have neither sons nor husband nor a father
Nor a brother. I am truly an orphan."
These words of yours still ring in my ears.
I have killed Duryodhana, drunk the blood of Dushyasana,
All humiliations heaped on us I have avenged;
Except for the guru's son, whose body only survives, all the rest
Have been laid to rest forever; the guru's son is a mad nomad!'
I said, 'Great Vrikodara, you have heroically fulfilled my
Desires and doused my burning anger; the world sees it in this
Crest jewel you have brought but let this decorate the person of
Dharmaja, why would I need it? There is within me all the time
A haunting sense of nothingness which will never leave me alone;
Yes, I have five husbands with me and Krishna too but
I have been an orphan and remain an orphan!
Sand lying spread in a vast desert will again, as
Dust rise into sky but like cells full of hidden energy will become

Atoms powerful, explode and announce the terrible end of
the world!
It will destroy the sky and the earth, push them into a
horrific void.
And then re-create all afresh! This is how I am full of
Anger desperate!
As Dharmaja was crowned King of Hastinapura and
Celebrations of the coronations were on Gandhari came and
told Krishna:
'Hey, Krishna, maybe you will defend your actions but the end
Of the clan of Puru is at hand; in another thirty six years
Your Yadava dynasty will be stamped out, root and branch!
Let the sorrow of the Kuru women befall on Yadava women too!
Let Dwaraka sink into the ocean and let this curse of a
Virtuous wedded wife come true!'

I do not know how she could curse the best of men! True,
There is within the maternal heart a great fund of love and
Compassion but beneath it there is adamantine hardness
which explodes
Because of sorrows which weigh on it; natural this is!

Kunti Devi listening to Gandhari said, 'Krishna! How could
A curse affect you or the Yadava dynasty without your
Leave! No, that is not possible! No curse will ever touch you
And let no enemy vanquish or kill you. You have the breast plate of
My prayers for you.'

Krishna smiled and said, 'No, in Gandhari there is strength irresistible;
Drunk Yadavas will squabble and fight among themselves and die;
This is true, the curse is but a pretext; once righteousness is
Established who can come in the way of my death? No, none can!
All our wives and relatives have to abide by the laws of time
Which never stops moving, none can call a halt to it. Listen,
There is the sound of the conch announcing the arrival of a new
Epoch, and the new will come with pomp and pageantry and that
Cannot be stopped!
The era of Treta reached its peak in the war of Rama and Ravana,

That was the high point of the age; now it is Dwarpara epoch,
And the descent has begun, and moving towards the evening of the setting sun!
Is it possible to make the high peak-point, of the ascession of
Sri Rama and Sita to stay eternally with us, in this world? No,
None can put a stop to the wheels of march of time! That
For which I appeared, saw it end in the auspicious happening
At the Kurukshetra field, the end of the Dwapara epoch
Has ended in Draupadi plaiting her sacred head of hair, the
Moving pilgrimage of the flaming tresses of Yagnaseni is now complete.
And all has ended!
Why be sorrowful? Mother Gandhari's, curse has a moving power which
Can never be stalled by anyone; this sorrow is futile!
We all have to bow to the god of all gods which is time; we
Can only do that and nothing else! This is a truth of all the
Truths of all epochs and how can we ever defy and stand against it?
Why undertake that adventure? An empty heart is a curse!'

Sri Hari whole heartedly accepted the strength and power of
Woman and the power he recognized has now become a blaze moving
Up, and has the thirst to devour the universe itself; its spreading
Flame desires oneness with creation, and dancing madly,
Plays around in intensity unbearable!
All sorrow and suffering merged with creation, and sent out a
Message whose life breath was a curse alone!

The Dwapara pilgrim's night of dreams and visions
Saw but a long stretch of murky and bloodied road!
Which could agur and witness the plaiting of the tresses of
Draupadi's sacred head of hair.

CANTO XXXVI

CHAKRA CHANDIKE ARE POWERS AUSPICIOUS IN THE UNIVERSE

When Kunti called, 'O, child, come!' Bhima came holding
His mace in hand, and stood; Partha came with his Gandiva
and I
Pushing aside my dream followed them running and consoled our
Mother, wiped the tears from her eyes; and with my hair
spread on my back
The eastern sun flooded the world with light,
And made the hill behind us warm and beautiful.

Disrobing me was an event which shamed the world!
It was transgression terrible of humanity and justice and it
Resulted in throwing up incandescent balls of fire full of
hatred and anger;
Living in the forests transformed my mind magically, and in a
Big way! How wonderful!
Five heroic husbands could not protect their wedded wife but
This epoch erected a green column of a light-house with a
bright light at its top to
Show the essence of the vision of woman-power lighting the
Path of the world! And it made it stand shining in the world!

'Mother Katyayini, you are the daughter of primeval
Jungles. Who can touch you when you are in yourself a
divine flame!
You are the protector of the five Pandavas, you the fire-born,
You who mount a lion and lead it, you, our mother, you who

Bear in your hands spears and swords, you Chandi-Chamundi,

Who else but you are the protector, preserver and destroyer
of mankind?
I bow and surrender to you, power beyond all powers divine!'

In this way I offered my prayer to Maya and submitted:
Born I was in fire and was made to pass through fiery tests and
At every step I had to wade through fire, and now I do not
Know what awaits me!
The seventeenth night is about to end and tomorrow
Surely there would be either victory or dark death! But
Why this division of humankind into classes and castes and clans?
Why segregate men as Brahmins, Kshatriyas, Vaishyas and
Shudras and Panchamas? Do they in this fashion divide
Fire and water? Why is a man's status made dependent on his
Birth? Accepted ways of life have broken down
And new values and views have made themselves strong.

Born in fire, I shall, through the pathway of fire, move
Forward; and whatever rocks of obstruction come in my way,
I shall have them all blasted to pieces; it matters not
Even if my blood is spilled or the body burned, there are few
who can destroy my thinking mind.
This chronicle of Mahabharata is a lexicon of morals for life:
Drona born a Brahmin became a revered Kshatriya;
The Karna by sheer courage became a brave Kshatriya;
Ekalavya broke through the net of untouchability and through
Practice uninterrupted became a heroic Kshatriya;
All are equal, one to the other; throw away the birth-mark,
And acquire knowledge and wisdom, and this will put an end
To divisions of caste and class and clan and gotras, and bring into
Being through education, a unity of feelings and thoughts and
Create a world of equality, tolerance and cooperative living!
Mahabharata is not a chronicle of unnatural, cross mingling of castes:
It builds a world of equality and fraternity and love,
It is a history of all human values, lived and demonstrated!

On that day when Dhritarashtra granted me three booms,
I, using one asked for the release of Dharmaja and through another
The freeing of the other four, but abjuring avarice did not ask for
The third boon. I lived my life for the sake of happiness of others
And for the establishment of way righteous but did not hear any
Word of consolation or appreciation! I was projected as the real
Mischief maker and blamed for everything and transformed into a
Character given to melodrama!
I dedicated myself to bring

In peace, and in the process, became a ladder for self-seekers, and
Was drowned in a sea of humiliation! When the Pandavas set
Out to cross the ocean, I became their life-boat, and managed to
Reach the other shore, what is left for me now?
True, I was the cause of their winning a kingdom but the
Largest share I had in it were the losses, pushed I was to live
in forests and suffer!
My daughters-in-law were happy with their husbands in
Their maternal homes but I stood like a rock by my five husbands;
O, Lord, who will ever listen to my cries of pain and shame
and torture?
Neither my husbands nor my brothers nor my parents ever
fought for me
Nor spared a thought nor saved me from the fire of humiliation.
Would you compare me with Janaki, the wife of Sri Ramachandra!
No, her exile caused her no hardships: for twelve years she lived
A life of happy contentment: Ravana did not torment her and
She did not have to endure humiliation fiery!

She did not become a maid-in-waiting, a sairandhri, a
Woman-servant; there was no Saindhava or Keechaka to heap
On her misery after misery! Ravana, learned in many shastras,
A devotee of lord Shiva, treated her with respect and dignity and
At the Ashokavana, Sri Rama, reverently following promise
made to his father and
Wedded but to one wife, honourably accepted her!
But I, the fire-born, daughter to King Panchala and wedded to

Five husbands and daughter-in-law to the home of Pandavas of
The lunar dynasty, and with parents and parents-in-law, I was
Abandoned by all, and remained truly an orphan! It is by
Sri Krishna's compassion that my honour was
Saved; from the torture of Keechaka and Saindhava, I was
Saved by Bhimasena's prowess;

The eastern sky rose colourfully and the champak trees
That were in the garden spread fragrance all around; cool breeze
Moved through the branches, and birds sang a song auspicious
for Hastinapura.
On the eighteenth day in Kurukshetra, on the battlefield were
Heroic warriors seated in their chariots and on the backs of
trumpeting elephants;
And there were horses gathered in great numbers, and
Shafts of sunrays made it all look lovely.

A single combat between Bhima and Dushyasana was but
Inevitable and the two, with their maces fought, and it was
like thunderbolts
Clashing, or like elephants fighting one another or like a live volcano
Bursting forth suddenly; but at the end Bhima with a heavy
blow from his mace
Brought down Dushyasana, and he fell like huge tree,
Torn from its roots, and he slumped to the ground mortally
wounded; but
Vrikodara, still vexed and discontented raised his mace, put his
foot on
Dushysana's limp body, and pressing it hard, broke his neck,
Tore away his arms and threw them skyward, and shouting in
Triumphent anger he looked an image of the terrible
Rudra himself!
And, then looked at me; my rich hair, for years on end, had not
Had a drop of oil, had not been combed, and was like dry earth
Which for years had not felt the falling rain from the sky, and
It was thirsty, and it was hungry for the blood of Dushyasana!
Then, Bhima roaring like a lion, laid Dushyasana in his lap,

Tore his body, broke his jaws and splitting open his heart, he
Caught the flowing blood in his cupped palms and drank it!
Savouring its taste, made noises terrifying, and sprinkled the blood
All over the earth as if in a sacrifice, and looked the spitting image
Of Shiva, the destroyer;

As I stood stock-still in fear and amazement he
Came dancing towards me and called out to me loud, 'Ah, you,
Woman among women, come, see I have ripped open the
bowels of wicked Dushyasana;
Come, sit on my lap, I shall oil your hair with his warm
Blood and with sharp teeth of his I shall comb your hair! O,
Lotus-faced one, now plait your hair; I shall ornament it with his
Red-lotus like intestines!'

He put the *kumkum* mark on my forehead with the bubbling
Blood of Dusyasana and shouted that he who had smashed the
thigh of
Duryodhana was alone victorious in the war! Hearing, his
ostentatious
Laughter, the flame of my anger slowly cooled down, and
went out!
'Yes, your vows you have completed and made me plait my hair;
Smeared it you have with Dushyasana's blood; you have broken
Duryodhana's thighs and you have become my dearest husband
And it is you who have won the war, and peace for us; you,
The hero among our warriors, have brought to a glorious close
The Sirimudi Parikramana, my flaming tresses are plaited now,
And made me free.'

This destruction is for the revival of fresh creation, and we,
As pawns in the game of time, have fought to stop the wheels
Of exploitation, come to a halt and brought into being a
A new world of refreshingly healthy culture, and this we did
And to all future wars and to establish values human,
And see that there would be a climate of love and tolerance and
Restraint. Yes, the plaiting of the flaming tresses is now complete!

Krishna is purusa and Krishne prakriti and the profound secret of
Life is a balanced combine of purusha and prakriti, of powers
Masculine and powers feminine; wars are fought for peace and
Peace is the desired object of war; the entire war of the Mahabharata
Is a prologomenon to peace lasting, and fulfillment of the wishes
Of Krishna and Krishne!
Let auspiciousness bless god-ordained order; Let it be victorious;
The auspicious powers of this world are Chakra Chandikes;
they, it is,
Who will make everything auspicious!
Glory be to purusha, glory be to prakriti, and glory be to all
That is auspicious; let glory be to all that makes for goodness
and virtue!
May the Veerappa Moily created The Flaming Tresses of Draupadi
be blessed with all auspiciousness;
Victory to the tradition of great epics in
Kannada! Let the earth goddess be blessed with auspicious greenery!

This great epic of the saga of Draupadi, of her flaming
sacred tresses
Is the vision, sweetly remembered vision of Yagnaseni; fire-born
And blazing like leaping fire; it destroyed nation-
Destroying attempts and created self-respecting woman-power
and transformed it into a live, pulsating metaphor ever alive!
Born a daughter to the King of Panchala and wedded to
Five husbands but rebelled against jealousy,
Took the path of devotion to Krishna and traversing it she
Understood the new epoch's desires and expectations and
fought a war
For a consolidation of the welfare of all men, she, with a
Vision for the future taught and reformed her companions all.
She got the unrighteous enemies killed and created a world
Fair and just and brought peace to men, the way a heavy
Downpour washes everything clean and leaves pleasant peace, like
Rain-washed early morning sun.

This is a legendary chronicle that presents the history of a woman

Hard as diamond and soft as the lotus, and who with her hair
set right
And wearing jasmine flowers in it, is the crest-jewel of her race.
This is history, this is narration of alchemical nature of
character,
And this has sprung from the heart's centre and is pure and sacred
Like the waters of Netravati, Tunga, Bhadra and Krishne;
This is the auspicious Ganga which invites the flowing–in
of Payasvini,
Site, Kapile, Kaveri, Yamuna and Saraswati!
As the flooded water sweetly plays and moves and stays
Seemingly still, Kannada words have flown with musical sound,
And doubling their strength present an unparalled story of
Woman-power which rings through the universe; this story
Has been mirrored in Kannada, which is but a mirrored-reflection of
Malati! Victory to you, the auspicious one, victory to you!

O, mother Yagneshwari, O, you the configuration of vital fire,
Agni; from time beginning, from time primal, you have within
Yourself kept all life alive and at the end of the dissolution of
The world, you again, make room for life in your womb; you are
The mother of the universe, bright as millions of suns born at once
In the firmament;
You, the killer of demons, you who have countless arms and
Eyes, you are the astounding, fiery Katyaini.
You encompass the sky
And the earth and are Lakshminarayani;
You are Shankari, Bhayankari, Draupadi, Brahamari,
Dharini, the stay of the world, you are Yugadosha Harini, the
Dispeller of all evil of all the worlds, you are the auspicious mother
Of Bharata, you are the yogini, the life-giver, you are sanjeevani,
You are Omkara itself, you are the nourisher of the great war
of Mahabharata!
You are Parashakti, the power beyond all power human and divine,
It is you who contain in yourself the five Pandavas as five elements;
You came to end exploitation of woman and was the centre
of strength

For all women and you stood as the lighthouse in the sea of women's tears!
Under compulsion from father, and from avarice for wealth and
Kingdom, you came as wife to an aged Shantanu; and the women of India are, look,
Ambe, Ambalike, Ambike, fish-smelling Satyavati and
Gandhari, Prithe, Dushaye, Shikandini, Bhanumati, Vaishali,
Satyabhame, Hidimbe, Chitrangade, Ulupi, Harita, Kripa Deva—
These, these are the women of Bharata!
The story of each is distinct; sad, pining mothers, widows and
Wives, and you are a metaphor for their cries and lamentation.
O, lady, the mother of Tamil people, the magic of the ritual of
Karaga dance, you, born of fire-sprung Vahni Kshatriyas, you are
The one who conferred on us dignity and respect;
It is you who brought all Bharat together and made us have
But a single path and a single aim, you truly are auspiciousness itself.
You set right the righteous Dharmaja, who was often caught in
Conflicting righteous ways; it is you who made Bhima's strength swell:
It is you who planted in Partha the desire for acquiring arms divine;
It is you who made Nakula and Sahadeva shed their diffidence;
It is you who impelled us to move from emptiness, from the void,
Towards realization of the fullness of our strength!

In sacrificial fire sacred, you were born; and in the presence
Of sacrificial fire made us wedded and conferred peace on the world!
Yagnaseni I bow to you again and again; you wiped the tears
From the eyes of the women of all our ages, and made them
See the authentic path of revolutionary revealing;
The wicked Duryodhanas and Dushyasanas;
The lustful Jayadrathas and Keechakas were wiped out; and
Those who suffered from humiliation, from loss of children and
Husbands dear—all these you filled with awareness new and
Made them stand up against injustice;
You became the harbinger of a world
Free of exploitation and violence.

You created a world full of confidence and self-respect.
Victory to you, Brahamari Durga Parameshwari,
Victory to Saraswati, Lakshmi and Parvati,
Victory to Prakriti, Victory to the famed Draupadi
The twin of Krishna, the daughter of King of Panchala,
Victory to the beloved of the Pandavas, victory to the
Bringer of all that is good and beautiful and auspicious.
To you, I bow, and pray to bless us all.

This epic, crafted by Veerappa Moily,
Is now complete, Om, Shanti, Om Sri Mangala Mahashree.

APPENDIX I

Dr M. Veerappa Moily belongs to that rare kind of achievers who achieve laurels in the fields of both active politics and creative literature. His contributions to Karnataka are varied in nature and have left an everlasting impact on several matters. They include: the help he gave to weavers when he was the Minister for Small Industries; establishment of Mangalore University and Gulbarga University, decision taken to conduct World Kannada Meet while he was the Finance Minister; establishment of Hampi Kannada University, education in mother tongue, CET unit for professional course, while he was the Education Minister and Electronic city, Vijayanagara Steel Factory, ITPL, Kannada Pustaka Pradhikara (Kannada Books Authority), Krishna Jalabhagya Corporation, provision for reservation in politics for the exploited class including women following the recommendations of Chinnappa Reddy Commission on Backward classes as the Chief Minister of Karnataka; establishment of permanent branch of High Court in Gulbarga and Dharawada, getting classical language status for Kannada, Ettina Hole Drinking Water Scheme for the ever drought-hit regions of Chikkaballapur and Kolara Districts, etc. as a minister in the Central Government.

He has penned two epics, four anthologies of poems, four novels, three plays and six other important works, and has thus become an important writer in Kannada. His novels *Kotta* and *Tembare* which bring before our eyes his in-depth study and beautiful pictures of Koraga, Nalke, Parava etc., communities that he has portrayed, have earned distinction in this genre of Kannada literature. His *Shree Ramayana Mahanveshanam* which aesthetically depicts the social changes and developments, struggle of third world countries like India against the economically giant nations in the 21st century, was the first Kannada work to be released in the House of Commons in London. That epic has already established several records and has also been translated into Hindi, Tamil and Telugu, and has drawn the attention of several thousand people. This epic has the honour of being the second Kannada work to get Murthidevi Award instituted by Bharatiya Jnanapith Organisation. It was also honoured with the Saraswati Samman.

Dr Moily has shared his thoughts and opinions through the character of Draupadi, who is the embodiment of energy in Mahabharata, and has presented the struggle of the people belonging to weaker sections, including women, in *The Flaming Tresses of Draupadi*. He is engaged in bringing out another epic on Bahubali, son of the first Jain Thirtankara Rishabha Deva, and who is also known for his renunciatory acts in the history of Jainism.

Dr K.R. Kamalesh

APPENDIX II

Ramayana and Mahabharata represent two important genres of poetry in the world of literature. While Ramayana upholds the values of life, Mahabharata is the story of the strife between opposite values in life. Both these works have engaged the Indian mind endlessly. The writers of Kannada literature have repeatedly encountered these and reconstructed them in the local idiom to suit the expectation of their times. Dr Veerappa Moily, who introduced the multi-faceted desi (local) culture in his magnum opus *Shree Ramayana Mahanveshanam* , has now successfully ventured to portray Mahabharata through the lens of modern times.

While in the original Sanskrit work of Vyasa there is no single protagonist, Pampa created Arjuna, Ranna posed Bhima, and Kumaravyasa idolized the ideal character of Krishna as their choice of the protagonist in their works and in doing so they reconstructed the work of Vyasa. Dr Moily has seen Mahabharata as the story of Draupadi, the coronated queen of Pandavas, and created a new Mahabharata, *The Flaming Tresses of Draupadi*. The very concept of this epic has given the author ample opportunities and possibilities with the main story. The political encounters are seen as the struggle between human relationships, which has given the original story a new look here.

For Dr Moily, a woman is the protective force who has the ability to question and challenge the system. Draupadi here is the union of these forces. The struggle that Draupadi had to undergo questions the customary beliefs that the male-dominated world has fostered within, for ages. It gives expressions to the subtle and delicate feelings of a sensitive person. *The Flaming Tresses of Draupadi* is not a story of a bygone era, but a live account of a daily struggle that each one of us is undergoing.

Dr Narahalli Balasubramanaya

ACKNOWLEDGEMENTS

It took more than seven years to complete this epic. I discussed with several scholars from all over India the tradition of Mahabharata prevailing in their part of the country. They also provided me a detailed account of the characteristics and lifestyles of different people. This posited on me a wide range of knowledge. I express my gratitude to all of them.

Several hands have helped in this accomplishment. To name a few important ones among them—Dr K. Anantaramu, guru of poetics, Dr Kabbinale Vasanta Bharadwaja, whom I consider my co-thinker, Sri J.N. Shama Rao, Smt. N. Bharathi, Sri Vasu, the Member of Legislative Assembly from Chamaraja constituency of Mysore, Dr B.A. Vivek Rai, Dr Chandrashekara Kambara, Dr Narahalli Balasubrahmanya, Dinesh K. Chitrapur, my personal assistant who typed this epic so beautifully, Sri Gregory Robert, who helped me in several ways, Sri Bagur Markendeya, the artist, Sri M. Krishnamurthy of Swan Printers, who printed this work, Hamsa V. Moily who presented a ballet, my children and my sons-in-law.

Dr K.R. Kamalesh is the catalytic force behind all my works and he made this book happen too.

To all these people I express my sincere gratitude.

|| May Kannada be victorious ||